UNE JEUNESSE QUE L'AVENIR *inquiète* TROP SOUVENT.

Obsolete Communism
The Left-Wing Alternative

Obsolete Communism
The Left-Wing Alternative

**Daniel Cohn-Bendit
and
Gabriel Cohn-Bendit**

translated by
Arnold Pomerans

AK Press
Edinburgh, London, & San Francisco
2000

The cover art and the poster reproductions found in the front and back inside pages are from photographs of the original posters. We thank the original unknown artists for their work and inspira-
tion, and the photographers for their donations.

Back cover photograph of Daniel Cohn-Bendit © Topham/The Image Works

Obsolete Communism: The Left Wing Alternative

ISBN 1 902593 25 1

AK Press   AK Press
PO Box 40682   PO Box 12766
San Francisco CA   Edinburgh, Scotland
94140-0682 USA   EH8 9YE

A catalogue record for this title is available from the Library of Congress

Cover and book design donated by:
fran sendbuehler
mouton-noir — Montréal
fran@mouton-noir.org

Book Dedication: Geoff Yippie!
The production of this book is dedicated to the memory of Geoff Meredith, AKA Geoff
Yippie! An alumni of the Bound Together Collective and lifelong anarchist, Geoff will be
missed by everyone who knew him except the authorities.

Author's Note

The author would like to stress that whereas he himself has been given VIP treatment by his generous publishers, no doubt in recognition of his help in greasing the wheels of capitalist production, his poor underpaid translator* has had to labour far beyond his normal call of duty. Not only has he had to read the author's illegible scrawl, to fill in the gaps and to make explicit what this text, written in such a hurry, has failed to do, but he must slave away day and night to meet the publishers' precipitate deadline. Perhaps he is consoled by the fact that, in this way, he is carrying the message right through the publishers' doors.

* The translator salutes the author. He would also like to express his deep appreciation of all those who have worked with him - day and night - on the English edition, and quite particularly of Rodney Strulo, Billie Peiser, Jean-Paul Villechaize and Michael George.

Publisher's Note

The publisher congratulates the translator, Arnold Pomerans, on the magnificent job he has done in translating this work in so short a time. He would also like to point out that while there are parts of this book which relate particularly to Daniel Cohn-Bendit's experiences and are therefore written in the first person the book, as a whole, is the result of the combined labours of Daniel and his brother Gabriel Cohn-Bendit.

Re-Publisher's Note

The book you hold in your hand is published by AK Press, who is not the publisher mentioned in the notes from the author, translator or publisher above. Those notes refer to Andre Deutsch, the original publisher of Obsolete Communism. Unlike Andre Deutsch, we're adept at neither sticking to precipitate deadlines nor greasing the wheels of capitalist production, and for that reason can be generous only of our time, not any more liquid asset. Our thanks to Daniel Cohn-Bendit and Arnold Pomerans who gave the reprint their enthusiastic support and to Donald Nicholson-Smith whose idea it was in the first place.

'Literary rogues great and small, have struck gold with the Commune, and have exploited it to the full. There is not a hack who has not churned out his slapdash pamphlet, book, or History ... 'There is a huge pile of Paris Burns, Paris in Flames, Red Books, Black Books ... *'Publishers are interested in nothing but the Communards these days ... Their writings titillate the minds of the bourgeoisie.'*

Lissagaray: Histoire de la Commune de 1871

Contents

Introduction

A writer is a productive worker not only because he produces ideas but also because he enriches the publisher of his books, in other words because he works for a capitalist.

Karl Marx: Theory of Surplus Value

Had I decided to write a book on the French political scene and on the chances of a revolutionary uprising only two or three months ago, no publisher would have taken the slightest notice of me. But such was the impact of the events of May and June and so wildly has the name of Cohn-Bendit been bandied about that, far from my having to go down on my knees to them, the publishers now come chasing after me, begging me to write about anything I choose, good or bad, exciting or dull; all they want is something they can sell — a revolutionary gadget with marketable qualities.

Strange, isn't it, this Cohn-Bendit myth, this legend of the 'cherubic Danton'. Strange that a movement opposed to all leaders should have ended up with one all the same, that those who shun the limelight should be singled out for the full glare of publicity.

In any case, all self-respecting publishers are falling over themselves to cash in on the May events. In our commercial world, individual capitalists are perfectly willing to pave the way for their own destruction, to broadcast revolutionary ideas, provided only that these help to fill their pockets. So anxious are they, in fact, that they are prepared to pay for the privilege through the nose in the short run (offering me a vast sum of money before I have written a single line). They do not even seem to be bothered by the fact that their cash will be used for the next round of Molotov cocktails. They hope, perhaps, that the revolution will be abortive — my readers may be among those to prove them wrong.

Why, then, did I decide to write this book? Who was I to refuse this golden opportunity of taking aim against our whole society, of saying what no one has been able to say for so long, of explaining the full importance of the French revolutionary movement, not only in the immediate past, but also in the future? For, as far as I am concerned, the revolution is not yet over. 'Ce n'est qu'un début, continuons le combat!'

I must also make clear what this book is not. It does not pretend to be an historical treatise, if only because the events are too recent for anyone to reconstruct them objectively. In particular, a true history of our movement cannot be based simply on the official statements of the authorities, of the opposition, the Trade Unions, or even of the revolutionaries themselves, as they were proclaimed from a thousand placards, wall-slogans and tracts, but must be a running commentary on the day-to-day practical and theoretical activities of the students and workers — of all those who believed our slogan 'Sous le pavé, la plage' — beneath the paving stones, the beach. This kind of history cannot be written in a couple of weeks (supposing it could be written at all).

Nor does this book pretend to give a simplified theoretical account of the events. Having participated in them and observed them at close quarters, I am unable to stand aside and take a detached view of the overall situation. The movement will have need of such a detached observer, there will no doubt be theoretical books and I do not wish to deny their necessity, but I, for my part, do not feel capable of producing one, and certainly not at this moment. Others will do it and no doubt far better than I could myself. This book claims to be no more than an attempt to participate in a continuing scene, with all its remarkable spontaneity. From the very outset, the movement succeeded in liberating our language from its bourgeois strait-jacket, and my book is but an echo of the great dialogue that was begun in the forum of the Latin Quarter. Both in form and content, it will try faithfully to reflect the mood of the movement. Finally, I look upon this book as a propaganda pamphlet, one that, thanks to the help of my benevolent publishers, will reach a far wider audience than it could in any other form.

The world identifies the recent revolutionary movement with the student struggle, the barricades, the occupation of the universities, and finally the general strike and the occupation of the factories by the workers. For me, the revolutionary movement was born much earlier and took the form of unofficial strikes, student unrest, the activity of tiny left-wing splinter groups, the so-called *groupuscles*. The events of May and June were merely an intensification of what went before, albeit on so vast a scale that they opened up an undreamt-of possibility: the prospect of a revolution. This book might, perhaps, be a brief moment of reflection in this great historical process.

That is why I do not address myself to a 'reader' or to the 'public', but only to those who were with us, might have been with us, or may be with us in the future, and quite particularly to the workers and peasants from whom the Establishment tried to separate us so assiduously. I know that the only chance of resuming the struggle is to put an end to the division between intellectuals, workers and peasants. Every revolution, every radical transformation of society, needs the conscious and creative participation of the working and peasant classes, and not simply their participation as a malleable mass whose only usefulness is their strength and numerical weight.

I know that there are many other ways of ending our division. However, since I happen to be writing a book, I shall try to use this particular method. Here, the problem of language becomes fundamental. The works of philosophers, sociologists, and professional politicians (sometimes quite outspoken, particularly after the elections ...) are written in a style which is not intended for the workers and peasants and which, in any case, they cannot understand. This is a danger I shall do my best to avoid.

Stilted language is not, moreover, a monopoly of the bourgeoisie; it also creeps into the writings of those Leftists who see themselves as the leaders, the self-appointed vanguard, of a working-class movement whose language they have ceased to speak and which, once it has become revolutionary as it did in May and June, is only too happy to dispense with leaders and a vanguard altogether.

I know that a theoretical language is necessary, and regret that the writings of Marx are, at least in part, hard going even for scholars and, in their present form, a closed book to most of the working class — which does not mean that they cannot be understood, once they are translated into simple language. But as it is, they are accessible only to the bourgeois intellectual — cultural inequality is no accident, but part and parcel of the oppressive structure of both capitalist and 'communist' societies and in fact ensures their survival. This is precisely what the revolutionary students were trying to say when they decried the universi-

ties and schools as 'factories of privilege': the present educational structure ensures that the majority of working-class children are barred not
only from the bourgeois society we are trying to overthrow, but also
from the intellectual means of seeing through it. No wonder that the
bourgeois directors of education are so hostile to university and school
reform.

True, we hear a great deal of talk about the subject today, but the real
purpose of the Fouchet plan* is clear: to turn people into ever more
profitable pack-horses.

'The ideas of the ruling class are in every epoch the ruling idea: i.e.
the class which is the ruling material force of society is at the same time
the ruling intellectual force. The class which has the means of material
production at its disposal, has control at the same time over the means
of mental production ...' (Karl Marx: *The German Ideology.*)

The division of society into manual and intellectual workers is a fundamental aspect of all exploitative societies. Every revolutionary movement must try by its actions and also by its very structure to narrow this
gulf, while remembering that only a socialist society can finally end it. It
is only by working for a socialist revolution that the exploited masses can
take control of their own future and that of society at large. No book can
help them to achieve this; they can only learn by their own revolutionary endeavours. 'In a revolution, when the masses erupt on to the political stage, their class-consciousness becomes practical and active. Hence
one year of revolution gave the Russian proletariat the kind of education
that thirty years of parliamentary and trade union struggle failed to give
the German proletariat.' (Rosa Luxemburg: *The General Strike.*)

This book will be divided into four main parts: (1) an analysis of the
principal factors of the May/June struggle (this for the foreign reader);
(2) an attempt to show how the French State dealt with the uprising and
to analyse the phenomenon of Gaullism; (3) an analysis of the role of
the French Communist party and its essentially bureaucratic nature; and
(4) a study of the failure of the revolution in Russia under the leadership
of Lenin and Trotsky.

True, no one writing about the French Revolution can explain why
the explosion came in May 1968 rather than in April: 'It [world histo-

---

* A government plan for transforming the educational system into a techno-
cratic one better adapted to the 'needs' of a modern society.

ry] would be of a very mystical nature if "accidents" played no part in it. These accidents themselves fall naturally into the general course of development and are compensated again by other accidents.' (Karl Marx, Letter to Kugelmann, 17 April 1871.)

For three or four years, the student movement has been recognized as a revolutionary force by all political observers, and it will therefore be part of my task to explain the history of this movement, to recount the major ideas proclaimed for more than ten years in the revolutionary study groups of Paris and elsewhere. These 'clubs', which were derided as 'splinter groups' by the official and patented representatives of the revolution (their letters patent were deposited by Maurice Thorez, the Son of the French People, with Joseph Stalin, the Father of all the Russias) — these groups, of which no one took the slightest notice, were nevertheless so effective that their ideas and revolutionary experience eventually spilled over into the streets and factories, and so helped to write a new chapter in the history of the revolutionary movement — the permanent struggle to end the exploitation of man by man.

This brings me to the question of the organization not only of capitalist or bureaucratic society — for this must be the starting point in any discussion of 'productive relationships' — but also of a non-authoritarian and non-hierarchical socialist society: should the new society be organized along Bolshevik lines or along the non-Bolshevik lines of the 22 March Movement?

This introduces the larger problem of the relationship between the revolutionary minority and the so-called 'masses'. What precisely are these masses, and why are there masses in the first place? How can the masses transform themselves into something more than an amorphous mass? And what sort of minority organization is capable of challenging an exploitative society and unmasking its real nature? To that end, I shall try to show how the 'masses' discovered the means of taking their own destiny in their hands, for example during the Paris Commune of 1871, during the Russian Revolutions of 1905 and 1917, during the Spanish Revolution of 1936, and finally during the Hungarian Revolution of 1956. These moments in the revolutionary struggle of the working class are more important than all the treatises that have been and will be written on this subject. This book, for one, does not try to do more than hold up to the working class the mirror of its own revolutionary experience, an experience that ran counter to all the tenets and practices of its would-be leaders. This experience and the chance that it may be widely copied are perhaps the most positive aspects of the May events as well. Thus while Lefort, Morin and Coudray are right to claim (*Mai 1968: la brèche*) that the month of May saw a breach of modern capitalist society and also of the old authority of the Left, it did far more than that: it represented a return to a revolutionary tradition these parties have betrayed. Hence the 22 March Movement was no 'brilliant invention' of a group of 'naive prodigies', but the result of arduous research into revolutionary theory and practice.

It would be wrong to think that what happened in France could only have happened there, just as it is a mistaken idea that concentration camps could only have occurred in Hitler's Germany or in Stalin's Russia. Revolution as well as counter-revolution are international, and much as the student movements in Spain, America, Japan, Italy, etcetera influenced the French student movement, so the French student movement, which was the first to spill out from the university into the factories, can serve as an example elsewhere.

The events in France have proved that revolution is possible in even a highly industrialized capitalist society. Those who argued that the working class had outgrown revolution stood convicted of theoretical and practical incompetence, a fact that suggests it is high time to discover why the working class has remained so passive for so long.

In conclusion, this book will necessarily interpret the events in the light of the author's 'Leftist' convictions — hence its title. The history of 'Leftism' is, in fact, the history of all that is truly revolutionary in the working class movement. Marx was to the left of Proudhon and Bakunin to the left of Marx. Lenin was a Leftist when he opposed social democratic reformism, and again when he opposed his own Central Committee and Politburo during the 1917 Revolution. After the Revolution, the 'Workers' Opposition', a group of left-wing 'deviationists' among the Bolsheviks, became the most revolutionary element inside the Party, while the Ukrainian anarchist Makhno represented the most revolutionary movement outside. This struggle between its 'Left' and 'Right' wings continues to divide the working-class movement to this day.

'As Lenin never tired of repeating, the masses are greatly to the left of the Party, just as the Party is to the left of its Central Committee.' (Trotsky: *History of the Russian Revolution*.)

The question of 'Leftism' became a major issue during the events of May and June. Who is the authentic representative of the Left today: the Fourth International, the Situationist International or the Anarchist Federation? Leftism is everything that is new in Revolutionary history, and is forever being challenged by the old. This new factor is what we must firmly defend in the present, lest it be crushed by what is obsolete in Leftism itself. Let the dead bury their dead.

The transformation and development of Leftist ideas reflect not only the transformation and development of capitalist society, but also the transformation and development of the Russian Revolution into a bureaucratic counter-revolution, sustained and defended by Communist parties throughout the world. I, for one, do not think that the French Communist Party betrayed its own principles during May and June; it simply acted in defence of its bureaucratic interests as a party, and of the bureaucratic interests of the USSR as a state.

No doubt this last remark will strike many people as a mere commonplace, but it is not yet, unfortunately, a commonplace among all sections of the people. Now, since I firmly believe that until they appreciate the true nature of Communist bureaucracy they will never be able to arrive at a revolutionary spirit, I think that it is essential to drive this 'commonplace' home. To that end, I could simply have compiled an anthology of the most incisive articles to have appeared in such radical journals as *Socialisme ou Barbarie, l'Internationale situationniste, Information et correspondance ouvrière, Noir et rouge, Recherches libertaires* and to a lesser extent in Trotskyist publications. But such an anthology would be of no interest to a publishing house that insists on a book signed by Cohn-Bendit. I find it most ironical that Lefort, in his book, should have seen fit to write: 'For my part, what I find in the speeches of some of the more rabid students and particularly of Cohn-Bendit, is a pinch of realism and a large dose of impudence.' Now, I have been hearing this sort of remark for many years, and can only say that the 'impudence' and the 'realism' are based, *inter alia*, on the theses which Lefort (among others) published in *Socialisme ou Barbarie*. The readers, unfortunately far too few in number, of this and other Leftist reviews, will appreciate how much this book owes to them. As for the rest, they ought to be told that 'Cohn-Bendit' is simply the anonymous author of all these reviews, and perhaps the journals *Action* and the *Cahiers de mai* as well. I am not, and do not want to be, anything but a plagiarist when it comes to the preaching of revolutionary theory and practice. I have simply had the good fortune to be around when the 'force of criticism was transformed into criticism by force'.

Postscript to the introduction

This book was written in five weeks and bears the marks of this scramble. I had intended to examine to what extent workers' control, as it has been applied in Spain in 1936, in Algeria, and today in Jugoslavia, could serve as a model for a new socialist society. It was also my intention to describe the direct action and forms of organization developed by the Russian workers in 1905 and 1917, by the German workers in 1918, by the Italians in 1920, and by the Hungarians in 1956. In the event, I have only had time to look at Russia. I have used this example to demonstrate the counter-revolutionary nature of the Bolshevik Party. As I wrote, I began to feel that my chief task must be to expose all those forces that stand in the way of revolution — from the State, the Trade unions and the Stalinists down to all the far-left splinter groups with a Bolshevik outlook. Once this was done I could proceed to examine the basic problems facing the modern revolutionary, and these, for lack of time, I could only outline in brief. Those who wish to be shown the royal road to socialism, or have a clear blueprint for the future, may take comfort from the words of Commandant Gaveau's indictment of the International Association in 1871, words which perfectly summarize my own point of view: 'To raze the old and build the new from scratch that is how the supporters of the International Association intend to construct a state that recognizes neither the government nor the army nor religion; that believes in legislation by the people for the people, in the collective ownership of all things, in the abolition of the right of inheritance and marriage; wants to disband the permanent army, and by breaking down all frontiers, to replace the Fatherland with the idea of international solidarity.'

I

The Strategy and Nature of the Revolutionary Movement

The accused who have been brought before you today have all taken a leading part in the insurrectionary movement that swept Paris from 18 March until 28 May, threatening to plunge the whole of France into the abyss of Civil War. Before determining the responsibility of each of the accused for this evil crime, we must first look at the origins of their movement, seek its causes ...

Indictment of the Communards *by* Commandant Gaveau

1. The Student Revolt

A spectre is haunting Europe — the spectre of student revolt. All the powers of old Europe have entered into a holy alliance to exorcize this spectre: Pope and Central Committee, Kissinger and de Gaulle, French Communists and German police-spies.

But now it has become world-wide: Berkeley, Berlin, Tokyo, Madrid, Warsaw — the student rebellion is spreading like wildfire, and authorities everywhere are frantically asking themselves what has hit them. The answer is really quite simple.

Let us take just one example: the student struggle at Berkeley in 1964 — four years before the events in Paris. How much just reading the newspapers might have helped the French authorities!

At Berkeley in 1964 — well in advance of Berlin or Paris — the students defended their right to participate in politics, and in particular to protest against the war in Vietnam, unhampered by internal rules and regulations.

It started with a decision by the administration to ban all fund-raising and propaganda for any political or social ideas of which they did not approve.

This inept move by the bureaucrats stung a small group of students into action, and their numbers rapidly increased as the administration tried with typical bluster to assert its authority. The students put their point of view in the bimonthly *Free-Speech Movement News Letters;* which brought hundreds, and later thousands, of students without previous political experience into the movement. The ensuing struggle taught them a few fundamental truths about the nature of the State, and in particular about the relationship of the university with the world of business, local politics and the police.

This student struggle at Berkeley was significant in that it helped to underline the dilemma of a rich but increasingly bureaucratic society.

The Berkeley model was copied at Berlin university a few years later, with Paris following suit soon afterwards. Here we shall look, therefore, not so much at the specific causes of the violent protest of the SDS (the left-wing German student Union) but at the way it influenced events in France.

In Germany, the call for university reform became a rallying cry for students and a strong one in the absence of an effective parliamentary opposition to West German capitalism. As a result, the German student movement became the standard bearer of resistance to both the German state and also to American atrocities in Vietnam.

While the German students were challenging the system, their French colleagues were becoming increasingly alive to the total failure of the reformist policies advocated by the UNEF (National Union of French Students). Unfortunately, the extreme Left was devoting all its energies to making scientific, Marxist analyses of the situation, which, despite their learned character, did little to mobilize the students for *their own* struggle.

However, as opposition to the Vietnam war assumed international proportions, French students, particularly in Paris, were increasingly involved in campus demonstrations, the more so as their hatred of this war went hand in hand with the dawning realization that their own universities were nothing but cogs in the capitalist machine.

'These students now insult their professors. They should be locked up ... For the moment this illegal agitation is being closely watched by the Ministry of the Interior' *(L'Aurore,* 26 November 1966).

This particular broadside was fired, not at the 'notorious' students of Nanterre, but at those of Strasbourg who, in 1966, had got themselves onto the local UNEF committee. Their unexpected election, though perfectly regular, was only possible because the majority of students were completely uninterested in the platitudes of student politics, and because the bureaucratic machinery of the old UNEF had broken down. The new committee decided to expose university life for what it really was. The result was what the press and UNEF called the 'Strasbourg scandal'.

The 'Strasbourg Scandal'

To begin with, the committee used a number of unorthodox methods to draw the students' attention to a pamphlet they were producing in collaboration with the Situationist International, a pamphlet that marked a great step forward in French student affairs. On 26 October 1966, A. Moles, Professor of psycho-sociology in the University of Strasbourg, was bombarded with tomatoes during his inaugural lecture. Soon afterwards, members of the AFGES (Federal Association of Strasbourg Students) started a bill-sticking campaign, partly to advertise their new pamphlet. They plastered the walls with a comic strip called 'The Return of the Durutti Column', in which they took a swipe at the old Communist student 'leaders'.

The pamphlet, 'On the poverty of student life considered in its economic, political, psychological, sexual and intellectual aspects and some means of remedying it' was handed out at the official ceremony marking the beginning of the academic year; simultaneously the new AFGES let it be known that its only 'student' programme was the immediate dissolution of the union. This prospect struck many people as horrifying; the *Dernières nouvelles* called it 'the first real sign of a revolt' (4 December 1966). *L'Aurore* (16 November) had this to say: 'The Situationist International, with a handful of supporters in all the chief capitals of Europe, anarchists playing at revolution, talk of "seizing power", not so as to take it, but simply to destroy it, and with it even their own authority.' And the good citizens, appalled that their own dear sons and daughters might keep company with this scum, quickly set its judicial machinery in motion, and proceeded against the students on a set of trumped-up charges.

'The accused have never denied the charge of misappropriating the funds of the students' union. Indeed they freely admit having made AFGES pay some 5,000 francs for the cost of printing and distributing 10,000 pamphlets, not to mention other literature inspired by the Situationist International. These publications express ideas and aspirations which, to put it mildly, have nothing to do with the aims of a student union. One has only to read their publications for it to be obvious that these five students, scarcely more than adolescents, lacking any experience of real life, their minds confused with ill-digested philosophical, social, political, and economic theories, and bored by the drab monotony of their everyday life, make the empty, arrogant and pathetic claim to pass judgement and even to heap abuse upon their fellow students, their professors, Gods, religion, the clergy, the government and political and social systems of the entire world. Rejecting all morality and restraint, their cynicism does not hesitate to preach theft, an end to all studies, the suspension of work, total subversion and world revolution with unlicensed pleasure as its only goal. In view of their basically anarchistic character, these theories and propaganda are socially noxious. Their wide dissemination in both student circles and among the general public, by the local, national and foreign press, is a threat to the morality, the studies and the good name of the University, and thus the very future of the students of Strasbourg.'

These remarks taken from the summing-up by the learned judge are extremely interesting. They substantiate the charge made by the pamphleteers themselves that students have been turned into mere spectators of social events, consumers of what scraps the system cares to throw their way. Moreover, the pamphlet shows clearly that in our 'wealthy' society, the student is forced to live a life of extreme emotional poverty. The writers have nothing but contempt for that class of students who take no interest in any problems except their own, who revel in their alienation which they vainly hope will attract the sympathy of a society indifferent to much more poignant suffering throughout the world.

The liberal university allows its students a measure of liberty, but only so long as they do not challenge the basis of university education: the preparation of a privileged minority for a return to the ranks of the ruling class from which they have taken temporary leave of absence. The university has, in fact, become a sausage-machine which turns out people without any real culture, and incapable of thinking for themselves, but trained to fit into the economic system of a highly industrialized society. The student may glory in the renown of his university status, but in fact he is being fed 'culture' as a goose is fed grain — to be sacrificed on the altar of bourgeois appetites.

After making all these points, the Strasbourg pamphlet goes on to examine the current wave of student unrest. It is not simply the perennial revolt of youth, but a revolt against the specific horrors of modern society. As products of that society, the students have but two alternatives: they can embrace it, or reject it totally — there is no middle way. An extreme example of the second alternative is the behaviour of the *blousons noirs*, who run riot in the streets without any apparent motive or object. They hit out wildly at modern city life, against the plethora of equally sterile choices of entertainment, the straitjacket of petty restrictions and police control. The *blouson noir* refuses to conform and yet expects all the goodies of capitalist society to fall into his lap: cars, electric guitars, clothes and records. But even if his way of acquiring these treasures — theft — is one that strikes at the very roots of society, once he begins to enjoy their comforts, the *blouson noir* is only too happy to settle down to a life of humdrum conformism.

The revolt of the Dutch *Provos* took place on a considerably higher plane, though they, too, failed to realize that the proletariat alone is capable of changing society. All the *Provos* are, in fact, opposed to is the increasing monotony of life in a capitalist country. They want to make life more colourful, but do not realize that while the system remains as it is any improvements can, at best, be only tinkering with the machinery, benefiting some sections but never the whole of society. Hence the *Provos* can only succeed once they integrate their struggle into the general fight against oppression.

The Strasbourg pamphlet then takes a brief look at the Berkeley student revolt against the social system as such, a system run by a hierarchy which is a tool of the economy and the State. The American students, they contend, made the fundamental mistake of considering themselves the spokesmen of the most exploited stratum of society.

Finally, the pamphlet mentions the Zengakuren (Union of Revolutionary Japanese Students), and the Japanese League of Young Marxist Workers (the only organization in which young students and workers had begun to fight for common objectives), two groups with no illusions, and determined to fight against Western capitalism and Eastern bureaucracy alike.

The Strasbourg pamphlet is a radical critique of the French far-Left, incapable of any real action because it keeps rummaging in the dustbins of history. It was accorded a very mixed reception:

'This paper, with its high tone, must be considered a systematic rejection of all social and political organizations as we know them in the West and the East, and of all the groups that are currently trying to transform them. *(Le Monde,* 9 December, 1966.)

Other papers were far less friendly and objective, the more so as the pamphlet brought student discontent into the open: it acted as a kind of detonator. And although we, in Nanterre, did not accept the Strasbourg interpretation of the role of minority groups, i.e. university students, in the social revolution, we did all we could in helping to distribute the pamphlet. Moreover, since many students were delighted to find their miserable condition brought to public notice at last, and since many lecturers were stricken with a bad conscience, we were able to air the whole matter in a number of sociology courses and elsewhere. As a result, an increasing number of students became aware of the existence of the journal *Internationale situationniste* and began to come to grips with the radical ideas expressed in it.

Libre Circulation — The Battle of the Dormitories

Hand in hand with this ideological break-through went an intensified attack on monastic university regulations and particularly on the prudish intervention in the personal affairs of students living in the universities. This struggle was, in fact, only the beginning of a general offensive against the university institution.

In 1967, there were constant clashes between the administration and a group of students who were determined to unmask the repressive structure of what goes by the name of a university but is, in fact, nothing but a mire of intellectual corruption. To begin with, the students called in family planning experts and, with their help and by drawing on the political, social and revolutionary theories of Wilhelm Reich, started a sex-education campaign on the campus. This culminated in male students forcibly entering the women's hostels and after this many of the petty restrictions surrounding these bastions of French purity and chastity were repealed. There the matter might well have ended, had it not been for the French scandal sheets which, having lied for so long about rape, hashish and hard drugs on the campus, now thought they had more tangible evidence against the students, and threw out hints of an even greater sensation. Twenty-nine students were arrested and threatened with expulsion from the university. Unfortunately for the authorities, two of those arrested, members of extreme left-wing groups, had been away during the 'scandal', and this attempt to discredit the Left merely served to spread the struggle to universities throughout France.

As a result, the restrictive hostel rules were repealed on 5 December in Clermont-Ferrand, on 21 December in Nantes, and by 14 February 1968 in most other residential universities.

The Boycott at Nantes

The fight at Nantes, in particular, revealed that the Rector is just another part in the repressive state machinery: when the students assembled outside his office on 14 February, his only answer was to call in the police, who immediately set about the student leaders. By behaving in this way, the Rector played directly into the students' hands: he demonstrated that the university was not only a dispensary of dead knowledge and routine information on a conveyor belt system — which most perceptive students knew anyway — but that it was ultimately prepared to use violent repression. And why? Simply because its only function is to condition students so that they will fit into the economic and social system, as mere puppets dancing to the tune of technocrats, of men busily organizing the misery of the underdeveloped countries and the affluence of the rest. And so disgusted were the students of Nantes when this point was at long last driven home to them that they decided to boycott their psychology lectures, on the grounds that though this discipline likes to call itself a science, it is simply another means of suppressing critical thought and individuality. The following rejection of contemporary psychology was plastered all over the walls of Nantes:

NOTICE

CONSIDERING

that psychology as such aims at the systematic subordination of individual behaviour to false social norms;

CONSIDERING

that psychology is increasingly being forced into the mould of American psycho-sociology, aimed at perfecting the system by conditioning the workers to consume more and more rubbish while acquiescing in economic exploitation;

CONSIDERING

that psycho-sociology is nothing but the justification of 'ideal' norms and a means of concealing the monstrous discrepancy between the ideal and the real;

CONSIDERING

that this type of psychology is being used on the one hand to subvert the workers' struggle and on the other hand is being disseminated by means of the universities, the professional classes, and the advertising media;

CONSIDERING

that many students have embraced psychology in ignorance of its true nature, and because they are seduced by its professional glamour;

CONSIDERING

that they have been deceived by a form of obscurantism hiding under a ridiculous pseudo-scientific cloak, and representing a vicious assault upon liberty;

CONSIDERING

that the total rejection of modern psychology is a reaffirmation of PERSONAL LIBERTY, of the INNOCENCE OF DESIRE, of the forgotten JOYS of CREATIVITY, PLAY, IRONY, and HAPPINESS ...

THE AGEN-UNEF* THEREFORE CALLS ON
ALL STUDENTS OF PSYCHOLOGY TO ABANDON
THEIR STUDIES.

This proclamation bore a remarkable resemblance to that of the 'rabid' students of Strasbourg. But the 'extremists' of Nantes refused to act as a closed group and called at all times for mass participation. Their agitation culminating in the occupation of the Rector's office, this was again copied by students throughout France.

But already people had begun to speak of Nanterre, and almost overnight this charming and ugly concrete annexe of Paris University, this 'model university' became a hotbed of dissent.

Agitation at Nanterre had become a semi-permanent feature of university life, difficult to describe to anyone who did not actually experi-

*The Nantes branch of U N E F.

ence it. Its chief purpose was to galvanize a conformist institution which, because of its fear of transformation, tried to protect itself by ideological and, when necessary, by physical repression. 'The university is traditionally a peaceful institution whose smooth working depends on the rejection of violence by all who attend it and on the collective acceptance of regulations' — so said the heads of the various faculties at Nanterre.

But, in fact, these regulations are simply means whereby the official dispensers of 'knowledge' consolidate their place in the hierarchy, and repel every attack on their own mediocrity.

The smooth running of a university presupposes acquiesence in its ideology and structure, i.e. acceptance of the part it plays in churning out trained recruits for the ruling class. But while the smug administrators and reactionaries of tomorrow eke out their boring days on the campus, many students resent the futility of life in what is at best a middle class ghetto. The more revolutionary among them are particularly resentful of the fact that their voice counts for nothing among the real policy-makers. Hence the sporadic outbursts by different student organizations throughout the world.

The Protest Grows

This process has been greatly accelerated by the war in Vietnam, which struck many students and intellectuals as utterly scandalous, not only because it represents an attempt by the Americans to dictate to the rest of the world, but also because the 'socialist' bureaucracies are prepared to stand by and let it happen. At first, student protest against the war was spontaneous and disorganized but as the United States became more blatantly and unashamedly aggressive, the CVB (*Comité Vietnam de Base*) was formed and helped to consolidate student opinion at large. Soon afterwards, students began to take direct action against the representatives of U.S. imperialism in France and organized rallies in support of the Vietnamese, like the one on 7 February 1968. This showed that French students were no longer prepared to stop at mere verbal protest. Then came the Tet offensive and with it a growing sense of frustration. In Vietnam, a small peasant country was withstanding the aggression of the greatest military power on earth, and here were we, unable to do anything to help. As resentment and guilt mounted, more and more students threw themselves wholeheartedly into the Vietnamese campaign. Though there was much to criticize in the National Liberation Front and in the régime of North Vietnam and, for that matter in Castro's Cuba, the defiant and unshakeable resistance of ordinary Vietnamese and Cubans alike had proved that a super-organized and super-armed capitalist society is not invincible.

The hard facts were thrust under the noses of students: repressive societies can only be challenged by revolutionary means. The response was world-wide.

Tokyo: The students and the young workers in the Zengakuren refused to countenance government complicity in the imperialist aggression against Vietnam. Battles with the police prevented Japanese ports from being turned into major American bases.

Madrid: Students openly challenged Franco's Fascism in the universities. Faced with violent repression, they made common cause with workers' committees in the fight for a social revolution.

Rome: By violent clashes with the university authorities and the police, Italian students demonstrated their contempt for a university that does not challenge capitalist society. The result was complete paralysis of the university system.

Warsaw: Students made common cause with intellectuals in an open challenge of the ideological and political dictatorship of a bureaucratic party.

Berkeley — Columbia — New York: Students, sickened by the imperialist policies of their country, especially in Vietnam, showed their solidarity with the Vietnamese peasants and workers and with the oppressed racial and economic minorities in their own country. They made known their refusal to become privileged members of the American bourgeoisie.

Agitation at Nanterre

So much for the events outside France. In Nanterre, the first term of the 'historic' year of 1967/68 saw a student strike which went far beyond the traditional political and union framework. Some 10,000 to 12,000 of us boycotted all lectures in order to force the authorities to improve our working conditions. This 'model strike' as *Le Figaro* called it, was not, in effect, anything but a protest against overcrowding, which had been exacerbated by the recent Fouchet reforms and the consequent re-organization of lecture halls. As a result of this strike, a series of departmental commissions was set up but these proved completely unproductive because of the authoritarian approach of the professors involved.

Let us note in parentheses that the UNEF committee in Nanterre did little more than try to lead the strike once it was already in full swing. The refusal by the ultra-Leftists to acknowledge the authority of this so-called student union, moribund throughout the country and a complete farce in Nanterre, simply reflected our determination to reject all bureaucracy. And, indeed, in this we were entirely successful.

The second term brought a series of incidents, most of them the spontaneous expression of widespread student dissatisfaction. The 'Missoffe affair' during the opening of the swimming pool at the end of January 1968 will long be remembered, because this banal incident had wide repercussions. An exceedingly stupid minor police official (whom we salute in passing) started extradition proceedings against D. Cohn-Bendit, who had accused Missoffe, the Minister for Youth, of talking like a Hitler Youth. By way of retaliation, the students stuck up photographs of plain-clothes policemen mingling with members of the faculty, and also denounced the administration and the Dean as so many 'tools of the prefecture'. A convincing demonstration of solidarity and of protest against the proposed expulsion of Cohn-Bendit ended in scuffles with the riot police whom the Dean had called in. A short battle, in which students bombarded the police with anything handy, ended in victory: the police beat a hasty retreat. But the students had felt the iron fist under the liberal glove of the university.

In fact, M. Grappin, the Dean, was not the 'Nazi' people made him out to be but a 'good' man of the Left. Our struggle was not one against Fascism as such but against *bourgeois* authoritarianism. The mediocrity of university teaching is no accident, but reflects the life style of a civilization in which culture itself has become a marketable commodity and in which the absence of all critical faculties is the safest guarantee of 'profitable specialization of university studies'. The only way to oppose this type of stupidity is to attack all those academic restrictions whose only justification is that they exist: curricula; tests; set lectures and competitive entrance examinations.

Why Sociologists?

It was against this background that the events of 22 March 1968 must be viewed. Towards the middle of March, students in the department of social psychology, finding their courses too academic, decided to boycott the examinations and they sealed their decision by singing the Internationale. At the same time, a leaflet was distributed on the campus. It was called: 'Why do we need sociologists?'

'Students often ask themselves what jobs there are in sociology and psychology.

'The facts are clear to one and all: there are many more students of social science than there are jobs waiting outside, and this even after elimination by the examinations. The concern which students feel about their future goes hand in hand with the concern which they feel about the theoretical position taken up by their lecturers, whose constant appeals to science only emphasize the confusion of their various doctrines.

'Moreover, student agitation since 1960, abroad as in France, has been rife among sociologists far more than among other social scientists and philosophers. Students from other faculties have been remarkably passive. As a result, university and general social problems were aired in only one department, numerically weak and of fairly recent origin.

'The case was similar in the U.S.A., in France, in Germany, and also in Poland and in Czechoslovakia.

'Why was student dissatisfaction in all these countries expressed predominantly by social psychologists? Why did they act while the rest followed at a distance?

'Why this theoretical questioning and why so much anxiety about our future?

SHORT HISTORY OF SOCIAL PSYCHOLOGY

'We can only outline what a more detailed study will no doubt fill in one day. *Meanwhile students are invited to boycott all sociology lectures.*

'We must re-examine the whole problem in its historical perspective. The first important date is 1930 with research at the Mayo Foundation and at Hawthorne.

'In drawing attention to the importance of group psychology and by developing new methods of adapting the worker to the industrial machine and thereby increasing his output, Mayo did more than open new vistas to sociology — it put an end to speculation and inaugurated the glorious new era of empiricism and of scientific method.

'Similarly, by lending its services to business management, industrial psychology opened the way for large-scale collaboration with the world bourgeoisie, thus helping to underpin a system which was still shaking from the crash of 1929.

'*The transformation of academic sociology, a branch of philosophy, into an independent study with scientific pretensions, corresponds to the transformation of competitive capitalism into a state-controlled economy.*

'From that point, the new social psychology has increasingly been used by the bourgeoisie to help rationalize society without jeopardizing either profits or stability.

'The evidence is all around us. Industrial sociology is chiefly concerned with fitting the man to the job; the converse need to fit the job to the man is neglected. Sociologists are paid by the employers and must therefore work for the aims of our economic system: maximum production for maximum profit.

'Political sociology, with its opinion polls, initiates vast inquiries, whose results are misleading in that they suggest that electoral choices are the only valid ones. Stouffer has proposed methods of improving American army morale without any concern for the basic problem: the role of the army in modern society. Advertising sociologists develop thousands of ways of conditioning the consumer, once again ignoring the social function of this advertising.

'Moreover, in dealing with the class problem in the U.S.A., American sociologists have discarded the very concepts of classes and the class struggle, substituting the theory of a continuous scale of increasing status. They assume that each individual starts off with the same chance of reaching the top — for, after all, America is a democratic country!

'Quite apart from the theoretical refutations of Mills and D. Riesman, the practical refutation by the existence in America of a sub-proletariat (e.g. the Negroes and the ethnic minorities), and by the struggle of groups of industrial workers against their trade union machine, clearly dispels this dream of successful social integration.

'Quite recently, the American Negro Rebellion has created such a panic that Congress has voted extra subsidies for research into "the problem of the cities and the suppression of the forces of Revolt" (quoted in *Le Monde*).

'Last but not least, we should mention that, when the U.S. Secretary for Defence launched his "anti-subversive" campaign in Latin America (the famous Camelot plan) he could think of no better way of disguising his real intentions than calling it a sociological study project.

'So much for the United States. In France the rationalization of capitalism was ushered in with the advent of the postwar plans, but did not become a serious business until the rise of Gaullism with its authoritarian structures. Now it is not by chance that Sociology degrees were first introduced in 1958. The fact that French capitalism lags behind U.S. capitalism has necessarily had repercussions on the academic level. All modern French sociology is a belated import from across the Atlantic, and as everyone knows, the best training for a sociologist is to read all the American pamphlets and magazines.

SOCIOLOGICAL 'THEORY'

We have seen what close links there are between sociological theory and the social needs of the bourgeoisie. The practical organization of capitalism produces a host of contradictions, which various branches of sociology are expected to remove. Some are set to study juvenile delinquency, others racism, yet others slums.

Each group seeks solutions of its particular problem and leaves it at that, thus adding its bit to the jig-saw puzzle of "sociological theories".

The resulting confusion is reflected in the interdisciplinary fragmentation of the social sciences, so widespread today (cf. Althusser). The incomprehension of each specialist when confronted with the research of his fellows makes them collectively incapable of any general statement beyond mere platitude.

And underneath it all is the conveniently forgotten absence of theoretical framework common to sociology and the other human sciences. Social psychologists are agreed on only one point: the need to develop technical methods of social adaptation and re-adaptation and of resolving social conflicts. Just look at the concepts which are currently popular: hierarchy, ritual, adaptation, social function, social control, equilibrium, etc.

The "theorist" is expected to explain the nature of local conflicts removed from their social context, in which, alone, their cause can be understood.

This allegedly impartial procedure is, in fact, thoroughly partial and biased: phenomena are studied in isolation whereas in fact they are inter-related (e.g. racism, unemployment, delinquency and slums), and the rational nature of the present economic system is taken for granted. Since the word "profit" has lost its respectability, sociologists now speak of "growth". But how does this "growth" arise in the first place, *who* organizes it, *whom* does it profit? These questions are apparently too speculative to interest a "pure" science.

It follows that the disquiet of sociology students cannot be understood without looking at the relationship between sociology and society. In our day, sociologists have chosen their side: that of management and the State. What, in this case, is the point of defending sociology, as some have recommended us to do?'

This general analysis explains the particular case of Nanterre. Here, too, the general crisis in sociology, anxiety about jobs, anger about teaching methods and the importation of doctrines made in the USA., were the basis of student agitation. Those who remained outside the empiricist-positivist mainstream found themselves isolated and impotent.

The two great 'hopes' of French sociology are the jargon of Parsons (author of 'The place of ultimate values in sociological theory') and the cult of statistics (at least a bit of real science, this); these are the keys to every problem. In short, sociologists by a *tour de force* have succeeded in taking out the political sting from their doctrines, which is equivalent to sanctifying the status quo. Sociology professors like to pass for Leftists, in contrast to the heads of other departments who apparently still hanker after the good old times. While the latter try to cling to their crumbling ivory tower, sociologists welcome 'modernization': *planning, rationalization and production of consumer goods in accordance with the economic needs of organized capitalism.*

In this connexion, it is important to refute the ideas of Crozier *(Esprit,* January 1967) and Touraine (series of articles in *Le Monde),* two professors of sociology at Nanterre. According to Crozier, the troubles in America are not, as is naively believed, due to the violence of the blacks driven to desperation by their living conditions, nor to the horrors of the imperialist war in Vietnam (this 'accident', this piece of 'folly', as Crozier calls it). Such explanations, he claims, are magical rather than scientific. Nor are the troubles the result of the moral vacuum in American society, where cash is the only thing that counts. In fact, since violence has always taken place in the U.S.A., the only thing that is new in the present situation, according to Crozier, is the spread of rationalization, and the need for people to adjust to it. So the professor's U.S.A. is not the scene of a real struggle between social groups fighting for different material interests and socioeconomic priorities, but a sort of puppet show where Punch, representing Anarchy, tries to get the better of the Policeman, representing A Rational Society! This sociological 'analysis' would not be worth the trouble of a refutation, were it not for the practical advice which Crozier offers to the Negroes — not to seek power, but to change their attitude (sic!) and soon all will realize the great American dream of a country peopled with dynamic personalities.

Touraine, for his part, has put forward the following thesis: the function of the university is to foster knowledge in the service of growth (once again!) and in so doing it necessarily challenges old ideas and produces conflicts that are fruitful to both students and professors. In fulfilling its function of stimulating society the university thus parallels the 'healthy competition of nineteenth-century private enterprise'. Of course this analysis by Touraine is so much hot air. It is quite untrue to say, for instance, that 'knowledge and technical progress are the main-springs of the new society'. In fact, knowledge and technical progress come bottom of the list in order of importance — far below competi-tion for a lion's share in the profits (i.e. for a monopoly), or the military and economic confrontation between East and West. Sociologists are not the disinterested spectators they claim to be, nor is science a glori-ous pursuit that seeks nothing beyond pure knowledge. If our analysis has shown anything, it is that the modern university is not the place for solving social contradictions, which can only be removed by the trans-formation of that society in which the university plays an integral part.

Students and Society

There are 600,000 of us; sometimes treated as mere children, sometimes as adults. We work, but produce nothing. Often we have no money, but few of us are really poor. Although most of us come from the bour-geoisie, we do not always behave like them. The girls among us look like boys but are not sure whether they really want to be boys. We look upon our professors as part father, part boss and part teacher, and can't quite make up our minds about them. Some of us are destined to control the nation, others will become poorly paid intellectual hacks — but every one of us is privileged for all that. There are 600,000 of us — the so-called 'students' of the military academy at St Cyr, the artists and the 'arties', the technocrats of the faculty of political science (the École Nationale d'Administration), and the rigid Marxist 'intellectuals' of the Sorbonne, of Nanterre and elsewhere. We include followers of *L'Humanité* and 'militant' journals, assiduous readers of *Le Monde,* and devotees of the sporting press or the cinema, beatniks, crammers, spoilt rich kids who never graduate, girls who will marry during their first year, but meanwhile study law, languages and even psychology, dunces, duds, future mathematicians and doctors. How can one 'understand' modern students? Only by trying to understand their place in society.

A modern university has two contradictory roles. To begin with, a university must churn out the trained personnel that is so essential for bureaucratic capitalism. The system needs an ever increasing number of engineers, technicians, scientists, teachers, administrators and sociologists to organize production, to 'rationalize' industrial methods, to run the gigantic state machine, 'to adjust the psychology of individuals and groups' and to preserve their sanity, even to 'organize' leisure activities. Now, since the bourgeoisie itself cannot provide enough student material from among its own ranks, increasing numbers of bright lads are recruited from the lower middle classes and even the proletariat and the peasantry. The 'right-thinking' Left concentrates its fire on the class structure of French higher education, but stressing that only 6 per cent of the students are the sons of workers, when, in fact, they should be attacking the social function of the university: the production of a managerial élite. If some self-destructive fit should seize the bourgeoisie overnight and persuade it to recruit students exclusively from among the sons of manual workers, the university would become more democratic only in its composition. To the extent that the development of new manufacturing techniques is increasingly eliminating the need for unskilled labour, it is inevitable that pseudo-democratization by the recruitment of working class children to the universities will increase. In the past, the economic depression of the working and lower middle classes meant that sending one child, let alone several children, to the university, imposed an intolerable financial burden on the family, but higher wages and government grants now make it more and more possible. And what all the reformists — be they Communists, Social Democrats or left-wing Gaullists — really mean when they cry for the 'democratization' of the universities, is that this process be speeded up.

But in any case it is obvious that, as capitalism increases its demands for graduates, not only the prize pigs, but more and more horses, sheep, even chickens, will all be pressed into the sausage machine. Now this is precisely where the contradiction in the system lies. The production of the maximum number of graduate workers in the minimum time calls for increasingly closer contacts between the universities and industry, for the ever greater adaptation of education to specific industrial needs. But at the same time, the university is supposed to be the supreme guardian of 'culture', human reason and disinterested research, of unalloyed truth and objectivity. In brief, the university is supposed to be the temple and eternal repository of the spiritual values of society. Now if, for 'spiritual values' we read the 'ideology and values of the ruling class', we are left with the role the university has played from the Middle Ages down to the First World War. We might say that during this period the 'social' and 'cultural' role of the universities more or less overlapped. Society needed a relatively small number of lawyers, doctors, philosophers and professors, and chose them almost exclusively from among the sons of the ruling class. These enjoyed a humanistic and liberal education and were prepared to condone the most glaring social contradictions, while comforting themselves with the thought that the bourgeoisie was a champion of liberalization, democracy, universal education, etcetera. Later, a measure of petty bourgeois radicalism began to filter into the university, but was contained at a purely theoretical level: the crisis of society had not yet really occupied the academies.

Today, it is the economic rather than the theoretical role of the university which is predominant. This explains why the universities have been split up into a set of technical high schools, so many appendages to the major industries. But the system is internally inconsistent — it can only function by trying to suppress its own logic. The 'cultural' function of the university is constantly assailed and has constantly to be re-affirmed. After all, even an alienated society cannot allow itself to become alienated to the point of psychosis. Even a totalitarian society, with its determination to subjugate every part of life to the will of the ruling class, group or party, cannot in the long run afford to suppress scientific *objectivity*, and without it, would quickly perish. For the strictest utilitarian reasons, modern societies need fundamental and 'disinterested' research — because advances in applied technology depend on them. This the American bourgeoisie has come to realize more and more clearly.

Hence the basic problem of higher education is, then, that, while it cannot completely ignore the old humanistic values, since, after all, scientists and research workers must be produced, only the fragmentation of knowledge can supply all the faceless managers and technicians that are needed.

We have seen that the students are a socially heterogeneous group. They are also a transitory one, and their variety of social expectations increases their heterogeneity. Depending on his subject and the importance of his family connexions, a student may end up with a job worth 30,000 francs a month, and quite a few students want nothing better than that.

Their studies take from three to seven years. Hence while the younger students are still irresponsible adolescents, their older colleagues are men with a profession. Nor do these extremes always understand one another.

And yet it was these very students, the most heterogeneous of all social groups, who succeeded in banding together for collective political action, as witness their resistance to war in Algeria and the events of May 1968. The student movement was, in fact, the only 'hard' reaction against the war in Algeria, what with violent demonstrations, and constant propaganda campaigns during the later years. It was always given out that 'only a minority' participated in these student protests, but this minority represented at least 25 per cent of the French student population. As for the rest of the country, their protests remained largely verbal. The absence of organized protest outside of the universities can be laid squarely at the door of the Communist Party — it was both unwilling and unable to organize effective opposition to the war and support for the Algerian revolutionaries. Only towards the very end, did the Communist Party see fit to hold a few demonstrations, including the one at Charonne Métro Station (Paris) where eight people were killed by the police.

The remarkable phenomenon of student opposition was due to several factors, chief among them what so many people call sneeringly 'the revolt of modern youth'. Now this revolt, which involves ever larger numbers of young people throughout the world, must not be confused with the old 'conflict between the generations'. The latter, as we know it, particularly in earlier forms of bourgeois society, reflected the impatience of the young to step into the shoes of the old. This impatience often took the form of an attack on the fossilized thinking of the older generation and sometimes crystallized into a liberal, radical or a reformist attitude. In the current revolt of youth, however, very much more is being questioned — the distaste is for the system itself. Modern youth is not so much envious of, as disgusted with, the dead, empty lives of their parents. This feeling began among bourgeois children but has now spread through all levels of society. Daniel Mothé *(Socialisme ou Barbarie* No. 33) has shown clearly how opposed young workers are to both the 'values' that capitalist society has to offer them and also to working class values and traditional forms of organization (political parties and trade unions). Factory work, trade union 'militancy', verbose party programmes, and the sad, colourless life of their elders are subjects only for their sarcasm and contempt.

The same sort of disdain is the reason why so many students have taken a radical stand, and have made common cause with young workers in the struggle against a repressive society.

Another factor in the student revolt was their own position in the system and the special problems it brings to light.

A minority of students accept the culture which is being dispensed to them, and the knowledge which is being ladled out, with the trust of small children. They have been completely taken in by what we have called the mythical secondary function of the modern university as the temple of values. They dutifully attend all their lectures, and try above all to pass off as their own their professor's ideas; their ambitions stop short at the coveted degree, or perhaps to become, if they are worthy of it, professors themselves. However, this fraction of student opinion is fast dwindling away — for reasons we shall examine below. Another fraction can see through the system, but keep their eyes firmly on the main chance: they are the opportunists, only concerned with their professional future. They realize that much of what they are taught is false, or at least inadequate, they have no illusions about the purely utilitarian function of their education, know that they will be fitted to hold down a 'good' job, and are willing to accept the official bribes of privilege, a car, holidays abroad, money, a house in the country.

This section can always be mobilized in defence of the system. More often, however, they simply sit back and watch their more militant colleagues fight battles from which all students will benefit: for less overcrowding, better facilities, etcetera.

But for a third and constantly growing group, university life itself raises a series of fundamental questions. And once they start to analyse their own problems, the logic of their conclusions drives them on ultimately to reject the whole of contemporary society. This is because, as an essential part of the social system, the university necessarily contains all the contradictions, conflicts and paradoxes that characterize society itself.

We have said a university is supposed to be a seat of learning and rational inquiry. Now what young economist, for instance, can seriously believe in the rational character of the contemporary economic scene, whether planned or not? And only a few diehards among their teachers still pretend that the system is even capable of rationalization. How can an economist talk seriously about the rational distribution of goods in view of the glaring contradiction between the affluence of the highly industrialized countries and the misery of the Third World? How can a young industrial psychologist help being led to self-questioning when he sees that the object of his discipline is to 'fit the man to the job' and that the job itself is deadly and quite futile? How can a young physicist ignore the theoretical crisis that is shaking the very foundations of contemporary physics and with it all its claims to be an exact science; how can he tell himself that his research is of benefit to humanity, in an age which has produced the H-bomb? Can he really avoid wondering about his personal responsibility when the greatest atomic scientists themselves are beginning to question the function of science and its role in society?

And how can students of social psychology possibly shut their eyes to their professional role: to help in the sacred interest of profit, to break in more workers to the conveyor belt, or to launch yet another useless product on the market?

If these doubts about the value of one's studies are examined, inevitably the system which organizes it is brought into question as well. Subjects for courses are picked out of the hat; there is no logic in the curriculum, other than keeping research subservient to the demands of industry or, perhaps, the professor's next book.

These lectures reduce the student to the role of a listener; he is there to record, to remember, to reproduce in his exam the lecturer's threadbare arguments, opinions and style. The more opportunist a student is, the more he will try to ape his teacher's every word, in the certain knowledge that his final marks will be high. However, many students are becoming increasingly disgusted and sickened not only by this system but by the very culture that produces and fosters it.

There is one last element which should be mentioned in the students' situation: it is the explanation both of the relative ease with which they become involved in political activity and of the often superficial nature of this involvement.

The student, at least, in the modern system of higher education, still preserves a considerable degree of personal freedom, if he chooses to exercise it. He does not have to earn his own living, his studies do not occupy all his time and he has no foreman on his back. He rarely has a wife and children to feed. He can, if he so chooses, take extreme political positions without any personal danger; in general, he is not subjected to formal sanctions or even reprimands. Now, these very factors have an inbuilt inhibiting mechanism: they far too often cause his engagement to lack consistency and force.

However, when a minority of students takes conscious advantage of their freedom to attack the established order, they can become a catalyst activating a larger section of the student population. It is at this stage, and only at this stage, that the struggle becomes transformed qualitatively, and the university authorities feel compelled to call in the police.

The ensuing struggle is especially threatening to the authorities as the student population keeps going up by leaps and bounds. It constantly exceeds the official estimates (the Fourth Plan foresaw 500,000 students for 1971; there were already more than 600,000 by 1968). Pressure is continually increasing: the time-and-motion study boys have already got out their stop watches to calculate how long it takes to teach the Theory of Relativity. Most students will end up as managers and administrators, toiling away amid millions of other workers at their narrow little tasks, without any chance of deciding their place in society, their work, in short, the pattern of their lives. The so-called 'liberal' professions will become less and less liberal as the values on which they are ostensibly based are increasingly perverted by the State.

For all that, we are not so much protesting that our education is out of touch with the needs of the future, nor complaining about the shortage of jobs, we totally reject the entire system. Our protest only turns into violent action because the structure of society cannot be smashed by talk or ballot papers. To dream of turning the university into an 'island unto itself', where every man will be able to work in independence and peace, is in any case an empty dream because the future 'intellectual worker' will not be able to accept the fragmented and alienated life which this dream entails.

As a result, the student movement has become revolutionary and not simply a university protest. It does not rule out reforms (its actions, in fact, provoke them) but it tries beyond its immediate aims to elaborate a strategy that will radically change the whole of society. This strategy will carry the student movement through success and failure, through periods of open conflict and apparent inaction, but as every year passes, and the educational system shows ever more clearly its ideological loyalties and its repressive nature, the student will find himself as alienated from the society in which he lives as the lowest wage earner.

The 22 March Movement

On Friday, 22 March, following the arrest of six militants of the National Vietnam Committee, a crowd of students assembled quite spontaneously for a protest at Nanterre. At the end of the meeting, it was decided to occupy the administrative building. That evening, more than 150 students, of whom at least 50 per cent were politically uncommitted, met in the Staff Common Room and carried on a heated debate until two in the morning (The Union of Communist Students, naturally washed its hands of the whole affair). The results of the discussion were summarized in a statement, 5,000 copies of which were distributed the next day.

'ACTION AND REACTION

'Following a demonstration organized by the National Vietnam Committee, several demonstrators have been arrested in the street or in their homes, and charged with organizing attacks on American buildings in Paris. Once again we have come face to face with the usual police repression. After the invasion of Nanterre and Nantes by plain-clothes cops — *the black lists.*

'After the arrest and imprisonment of thirty workers and students in Caen;

'After continuous raids, searches and arrests of students inside the university, a further step — *the arrest of militants no longer stops with the end of demonstration, but is continued by house arrests.*

'For us this is no mere coincidence. The authorities have been driven into a corner; capitalism is badly in need of repair. To achieve this end, the ruling class has seen fit to tighten up the reins. It now:

– challenges the workers' right of association

– nibbles away at social security

– tries to run society like an army

– introduces psychosociological techniques into industry in a desperate attempt to play down class conflicts (some of us are being trained for this very task).

'CAPITALISM CAN NO LONGER CONCEAL ITS HAND

'*We must* stop challenging capitalism by means of *outdated* techniques.

'The Socialist Wilson has clamped down on England and now de Gaulle is clamping down on us. It is too late for the kind of peaceful procession organized by the SNESUP (University Teachers' Union) for next Thursday.

'We have to thrash out the problems inside the university and act right where we work.

'We call on you to transform the 29th into a vast debate on:

– *Capitalism in 1968 and the workers' struggles*
– *University and Anti-University*
– *The Anti-Imperialist Struggle*
– *The Workers' and Students' Struggle in the East and the West.*

'We shall accordingly occupy Block C and divide for discussions in the various lecture halls.

'As the authorities are becoming more and more brazenly brutal we are forced to become increasingly militant ourselves. We shall demonstrate our determination not to be cowed by holding a demonstration outside the Prefecture of *Hauts-de-Seine.*

'Resolution passed by 142 students, occupying the Administrative Block of Nanterre with 2 against and 3 abstentions.'

On reading this proclamation, the university authorities took fright and their fright turned into panic when, by way of preparing for the 29th, we plastered the walls with tracts, placards and slogans, some of which caused a real sensation.

'Professors, you are past it and so is your culture!'

'When examined, answer with questions!'

'Please leave the Communist Party as clean on leaving as you would like to find it on entering.'

The challenge of these slogans was one which forced people to take a stand. The authorities, no less than the Stalinists, were furious and tried to incite the staff of the faculty against the 'terrorist minority'. The library was closed in order to stop alleged thefts; there was a stay-in strike by the maintenance staff.

Under pressure from above, from neo-Fascist groups who had sworn to exterminate the revolutionary 'rabble', and from reactionary lectures, the Dean, on Thursday, 28 March, one week after the closure of the University of Warsaw, ordered the suspension of lectures and of laboratory work until the following Monday. Three hundred students assembled immediately after this announcement and decided not to leave but to spend the next day drafting a political manifesto to be published on 2 April. Having made up our minds to introduce politics into the campus, we were not going to retreat like a flock of frightened sheep at a bark from the sheepdog.

The weather helped us — the 29 March was a glorious and sunny day. A large police guard ringed the campus, while five hundred students divided into discussion groups on the lawn in front of the closed faculty doors. The gentlemen of the press were completely at a loss to understand what was going on; they had been led to expect a small band of anarchist bomb-throwers with long hair, and what they found instead was more than five hundred students seriously discussing the fundamental problems of our age.

On Monday, 1 April, second year sociology students decided, after a vote, to boycott their current examinations. Then they passed a resolution condemning sociology as a capitalist fraud. Meanwhile the professors themselves were at loggerheads, for while some (particularly in the Faculty of Letters and Social Science) were in favour of opening one of the lecture halls for political discussions, others (Faculty of History) wanted the 'ringleaders' arrested.

Tuesday, 2 April, was a great day for the students. We turned down the small room put at our disposal by the Dean and faced the administration with a *fait accompli*: we took over the large lecture theatre for our inaugural meeting, which was attended by more than 1,200 students including Karl-Dietrich Wolff representing the German SDS.

'On 22 March, when there were only 142 of them, they symbolically "took power" by occupying the lecture hall. After this event, which caused quite a stir, the authorities took a "liberal" decision: they officially allocated a lecture hall with four hundred seats to the students. But meanwhile the original 142 had swelled to more than a thousand and their ranks were still increasing.

The situation became explosive when the students continued to be barred from using the larger lecture theatre. Thus while pretending to be liberal, the authorities tried to constrict the movement, and merely succeeded in accelerating its growth ...' (Guy Michaud, Professor of French Literature at the Faculty of Nanterre in *Nouvel Observateur*, 15 May 1968).

The students' committees continued their deliberations for the whole of that day, and eight hundred of them and several assistant lecturers assembled in the evening to hear the various reports. After this they decided to publish a manifesto.

The Easter holidays intervened, but as soon as the university re-assembled in mid-April, the struggle was resumed. It all started with a meeting in support of the German student attack on the Springer trust, that mini-Fascist publishing empire whose newspapers were pulling the wool over the eyes of the German workers. At about the same time we heard that an attempt had been made on the life of Rudi Dutschke, the spokesman of German revolutionary youth.

The students immediately published a pamphlet in which they said, *inter alia*, that the Fascist who was arrested for shooting at Dutschke was surely not the only culprit. 'Directly responsible for this assassination are all those in Germany who for months have been carrying on a monstrous slander campaign against students fighting in support of the Vietnamese revolution. The German bourgeoisie is scared to death of this movement. It has done all it can to suppress it, and in particular to prevent three thousand young people from demonstrating in Berlin on 18 February for victory in Vietnam.'

Only too happy to see student agitation develop outside its own frontiers, the Gaullist authorities made the mistake of giving it extensive coverage, particularly on television. Thus Peyrefitte, the Minister of Education, declared over the air that the insignificant demonstrations at Nanterre were in no way comparable to the student troubles abroad. And this at the very time that five thousand French students were declaring their solidarity with the SDS and Rudi Dutschke!!

In fact, the action of the German students had repercussions far beyond the borders of the Federal Republic. One result was the '22 March Movement '– for the first time French students found a common platform and forgot their factional differences. They ceased hurling invective at one another, and tackled the serious business of building a common front, for testing their theories in practice. And when they did so, it immediately became clear to them that all the old verbiage had done was to impose fetters on their thinking rather than help serious discussion of actual political issues.

Meetings were held almost daily, committees were constantly in session, there were heated debates on the workers' and students' struggles. Our posters were the focus of attention throughout the university. Moreover, the boycott of the examinations became an increasingly important issue. It was talked about everywhere; discussed, explained, and its chances of success evaluated. We felt that the examinations were simply a means of perpetuating a system of selecting new captains of industry and that it was our duty to reject the degree, that badge of holy office in the hierarchy.

On 2 April, we decided to set aside 2 and 3 May for the study of imperialism, with special film shows, discussions in committee and in general assembly, etc. But it did not work out like that. Threatened by an attack from such semi-Fascist groups as *Occident,* we had instead to see to our defences, and arm ourselves with stones and other improvised weapons.

Panic-stricken, misinformed and above all under pressure from some of the professors, the Dean ordered Nanterre to be closed once again. Moreover, seven of the most militant students of the 22 March Movement together with a prominent member of the Trotskyist Federation of Revolutionary Students were ordered to appear on the following Monday, 6 May, before a disciplinary board at the Sorbonne. We decided to go along to the hearing *en masse,* and called on all students to assemble on that Monday at 9 o'clock to march on the Sorbonne.

By their disciplinary action the university administration had hoped to strike our movement a fatal blow. They had calculated that student agitation must surely subside in the third term, what with the crucial examinations only four weeks away. As the Rector himself put it on 9 May:

> 'The systematic disturbances brought about by a small gang of students who have been trying, on their own admission, for some time to paralyze our lectures, and now threaten to stop the examinations, have forced us to take strong measures. We intend to preserve the freedom of all to sit for their examinations in

order that the vast majority of students can derive legitimate recognition for their work.'

Now, at the time, the politically conscious students were, in fact, still a minority, and they knew it. Hence they never set themselves up as champions of the 'common interest of all students', but simply demanded the right to express political opinions within the campus and without police interference. They realized full well that the main body of students were far more interested in furthering their careers than in social justice.

It was because of this that the Communist Party has accused us of despising the students. In fact, we only despise the sons of the bourgeoisie who, not only content with belonging to a privileged class, clamour for its privileges and are ready to defend them. Students differ in their political opinions as in everything else. Moreover, they are not a class, and they have no objective interests to defend. In a truly democratic society, higher education will be open to all, and students will cease to be a group apart. We do not, therefore, despise students as such but only those who applaud the men with the whip, who move in against every revolution.

But let us return to the events themselves. It was the action of the authorities that opened the eyes of many previously uncommitted students. Our 'provocation' daily brought the latent authoritarianism of the bureaucracy into the open. As soon as any real problems were brought up, dialogue gave place to the policeman's baton: in Berkeley and Berlin no less than in Paris. The pathetic excuses put forward by the university dignitaries, who thought every pussy cat was a tiger, have left many a liberal observer perplexed.

'Was it really necessary, on account of a handful of trouble-makers, to suspend all lectures in two faculties? It seems that the authorities lacked sang-froid. It is certainly true that small groups of the extreme Left, or at least several among them, have turned provocation into a weapon of war. Loving absolute truths and even more the fear they arouse in the "bourgeoisie", they claim that examinations help to perpetuate an archaic and meaningless system of education. But do we really have to take them so seriously?' (B. Girod de l'Ain in *Le Monde,* 6 May 1968.)

If we ignore the paternalistic tone of this and similar articles in the liberal press, we must admit that there is a great deal of truth in them. In reality, everything hangs on the use of provocation in the crystallization of thought and latent emotion. Provocation is not a 'weapon of war' except in special circumstances. It can only be used to arouse feelings that are already present, albeit submerged. In our case we exploited student insecurity and disgust with life in an alienated world where human relationships are so much merchandise to be used, bought and sold in the market place. All we did therefore was to 'provoke' students to express their passive discontent, first by demonstrations for their own sake, and then by political actions directly challenging modern society. The justification for this type of provocation is its ability to arouse people who have been crushed under the weight of repression. Now, to speak of 'repression' in the case of an institution such as a university which has no physical means of repression may seem ridiculous. But repression lies in the very function of that institution, in its blinding of the student to the fact that he is daily being spoon-fed with poisonous rubbish. Most students, as we saw, are willing to swallow it all, for the sake of a privileged position in the future, and because they believe that a rigid hierarchy is necessary for the efficient functioning of society. As a result, they lose all real desire, every ounce of creative spirit, all expression of life. The use of provocation is to drive this point home to them and to show how empty their lives have become.

We show them first of all that the petty hostel regulations are an impertinent infringement of their personal liberty, that learning is no substitute for the warmth of human companionship. In learning to question these regulations, the student is forced to explore repression in general and the forms it takes in the modern world. Open physical repression with the point of a bayonet, as it was seen in the nineteenth century, is now reserved strictly for the suppression of the Third World. A complex and sophisticated industrial bureaucracy cannot function efficiently with a resentful proletariat. What it needs is apathy — just this apathy against which we are agitating. If we in the universities can show factory workers how authoritarianism and the official hierarchy can be overthrown in our own institutions, they will not be slow in applying similar methods to theirs. Hence the panic of the authorities — they do not mind criticism, however radical, but they cannot afford to let us express our disgust in action. Our threat is that we offer students real liberty by overthrowing, not only in theory, but in practice, the class-based university system. We do this by our boycott of lectures dispensing 'pure' and 'objective' knowledge and, worst of all, by our determination to carry the debate from the lecture hall into the streets and the factories. Our first task is to make the students themselves more politically conscious. In practice, this means developing new ways of communication: improvising meetings in the various faculty common rooms, occupying lecture halls, interrupting lectures with denunciations of their ideological basis, boycotting the examinations, sticking up posters and slogans, taking over the public address system — in short taking any action that openly challenges the authorities.

The university bureaucracy cannot really cope with student power. True, it made an attempt to let the movement run its course for a while, but soon afterwards Rector Roche or, rather, the government felt impelled to take a strong line.

Following our distribution of a pamphlet calling for the boycott of examinations, the Dean put out the following notice: 'The Dean and Professors of the Faculty of Letters of Paris would like to remind students that the examinations (May and October) will take place on the usual days, and state categorically that no supplementary arrangements can be made under any circumstances.'

The Dean, moreover, proscribed the distribution of our pamphlet which said, among other things:

'In the present circumstances ... any attempt to test the qualifications of students by competitive exams is little more than a sham. All candidates ought therefore to be considered as having passed the examinations.'

Monday, 6 May, was the official day for the competitive examinations. It is at this point that the Rector's 'lack of sang-froid' seems to have degenerated into complete panic. Instead of proceeding with his 'sacrosanct examinations', he decided to close the Sorbonne and to put it under the protection of the police.

Part of the explanation for his actions was that, whereas the most militant students were at the Sorbonne, the vast majority of 'good' students were at home feverishly preparing for their examinations, so that this seemed a golden opportunity for crushing the enemy's 'shock troops'. How badly he miscalculated was shown by subsequent events.

The Battle of the Streets

Paris had known many recent demonstrations at the Place de la Bastille and Place de la République — some for higher wages, others against American aggression in North Vietnam. The authorities knew the strategy of the traditional Left and felt confident that, if they could deal with militant workers, they would have little trouble with a lot of 'mere children'.

The police were in full control of the streets, and the political battles were being safely fought in the ministries, and in parliamentary committees. Hence it seemed a very simple matter to send the forces of law and order into the Sorbonne, occupy all the faculties and arrest four hundred students. Emerging from their libraries, from their lectures or simply strolling back to college along the Latin Quarter, students suddenly found themselves face to face with riot police (CRS) blocking the gates of the Sorbonne. Their reply was immediate, spontaneous and quite unequivocal, and it was not even the students with the strongest political convictions who were the first to explode. Suddenly the walls were covered with such slogans as 'Stop the repression', 'CRS = SS', while the ranks of demonstrators swelled to unprecedented proportions. All hell broke loose when the first police vans left the Sorbonne filled with students being taken off for questioning.

'In the Latin Quarter at about 6 p.m., violent incidents occurred as students joined battle with police contingents' *(Le Monde,* 5–6 May 1968).

All night, special police squads poured into the district, every civilian was stopped, and anyone who even vaguely resembled a student was clubbed down mercilessly. More than one passerby who had nothing whatever to do with the demonstration spent an uncomfortable night in the police cells.

Hence the 'riotous scenes' everyone talked about that night. What was so remarkable about the events of 3 May was the spontaneity of the resistance — a clear sign that our movement does not need leaders to direct it; that it can perfectly well express itself without the help of a 'vanguard'. It was this day that really mobilized student opinion; the first great ripple of a swelling tide. And not unexpectedly, the Communist students, bound to their party, like Oedipus to his fate, did their utmost to stem that tide:

'Irresponsible Leftists use the pretext of government inefficiency and student unrest in order to subvert the work of the faculties and to impede the mass of students from sitting for their examinations. These false revolutionaries behave, objectively, as allies of the Gaullist authorities and represent a policy that is objectionable to the majority of students, above all to the sons and daughters of the working class.' Clearly the Communists would do anything rather than try and understand the real issues.

I have said that the events of the day brought about an awakening of political awareness in many students. Take this eye-witness account published in the June issue of *L'Evénement*:

"Are you a member of the 22 March Movement?" they asked me.

'I was still a little embarrassed, the speakers had talked of Marx and someone called Marcuse, of whom I had never even heard. The first time they mentioned that name I asked them to spell it for me. I looked him up in Larousse, but I could not find him there.

'I was told: "The movement has proved its strength by boycotting the examinations." But to boycott partial examinations is something anyone can do — you can always sit them again. And in any case, I was quite happy to give mine a miss for personal reasons. And then one day, quite suddenly, I felt like jumping on to the platform and shouting: "I have been an imbecile. I always thought that personal revolt was the only way of telling the authorities to go and jump in the lake. But you have shown me that we can all stick together in Nanterre, that we need no longer be alone, and that no one has to wield the big stick to make us act in unison."

'There were no membership cards, no followers and no leaders. From then on everything went like greased lightning. Meetings, leaflets, and then we went out among the workers in Nanterre ...'

The unwelcome presence of the police on the campus gained the students the support of the University Teachers' Association (SNESUP), and also of four professors in Nanterre: Messrs. Lefèvre, Michaud, Touraine and Ricœur, who declared themselves willing to undertake the defence of those students who had been summoned to appear before the Disciplinary Committee in the Sorbonne on the following Monday. Their moral support took the press completely by surprise and did much to gain the students fresh sympathizers.

On Saturday, 4 May, the police swooped again, and on Sunday, 5 May, an emergency court sent six student demonstrators to gaol. Proclamations in the press and over the radio then made it known that the demonstrations in support of the condemned students which had been called for Monday at 9 o'clock were officially banned.

'On Monday, Paris saw its most impressive and threatening demonstration for many years. Even during the Algerian war there has never been a movement of such breadth and above all of such staying power.' *Le Monde,* 8 May 1968.

'We cannot allow those who are openly opposed to the university to seize that institution. We cannot tolerate violence in the streets, for violence is no way of starting any kind of dialogue.' Charles de Gaulle, 7 May 1968.

Many people have asked themselves how it was possible that so vast a movement should have erupted from what was apparently so unimportant an event as the closure of a university and the intervention of the police in student affairs. It is therefore important to explain how a relatively small number of students succeeded in broadening the struggle against police repression to such an extent that it culminated in the occupation of the universities and the total rejection of its function in capitalist society. Learning through action plays a basic part in the genesis and growth of all revolutionary movements. From analyzing what is closest at hand, we can come to understand society at large.

The complexity of modern life and the frustration it brings in its wake are such that we are forced most of the time to submerge our deepest aspirations. Students, who have to swallow humiliation every day, are particularly subject to these frustrations, and so react all the more violently once they are aroused. Lull them with sweet promises about the future and they may be prepared to put up with petty restrictions, false values, hypocritical doctrines and the lot, but bring out the police against them and you will find that you have stirred up a hornets' nest. The students started demonstrating at 9 a.m. and by the time they dispersed fourteen hours later, a mere trickle had swelled into a torrent, and 'barricades' had sprung up in the streets. The students' determination, and above all their willingness to take on the police, were truly astonishing. They asserted their right to enter their own university, and to run it themselves for the benefit of all. The almost continuous confrontation with the police merely hardened their determination not to go back on their first claims: the release of all the imprisoned demonstrators, withdrawal of the police and re-opening of the faculties. I must add in parentheses that during the 'Long March' of 7 May, and during the demonstrations at the university annexe at the Halle aux vins, the various factions of the Left tried desperately to insinuate their own marshals in the vain hope of taking control. There were some 35,000 demonstrators present in the Champs Elysées alone and — *mirabile dictu* — they managed without any leaders at all. Unfortunately, the bureaucratic officials of UNEF, that moribund Student Union, who had been frustrated in their earlier attempts to take over the movement, now called in the help of the trade union bureaucrats who, at the Halle aux vins and in the demonstrations that followed, were able to divert the movement away from its original aim: the recapture of the Sorbonne. I do not want to pass an opinion on the strategic and tactical possibilities of capturing the Sorbonne at this point, but merely to show that all hierarchical and bureaucratic organizations must necessarily pervert all activities in which they participate to their own ends. Thus Alain Geismar explained to the General Assembly of the 22 March Movement on 8 May how trade union officials had used every trick in the book to force the student movement to opt for a programme that would divert the struggle into purely reformist channels. In this they were greatly helped by Communist students and lecturers, who played a particularly treacherous part on 8 May at the Place du Luxembourg, when they called upon the students to disperse. This might well have spelled the end of the movement, long before it had a chance to express its real demands: the overthrow of repressive society. Luckily the revolutionary students were not taken in; they realized that they themselves had the power to beat repression, even in the face of Communist Party and other bureaucratic obstruction. Indeed, UNEF, by launching appeals to 'reason' and issuing communiqués through the press, merely mobilized an ever larger number of demonstrators. And so when Roche announced he would re-open the Sorbonne under police protection, the students replied with an improvised 'teach-out', assembled in their thousands and completely stopped the traffic in the Boulevard St Michel. This teach-out was the first attempt to turn the Latin Quarter into a 'public forum'. Those responsible for the dispersal of the students in the Place du Luxembourg during the previous night were severely taken to task and asked to explain their actions. Direct democracy was being put into effect — under the very noses of the police. All the political and strategic problems of the past few days were brought up for discussion and thrashed out, not least among them the role of the university of the future. As the students stood talking they were joined by scores of passers-by, among them Louis Aragon, that venerable bard and prophet of the Communist Party, the man who had sung paeans of praise to OGPU and Stalinism, and who had come to take his place among those who 'remind me so movingly of my own youth'. A group of students recognized him and greeted him with cries of 'Long live OGPU! Long live Stalin, the father of all the people!'

The Aragon episode, in itself banal and without political importance, nevertheless shows how politically aware the young demonstrators had become. They would have no truck with members of a party whose official organ, *L'Humanité* had launched what could only be called a smear campaign against French youth. The revolutionary movement did not deny the importance, and even the necessity, of a dialogue with the rank and file of the Communist Party, but it did try to unmask the opportunist strategy and counter-revolutionary attitude of its leaders, including Louis Aragon, the poet laureate of the personality cult. He could not make himself heard simply because those participating in the 'teach-out' knew that he had nothing in common with them. His bold assertion that he was in the Party 'precisely because he was on the side of youth' merely turned him into a laughing-stock. By refusing to act honestly for once in his life, and to denounce the machinations of his Party, he threw away his chance to join the student movement, and incidentally saved his leaders a great deal of embarrassment.

Luckily the dialectic of events did not have to wait on an Aragon: we knew that the issue would be decided by the demonstrations called for next day and not by some Party demagogue or other. The people were clearly sympathetic, the National Assembly was divided, and we saw our chance to prove that the power of General de Gaulle would collapse like a house of cards if we went about it the right way. And here the police force itself came to our aid: by barring the route we had planned to take, they forced us into the Latin Quarter. Once there, we were determined not to disperse until all our demands had been met. And so we found ourselves drawn up in front of the CRS, facing their clubs, 30,000 of us standing united and ready for action, but with no definite plan. No one seriously envisaged attacking the Sorbonne, no one wanted a massacre. All we knew was that we had to defend ourselves where we stood; we split up into small groups, so that the police services were unable to launch a single, directed attack. Every barricade became a centre of action and of discussion, every group of demonstrators a squad acting on its own initiative. Barricades sprang up everywhere; no one felt the lack of a general in charge of overall strategy; messengers kept everyone informed of what was happening on the other barricades and passed on collective decisions for discussion. In our new-found solidarity our spirits began to soar. For the first time in living memory, young workers, young students, apprentices and high school pupils were acting in unison. We could not guess what turn the events were going to take, but that did not bother us — all that mattered was that, at long last, we were all united in action. The Gaullist régime proved completely helpless in the face of this youthful demonstration of strength, and this was only a beginning! None of the lies that have been told since, nor yet the final sell-out by the CGT, can detract from this achievement. In a society which seeks to crush the individual, forcing him to swallow the same lies, a deep feeling of collective strength had surged up and people refused to be browbeaten. We were no longer thousands of little atoms squashed together but a solid mass of determined individuals. We who had known the nagging ache of frustration were not afraid of physical hurt. This 'rashness of youth' did not spring from despair, the cynicism of impotence, but on the contrary from the discovery of our collective strength. It was this feeling of strength and unity which reigned on the barricades. In such moments of collective enthusiasm, when everything seems possible, nothing could be more natural and simple than a warm relationship between all demonstrators and quite particularly between the boys and the girls. Everything was easy and uncomplicated. The barricades were no longer simply a means of self-defence, they became a symbol of individual liberty. This is why the night of 10 May can never be forgotten by those who were 'there'. For bourgeois historians the barricades will doubtless become symbols of senseless violence, but for the students themselves they represented a turning point that should have its place among the great moments of history. The memory of the raids, the gas grenades, the wounds and the injuries will surely remain, but we will also remember that night for the exemplary bravery of the '*commu-*

nards' or '*sans culottes*' of the rue Gay-Lussac, of young men and women who opened a new and cleaner page in the history of France.

So great was their impact, in fact, that the trade unions and parties of the Left were forced, willy nilly, to call a general strike for 13 May 1968, in an attempt to take the political sting out of the student movement. But, having demonstrated their solidarity with the working class throughout the day, the students did not meekly disperse — that very night they took the Sorbonne. Students were suddenly freed from their intellectual imprisonment, and communication, discussion, explanation were, all at once, easy and meaningful. The Sorbonne became a spectacular focus of intellectual liberation, and one that, unlike the Liberation of 1945, refused to be gagged by the authorities. Moreover, something quite unprecedented had happened: the science faculties had declared their solidarity with the revolutionary students and joined in the general debate. Now, unlike Nanterre, the Faculty of Science (36,000 students) had never been a centre of protest, though students there, too, had been perturbed when Dean Zamansky proposed to introduce a more competitive system, and when the Fouchet reforms threatened to make the curriculum even more arduous than it already was. Still, their reaction had always been limited to pressing for purely internal reforms. Since 3 May, however, lectures had been cancelled in a few departments at the direction of some of the more decent professors, including Professor Monod, the Nobel Prize winner, in protest against the police brutalities. The students used the opportunity for holding meetings with their teachers, many of which were attended by more than 600 people. It must be said that these discussions dealt primarily with the problem of the examinations which were to begin on 15 May, but they very quickly ran on to questions of general policy. In other departments run by reactionary professors, attempts were made to continue the normal lectures, but students kept interrupting the lecturers and provoked discussions to be pursued elsewhere. While, previously, it had been impossible to fill a lecture hall for a serious debate of any kind, and anyone who spoke of politics, capitalism, etcetera was whistled at, the majority of students now listened and participated even if only to express their opposition to the movement.

On 10 May, a strike committee consisting of a few dozen students met and decided to take over the entire science faculty, and to stop all the official lectures that were still going on. The committee was formed quite spontaneously, and grew rapidly in strength, while most of the official political organizations stood to one side or even put up obstructions.

After the night at the barricades, members of SNESUP formed a strike committee of their own, which quickly fused with the students' committee.

The following parallel 'lines of power' now existed within the university: (1) laboratory committees answerable to the laboratory staff; (2) general student committees charged with carrying out decisions taken by a general assembly in the lecture theatres and answerable to the assembly; (3) staff committees made up chiefly of lecturers but also including several professors; (4) the strike committee; (5) the provisional commission comprising student and teachers' delegates (the Dean himself appointed a number of professors to sit on this commission) and (6) the regular university authorities. All these powers more or less co-existed as the movement grew, and there was little the Dean or his friends could do about it. It was not a coincidence that, after the speech by de Gaulle on 30 May, the attitude of the reactionary professors hardened, and they refused to continue to serve on the commission.

This decision helped to cement the unity between the remaining students, research assistants and assistant lecturers, who in their place elected new members to the commission. The entry of the police into the faculty is probably not unrelated to this new situation.

The strike committee also decided to follow the example of other faculties and set up a 'summer university'. The more radical members felt that this university should be open to all, and that workers in particular should be invited to attend. A Central Bureau of the Summer University was elected and given the task of (a) developing new teaching methods; (b) running political seminars, and (c) organizing art exhibitions, cinema shows, book sales, etcetera.

The creation of the summer university, which tried to bring knowledge down to earth from its academic ivory tower, was, without doubt, one of the greatest achievements of the student movement. But it proved extremely difficult to arrange, the more so as the strike committee had to waste most of its energy on keeping the lecture rooms open in the face of increasing pressure by the authorities. It goes without saying that the government could not let things like this continue in Gaullist France for long, and one of the first policemen who invaded the faculty on 5 July admitted quite frankly that his job was to 'put a stop to all this nonsense'. In any case, the summer university provided concrete proof of the movement's strength of purpose: the official hierarchy was simply ignored and replaced by collective effort, in accordance with the needs and wishes of the students. Undergraduates in the science faculty had been much slower to question the value of their studies than those from other departments, but once they began to ask the right questions, they were inexorably led to a radical critique of the aims and objects of modern science. And since this inquiry went hand in hand with an attempt to open the university to the people, it also forced them to question the entire social system and to make common cause with the working class. This must have been the real 'danger' the authorities referred to when they attacked the students for occupying the university.

Not a train was running on the main lines or underground, not a letter, not a telegram could be sent, not a car or a ton of coal was being produced, workers in every industry, from every branch of the state, had joined the students. Even the football clubs were taken over by their players! Just as the strike itself came about spontaneously, without specific grievances, in the wake of the student revolt, so, now, new forms of organization of society were being discussed everywhere. Passionate and entirely novel ideas were being mooted throughout France.

It was at Charlety Stadium on Monday, 27 May, that Barjonet, recently resigned from the CGT, openly confessed that a revolution was possible after all. Barjonet only expressed what hundreds of other trade union militants had suddenly come to realize.

Perhaps the most concrete expression of this new sense of purpose was the occupation of the Sud-Aviation works in Nantes. The workers, by 'imitating the students', were rediscovering a form of action that they had far too long discarded while playing the parliamentary game of the reformists and Stalinists. The applied psychoanalysis of the revolutionary students was clearly bringing on a general cure; on 20 May, even the most apathetic joined in, the Citröen works were occupied and a host of others followed suit soon afterwards.

Recourse to direct action changed the whole tenor of the struggle, for the workers' self-confidence is enormously increased once they act without delegating any of their power to political parties or trade unions. 'The factory is ours, so do we need to start working for the bosses again?' This idea arose quite spontaneously, not by command, or under the aegis of the so-called vanguard of the proletariat, but simply as a *natural response to a concrete situation.*

Discussions took place everywhere — there was hardly a factory where the question of 'workers' control' was not raised and debated, so much so that, on Tuesday, 21 May, Seguy, speaking officially for the CGT, felt impelled to inform a press conference that 'self-management is a hollow formula; what the workers really want is immediate satisfaction of their claims'.

The revolution burst the old dams, its force took the entire world by surprise, and, of course, no one more so than the French authorities and bureaucracy of the CGT. The CGT realized that it was no longer sufficient to fight Leftism with invective in *L'Humanité* and a bit of character assassination in the factories. It had somehow to intervene on the shop floor if it was to stop the rot. And in this field the CGT was a past master — it had played the same part in 1936 and 1945 and, in a smaller way, in daily practice.

On 22 May, the government, in a desperate attempt to quieten things down, voted a general amnesty. But if they hoped to stop the movement in that way, they were badly mistaken. The movement was no longer restricted to the students, it had assumed wider proportions.

During this period everything was still possible, authority no longer existed except as a threat, and even part of the professional army was known to be sympathetic to the strikers. Moreover, the government no longer enjoyed the confidence of the public and finally it could not count on enough genuine, sick Fascists to carry out a counter-revolutionary coup.

The various police forces were dispersed in the streets, in the factories and even in the fields, since even the peasants had begun talking socialism and revolution. As a result, the police stations were unmanned and the administration left to its own, diminishing, devices. At this moment, I repeat, everything was still possible.

It was against this background that de Gaulle delivered his speech on 24 May. After blackmailing us with the threat of civil war (by whom against whom?) the Head of State graciously gave us permission to vote for a new set of laws and to give him a new mandate.

This generous offer fell spectacularly flat. Moreover, two hundred thousand peasants downed tools in various parts of France, blocking the roads and organizing mass meetings.

Then came the night of the 24th, which could have spelled the end of de Gaulle, but merely revealed a lack of political awareness among the masses and the narrowness of outlook of the different left-wing splinter groups who, instead of making common cause, tried to bend the situation to their own petty ends.

That day the CGT organized two marches in support of the strikers in different parts of Paris. These marches were restrained and highly organized — they were meant to pass off 'in calm and dignity' and not to provoke the police. The whole idea was out of touch with the spirit of the more militant workers, and also with the advanced stage we had reached in our struggle: we were on the brink of overthrowing the government, and felt no need for appeasement.

And so we decided to let the procession take their peaceful course, while we ourselves would spill out of the Latin Quarter and plant the banner of revolution over the rest of Paris. Unfortunately the way we of the 22 March Movement saw things was not the way the other student groups saw them. UNEF and PSU (United Socialist Party) were opposed to the whole idea, while the Trotskyists felt that no final push could be made before a revolutionary party was ready to step into the shoes of the bourgeoisie. As far as they were concerned we were simply a 'band of irresponsible adventurists'.

Nevertheless, they joined our appeal for a massed assembly at the Gare de Lyons. With the help of scores of action committees, in which high-school pupils played an important part, we organized five assembly points from which we would converge at 5 p.m. on the Gare de Lyons.

During the day, we got the Action Committees to distribute the following pamphlet:

Toilers, it is time we looked after ourselves! To ten million strikers! To all workers!

– No to all parliamentary solutions! De Gaulle may go but the bosses will stay!

– No to negotiations which only prop up capitalism!

– Enough referendums, no more circuses!

No one can speak for us. We ourselves must remain masters of our factories! The struggle must go on! The factories must support all those who are now engaged in battle.

This is the time to plan our rule of tomorrow –

Direct supplies of food, organization of public services, transport, information, housing, etcetera.

In the street, in the committees, wherever you may be! Workers! Peasants! Students! Teachers! Schoolboys! Let us organize and coordinate our struggle: For the abolition of Bosses! All power to the Workers!

The campaign had been launched. The CGT demonstration in the afternoon collected more than 200,000 workers, that of the 22 March Movement and the Action Committees started with far less but very quickly grew in number, for as we marched through the various quarters, the people fell in behind us. At the Place de la Bastille and elsewhere, many from the CGT demonstration who had refused to disperse joined us as well. In the end, more than 100,000 people assembled at the Gare de Lyons, while several thousand others were demonstrating in other parts of Paris. The atmosphere was electric. We then marched on the Stock Exchange as we had planned (the Hôtel de ville, another objective, was too well defended by the CRS and the army), captured it with remarkable ease and set it on fire. Paris was in the hands of the demonstrators, the Revolution had started in earnest! The police could not possibly guard all the public buildings and all the strategic points: the Elysée, the Hôtel de ville, the bridges, the ORTF (the French Broadcasting Service).... Everyone felt it and wanted to go on. But then the political boys stepped in. It was a leader of the far-left JCR (Revolutionary Communist Youth) who, in the Place de l'Opéra, took charge and turned us back towards the Latin Quarter — when most of us thought we had done with the fatal attraction of the Sorbonne. It was officers of UNEF and PSU who stopped us taking the Ministry of Finance and the Ministry of Justice. These 'revolutionaries' were quite incapable of grasping the potential of a movement that had left them far behind and was still gaining momentum. As for us, we failed to realize how easy it would have been to sweep all these nobodies away. We should never have allowed them to divert us, should have occupied the Ministries and public buildings, not to put in a new lot of 'revolutionary' bureaucrats, but to smash the entire state apparatus, to show the people how well they could get on without it, and how the whole of society had to be reconstructed afresh on the basis of workers' control.

It is now clear that if, on 25 May, Paris had woken to find the most important Ministries occupied, Gaullism would have caved in at once

— the more so as similar actions would have taken place all over the country.

It has been said, and rightly so, that for the first time in history a revolution could have been made without recourse to arms. And people have pointed out that one of the first steps we should have taken, and failed to take, was to capture the radio stations.

Even if the ORTF in Paris was well guarded, the authorities could not have defended or re-occupied the radio stations of Lille, Strasbourg, Nantes, Limoges and elsewhere.

It is clear that control of the communications media is of vital importance in any revolution: thus when one station announced a demonstration at 3 p.m., 20,000 people gathered in the appointed place two hours later. The broadcasting of newsflashes direct from the 'barricade units' was responsible for much of the cohesion of our forces. Moreover, the authorities realized this danger and, from the next day, the 24th, forbade any live broadcasting of news, only to re-authorize it again during the Gaullist demonstrations.

Here is a point to remember for the future and one that we will be sure to take care of.

When the 24 May drew to a close, a revolution was still in the cards — nothing seemed settled either way. But by the 25th, our failure to take the Ministries enabled the state and the trade union bureaucrats to rally from the blows they had been dealt the night before.

Pompidou declared that henceforth demonstrations would be more energetically dispersed. At 3 o'clock, representatives of the State, the employers and the trade unions met at the Ministry of Social Affairs in the rue de Grenelle, to thrash out what became known as the Grenelle Agreement. Those present knew full well that the alarm had been sounded and that it would take very little more for everything they held dear to be swept away — hence the speed with which they struck their bargain (guaranteed minimum wage, trade union rights, improved social security benefits, etcetera).

The political top brass, too, came out of hiding, and the Communist Party proposed to the Social Democrats and the the trade unions that they launch a joint campaign against the monopolies.

On Monday, 27 May, the CGT called twelve meetings in Paris to render an account of the state of the Grenelle negotiations. One of the speakers was Seguy, who declared:

'Much remains to be done, but our most essential claims have been met and we will not go back on what we have agreed ...'

At the same time the mass meeting in Charlety Stadium, to which we have already referred, gathered to express its determination not to be put off with what sops the CGT and the bosses were graciously prepared to throw their way. Fifty thousand people piled up the stadium steps, when the CGT had been unable to attract more than a handful of the faithful to their own meetings.

Alas, the Charlety meeting, too, ended in a complete fiasco. It was turned into a great salvage operation by the official parties of the Left, and ended with the sanctification of Mendès-France, the ex-Stalinist Barjonet and the reformist Astre.

Each one in turn went up to the platform to harangue the crowd, which had become sullen; each delivered an ultra left-wing speech, and each repeated the perennial call for the union of all progressive forces. The crowd had been cowed at the beginning of the meeting with an impressive show of force by the marshals of the PSU and UNEF (the very ones who had tried all along to shackle the movement ...), then bludgeoned by National Assembly-style speeches, and finally bedazzled by the revolutionary slogan-mongering of the new 'leaders'.

Worst of all was the cowardice of the various left-wing splinter groups (JCR, Fourth International, FER and OCI), who no longer felt the urge to explain themselves in front of the masses.

And so, instead of voting in favour of continuing the struggle, the crowd dispersed and left the future in the hands of a Mendès-France, a Barjonet and a Sauvageot. No wonder that the latter proclaimed proudly in an article:

'After the rue Gay-Lussac, our greatest hour was at Charlety! Not a policeman was in sight anywhere, and so there was no violence. If the police had been there things might have turned out differently. As it was, the marshals helped to disperse the crowds by guiding them along different routes away from the stadium, and so everything passed off quietly. This was because, at Charlety, people had come to realize that something new was happening, that this demonstration had achieved much more than the barricades ...'

How right he was — things *would* indeed have been different if the police had been there! It would have provoked a battle we might easily have won. And so the bourgeoisie relied instead on their Trojan horse — they would no more have dreamed of using the police to prevent the Charlety meeting than they would of proscribing the CGT.

Next day, Mitterand offered himself as candidate for the Presidency of the Republic, and at the same time Barjonet, Vigier, Mury, the JCR, *et al.* made an attempt to turn the revolutionary student movement into a more 'respectable' body — under their leadership. The resulting MUR (Revolutionary Union) carried no conviction at all; the masses disowned an organization that had been built up over their heads, and that, when all was said and done, was the old Bolshevism adorned with a liberal sash. Perhaps I should have said a black sash, for their machinations put paid to the promise of 24 and 27 May, and gave the government and the trade unions a much needed breathing space. The CGT called for an end of the strikes, the acceptance of the Grenelle Agreement, and election of a 'popular government'. De Gaulle disappeared for the entire afternoon of 29 May to confer with his army chiefs. Then, on Thursday, 30 May, he delivered a speech that would have been unthinkable only a week before. In effect, he brandished the spectre of Stalinism and Soviet concentration camps which would have carried no weight at a time when the Communist Party was known to be bitterly hostile to the student struggle. But the very moment the Communist Party officially entered the arena with the call for a 'popular government', the struggle became one between Stalinism and Gaullism, and few Frenchmen wanted to have any truck with the former. And so de Gaulle's blackmail took effect — shortly after his speech hundreds of thousands of Gaullists assembled in the Champs Elysées and demonstrated against the alleged threat of a Communist dictatorship.

The CGT hastened to take up the General's challenge, and at once published the following declaration: 'The CGT will in no way obstruct the course of the forthcoming referendum. It is in the interest of all workers to express their desire for a change of government.'(Seguy)

And the bourgeoisie took a deep breath of relief. ... Petrol, which had been almost unobtainable, now flowed abundantly from the pumps. Thousands of Parisians recovered their serenity in the countryside that Whitsun week-end, as they made their usual mass exodus from the capital.

On their return, they started slowly to drift back to work, not *en masse,* but sector by industrial sector. We decided to take what counter-measure we could.

The situation was as follows: the general strike was collapsing but a host of factories were still holding out and were faced with concerted attacks by organized blacklegs and special police contingents. For instance, at Rennes, the Post Office workers were engaged in a two-hour long battle with the CRS.

The 22 March Movement accordingly decided to render active help to the workers in their factories. By means of Student-Worker and 'Support and Solidarity' committees we were able to mobilize permanent squads to reinforce strike pickets and also to get supplies through to the striking workers. We had at all costs to prevent the factories from being picked off one by one. Permanent liaison groups enabled us to circulate news and information from factory to factory, and thus to keep the workers informed of what was happening in the many remaining 'islands of resistance'.

We could not do all we wanted because there were not enough of us to go round. Even so, our achievements were not negligible, and we certainly helped to hold the fort in a large number of postal and transport depots and in several big stores. Above all, our intervention helped to prepare for our last great effort: the defence of the Renault workers in Flins against a concerted attack by the CRS. On 7 June, at 3 a.m., Flins was occupied by the police. This particular objective had been chosen by the government because it seemed to offer two advantages: first of all it was a large and prominent factory of some strategic importance, and secondly it had a small CGT membership and a high proportion of foreign workers. Moreover, only 250 out of a total 10,000 employees were holding the factory. Some thirty light armoured cars and half-tracks drove at the factory gates at high speed and quickly smashed through the barriers. The CRS followed close behind and drove out the pickets by threatening them with machine guns. The state had decided to show its hand and now wanted everyone to know who was master.

The only reply by the trade unions was to call a protest meeting at Mureaux, six kilometres from the factory, for 8 o'clock next morning. Now, by that time, two shifts of 1,500 and 6,000 workers would have clocked in under the protection of the police, and the protest meeting would have been so much hot air. It was in these circumstances that we called for a show of force outside the factory gates at 5 a.m. Twelve hundred students turned up, stopped cars, and explained to as many workers as possible that to go back to work under these circumstances was an act of rank betrayal. While no more than 40 workers showed up at the CGT meeting in Mureaux, hundreds of workers gathered outside the factory. The CGT accordingly decided to abandon its own meeting and to harangue the larger crowd. By then some three to four thousand people had collected only a few yards away from the CRS. The temperature rose rapidly and several young workers who had been there since the early morning now demanded that the CGT officials shut up and that a student be allowed to speak. The workers then started to move against the factory gates despite desperate appeals by the CGT delegates; the first grenades burst, and fighting started in earnest. For the next three days, young students and workers kept up a running battle with the CRS in all the surrounding fields and woods. The CGT tried to call them back, but in vain. The local population were clearly on the side of the young, gave them shelter, fed them and looked after them in every way they could. A shopkeeper who denounced a student to the police had his business smashed up and was afterwards boycotted by most of his old customers.

The resistance at Flins raised the flagging courage of workers throughout France. The metal industry as a whole refused to give in, the ORTF decided to stay out on strike, while practically everywhere barriers were being put up, notably at Renault-Billancourt and at Citroen. Unfortunately these defences were never used — the trade unions had them dismantled just before the general return to work.

On Monday, 10 June, the students once again mobilized in response to a call from the factory. At 6.30 a.m. a hundred or so of us were arrested while assembling in the offices of the CFDT, the only Trade Union that did not bar students, and there was a veritable 'rat hunt' in the entire neighbourhood which, in the evening, ended in the death of Gilles Tautin, a schoolboy.

This is how the CGT later spoke of the students' attempts to help the workers' struggle:

'Rigorously oppose every attempt to mislead the workers' movement.

'While negotiations are proceeding in the metal industry, and while consultations prior to a return to work continue in various other branches, dangerous attempts at provocation are clearly being made. These take the form of questioning our undoubted achievements and misleading the workers into adventurist escapades.

'It was at Flins that the most recent attempt of this nature took place this morning. After the government had decided on the occupation of the factory by the CRS, and while the workers were assembled in perfect calm, groups who are strangers to the working class, led by Geismar, whom we can see more and more clearly as a specialist in provocation, insinuated themselves into the meeting and tried to incite the workers to re-occupy the factory.

'These squads, trained in para-military fashion, who have already appeared in operations of a similar nature in the Paris region, act visibly as agents of the worst enemies of the working classes. It is difficult to believe that the arrogance of the employers in the metal industry, the support which they enjoy from the government, the police brutalities against the workers, and these attempts at provocation are not all of the same kind.'(CGT, Paris Region, 7 June)

On the night following the death of Gilles Tautin, a demonstration, quite spontaneously, spilled into the Latin Quarter, attacked the Police Commissariat of the Fifth *Arrondissement* and continued to remain in the streets until 2 o'clock in the morning.

But that was not the end of the story. The next act was played out near the Swiss border. On Tuesday 11 June at Sochaux round the Peugeot factories, which the CRS wanted to occupy, there took place what were probably the most violent scuffles of all in those months of May and June. They claimed the lives of two victims.

But while we struggled on, factory after factory returned to work and we realized that the first round had to be conceded. Even so, Flins and Sochaux remain two shining monuments to real, living solidarity, rays of light in the dark betrayal of the working class.

Another result of our solidarity, perhaps less spectacular but even more important, was the spontaneous emergence of Action Committees.

Whereas for decades the 'Left' had lamented the lethargy of the masses, while splinter groups had vainly kept drumming on the factory gates, haranguing the crowd outside the Metro, or in university cafés, here we suddenly saw thousands of militants joining together without any outside prompting, all of them active, informed, aware and responsible. Thousands of people discussed democracy, the class struggle, the next action, and all this without having learned to recite the magic spells put out by the Central Committee of the Communist Party; without even knowing that there are five different wings to the Fourth International, or whether the PCMLF or the UJC(M-L) support Mao Tse Tung. They refused to admit that they were as nothing without the brilliant leadership of that great revolutionary vanguard of the proletariat which would one day seize the reins on their behalf, much as it had already seized the reins in the 'Workers' Fatherland'. Nor did they appreciate that every splinter group expresses at the top what the gagged proletariat thinks at the bottom. A profusion of journals, of pamphlets, of reviews, poured from the private presses proclaiming the word: 'Truth', 'The Way', 'The Proletarian', 'Revolt', 'Workers' Struggle', 'Communist Struggle', 'People's Struggle', 'Workers' Power', 'Workers' News', or sometimes 'To Serve the People'. Before so much good will and so many good offices, it is indeed astonishing that the working class should have chosen to take its own destiny in its hands rather than acclaim any of the great messiahs competing for their favour.

If lack of political understanding means the rejection of bureaucracies big (e.g. the Communists and the Social Democrats) and small (e.g. the Trotskyist splinter groups), and the denial that the workers must be led by a revolutionary élite; if lack of political interest means being bored with platform rhetoric, with theories that have no practical application, with resolutions, petitions, marches, congresses and annual dinners; if lack of political interest is the rejection of all the phoney alternatives (Communists *vs.* Social Democrats; London *vs.* Paris; Mendés-France *vs.* Mitterand; Mali *vs.* Guinea; gin and tonic *vs.* tonic and gin; the King in his palace *vs.* the palace in King Street; the Six *vs.* the Common Market) — if lack of political interest means all this, then indeed most young workers and working intellectuals have become eminently apolitical. The origins of our movement, the absence of officials in the district and factory Action Committees alone demonstrate that no professional agitator or theoretician was ever seen or ever needed. Better still, the Action Committees stopped such people meddling in practice. All that was most effective at Nanterre and in the fighting — our ability to rally where the action was hottest, and to take common decisions without consulting the 'leadership' of the splinter groups — all this went into the creation of Action Committees. They were born for the purpose of solving concrete common problems and sharing life in battle, rendering aid to the strikers, and helping wherever help was most needed. All individuals and splinter groups involved in the student struggle or the strike movement felt the urgent need to unite for the sake of greater efficiency. Solidarity became not an ideological slogan but a necessity. Almost overnight, atomized individuals turned into vital groups, into genuine communities (for several weeks in Sorbonne, and at the new annexe in the rue de Censier, members of various Action Committees lived together almost continuously).

The petty life of yesterday was left behind; gone the dingy office, the boredom in a tiny flat, with a tiny television and, outside, a tiny road with a tiny car; gone the repetition, the studied gestures, the regimentation and the lack of joy and desire.

The organization of the local Action Committees did not precede the events but followed them step by step. New forms were evolved as we went along and as we found the old forms inadequate and paralyzing. Organization is not an end in itself, but an evolving means of coping with specific situations.

When we discovered that it was impossible to get any real idea of what was happening from the radio, the press, and the television, or rather from their deliberate silence concerning the course of the student struggle and the gradual spread of the strikes, our spontaneous answer was the publication of wall newspapers. They were stuck up in the street, in squares, in the markets, and in the Métro: particularly at Gobelins Station in the Thirteenth *Arrondissement* and at Château Rouge in the Eighteenth. This collective experience of moving into the streets and squares was a new one, and no preconceived idea, however brilliant or 'correct', had any part in it. In fact, in our experience of occupying the streets we overstepped all theories, just as we thrust aside the official prohibition of meetings and also the machinations of the Communist Party, which failed completely in its attempts to divert us by creating stiff-born action committees of its own.

Moreover, the large crowds that gathered permanently round our wall newspapers, the physical presence of hundreds of people in the street, made the impact of our movement felt as never before. People first of all exchanged information on what was happening in the universities or in the factories, but soon they would get involved in deeper questions and explanations. What do the students want? Do they all want the same thing? Why the revolt? In whose interest? And who started all the violence? And what do the strikers want? A real debate was begun, and gone was the habit of accepting biased information from a single source. People began to take a cool look at the monopoly of news and the specialists of information. Nor would they any longer accept the threadbare explanations of the official party theorists who know everything, predict everything, and must needs organize everything. The splinter groups dissolved in the mass; they were clearly seen to be directing nothing at all. The high priests of the revolution barely knew on what page to open their Holy Bible (who had the time to wait for them to finish their logic-chopping?), or what particular verse to apply to the changing situation. They no longer even dared show their badge of office — they hid their revolutionary dog-collars under a pullover. The time for making fine Marxist points was clearly over.

The Action Committees

Never before had the local population been so actively involved in real political decisions; never before were their voices heard so clearly in the public forum. Democracy sprang from discussion of our immediate needs and the exigencies of the situation which demanded action.

What did the Action Committees do? And precisely how did they function?

Among the hundreds of such committees formed all over Paris, we shall choose those of the Thirteenth and Eighteenth *Arrondissements* as particularly good examples of what went on.

To begin with the activities of these committees had to be geared to the vagaries of the battles raging in Paris itself and sometimes as far away as Flins. To that end, we had to make sure that information was passed on quickly and efficiently. The only way in which the students involved in the struggle could spread their message and break out of their isolation was to communicate with as many of the local people as possible. Now, once the people had seen the police at work, they were only too anxious to express their solidarity, and to participate in future actions. To begin with, they helped to tend the wounded, collected funds, and above all saw to the provisioning of the stay-in strikers: in the

Thirteenth *Arrondissement* alone, almost two tons of fruit and vegetables were distributed each week. We also ran solidarity meetings and gave direct support to the strikers, by reinforcing their pickets, and by printing posters for them.

At the local level, we carried on with permanent information and discussion centres in well-known places. Every day, people who had been out on demonstrations gave an account of what had happened to them personally, of what was going on in the rest of Paris, and of how the strikers were faring. There were announcements of solidarity meetings, of public discussions on various topical subjects, and of the work of other Action Committees. Pamphlets were written and distributed, technical tasks allocated (typing, duplicating, printing, etc.), lists of factories to be contacted were compiled, food distribution teams set up and sent out, etc.

The Action Committee usually met once a day at a fixed hour and place and its deliberations were open to all. Each local Action Committee was in contact with the wider *Arrondissement* Committee, which in turn was in contact with the Paris Action Committee. However, the local Action Committees consistently refused to allow this coordination to degenerate into a kind of political direction. They reserved the right to take whatever steps they saw fit on both the local and also the national level, and rotated their delegates, who had no mandate and merely acted as go-betweens. At the central meetings, two major trends emerged: while the majority contended that they should concern themselves exclusively with the coordination of the day-to-day struggle rather than work out a political programme, the minority felt that only such a programme and a centralized leadership could carry the struggle to its successful conclusion.

The supple structure of the Action Committees favoured the formation of horizontal relationships, whose power of united action was in no way diminished by the absence of leaders at the top. When necessary, several thousand militants could be assembled within an hour (between 2,800 and 3,500 were called out by the Permanent Factory Mobilization Committee at 9 a.m. on Monday, 3 June, and stayed until 1 p.m. on Wednesday, 5 June). The basic working unit, however, remained the local Action Committee — in the Eighteenth *Arrondissement* for instance, there were five such groups, each with a specific geographical area of responsibility. It was these which did most of the real work, the

Arrondissement Action Committee itself acting chiefly in a coordinating capacity (relaying information, etc.). The division into geographical sectors was often arbitrary and provisional, and had to be modified from time to time according to the specific task on which we were engaged. Moreover, the internal organization of the local groups also varied according to the role they were playing at a given moment. There was one thing, however, on which everyone was agreed: the preservation of autonomy.

During lulls in the struggle, the Action Committees organized public discussions and study commissions on such themes as the economic situation, the political situation, workers' control, etc. To that purpose they made use of large public halls, and if none such were to be had in the immediate vicinity, of schools, colleges, and office buildings. Most Action Committees had their period of keenest discussion during the power-vacuum which occurred from 24 to 30 May. Unfortunately, the public debates that went on almost continually at the time showed that the majority were not yet ready to manage their own affairs. The most frequent question asked was 'What is going to happen?' and not 'What are we going to do?'

Then as police repression was stepped up, as the problem of taking food to the workers and their families became more acute, and as protest grew, the 'they' of resignation gave place to the 'I' of responsibility. This was demonstrated most clearly at the Lebrun Depot, and again at Flins, where, by united action, the young workers, students and teachers won a victory over the police, the state and the bosses. Actions of this type helped to bridge the gap between different sectors of society, and threw people of all kinds together in a common struggle.

But it must be frankly admitted that these remained isolated incidents, although this was surely not for lack of courage on the part of the workers, or from fear of the CRS. The authorities had been reduced to utter helplessness, the workers knew it, and yet failed to seize their opportunity, overwhelmed no doubt by the unexpected vistas that had suddenly opened up before them. Still, they did make a beginning by posing the real problems instead of being diverted into idle parliamentary debates, and they did have a foretaste of what self-government can achieve in practice.

Today, the workers are back in the factories, and the struggle has ceased — for a time, at least. Once again, the bands of hope stand at the corners chanting their old litanies, telling the workers that only by heeding the call of the 'vanguard' will they ever achieve their emancipation. Words are apparently more important than deeds once again.

But the message of the Action Committees will surely drown these discordant voices, once the workers begin to flex their muscles again. Let us therefore see what precisely this message was.

ACTION COMMITTEE OF

THE THIRTEENTH ARRONDISSEMENT

Political programme adopted by the General Assembly

of 25 May

We are not a political party, but a group of militants with various political and trade union backgrounds. Our ideal is a united movement in which sectarianism and bureaucracy are replaced by the greatest possible measure of democracy. The Action Committees are the political expression of the fundamental democratic needs of the masses. The committee can only take decisions on specific political and organizational issues and is answerable to the general membership. The Committee of the Thirteenth *Arrondissement* is a part of the Combined Action Committee Movement; the assembly therefore can decide to associate itself with any Parisian or national political initiative.

Why have we combined into Action Committees?

Because we wholeheartedly endorse the struggle, waged first by the students and, today, by the workers as well.

Because we feel it is not enough merely to support this struggle, but that we must ensure its maximum extension, and further the political expression of its revolutionary message.

Because we think that we have much to learn from the students and workers whose courageous struggle offers new prospects of overturning the bourgeois order. The students have shown that it is possible to send the government packing in the streets; the workers must now show that they can flush it out of office.

The students, by their direct confrontation of the authorities, have shown the futility of the traditional policies and parliamentary procedures with their marches, petitions, censure motions and election campaigns.

But the struggle of the students against repression is only one aspect of the frontal attack by the whole of the working class on the social and economic structures of capitalist society.

It is not by pointless negotiations that the students have succeeded in paralyzing the university system and in throwing out the Fouchet plan, but by fighting for, and taking over, their own institutions.

It is not by means of Toutée or Grégoire commissions, or with the help of economic and social councils, that the workers launched their battle, but by occupying the factories, by direct action, by meeting violence with violence, and by fighting against all forms of repression, conscription and collaboration with the bourgeoisie.

These struggles have opened up new horizons to workers throughout the world — the bourgeoisie can be beaten provided we are prepared to do battle rather than shout the old slogans ...

The struggles have shown that when they begin to question the very basis of the bourgeois order, students and workers speak a common language. By themselves, the students, however resolute, can never hope to topple the Gaullist régime. Only the proletariat can bring this about, by seizing power from the bourgeoisie, a class that is, by its very nature, incapable of granting the workers a decent life or the students a decent education.

In the present situation, the authorities can try to undermine the movement with limited economic concessions and promises to discuss all outstanding claims at board meetings, or else with vicious attacks on the most dynamic and radical elements in the movement. It can also combine these two forms of attack and use the good offices of political parties ready to accept minor reforms, but basically in agreement with capitalism itself.

What unites the revolutionary militants of the Action Committee is their refusal to be cowed by the authorities, and their determination to eschew all forms of class collaboration. What unites them is their will to pose the question of power, and develop the struggle in action, by confrontation in the street, and in the factories.

Action Committees should be created wherever they are needed to advance the struggle.

It is because we believe that a revolutionary reappraisal of French society is possible today, that we think that these committees should be set up everywhere with the express purpose of involving the masses in political and active struggle, of supporting the workers, and of rendering aid to all those who are fighting at this very hour.

FRIEND, WILL YOU BE WITH US TOMORROW?

For a month and a half we have been battling in the universities and factories, in the streets and the squares. We have a short respite now, let us profit from it.

When the workers realize that they are being swindled out of their wage increases by rising prices, when they see that the same docile parliamentarians cannot stop playing their game of endlessly discussing decisions they themselves have never taken, when the top brass get round to imposing on students the educational reforms that have been worked out by some official in the Ministry of Education to ensure everbetter NCO's for the future:

WE MUST BE READY WITH THE ANSWER

The Action Committees propose:

– to inform the population of the real political and social situation and the prospects opened up by the May crisis:

– to explain that the elections merely divert the struggle of the masses into the parliamentary field, mined by the enemy, and in which the political parties will once again prove their ineffectuality;

– to help the people to organize themselves, to construct a political system in which they themselves will take charge of the management and administration of their own affairs;

– to participate in all the struggles which are being waged and to support the factory strikes by fighting the repressive measures of the authorities (expulsion of foreigners, Gestapo style raids, banning of revolutionary groups, etc. ... and by organizing for self-defence.

The Action Committee want:

– to oppose the creation of any new political party on the lines of those we know already, all of which must sooner or later fit into the existing system;

– to unite in the streets, in the factories, and in the suburban communes, all those who agree with the above analysis and who realize that the struggle begun on 3 May can end in the overthrow of the capitalist system and the installation of a socialist state;

– to coordinate resistance at the Paris level and then at the national one, to fight in the front lines of the revolutionary movement.

This, then, is the current position of the Action Committees.

It is on this basis that they will intervene during and after the election campaign.

NOW MORE THAN EVER
THE STRUGGLE CONTINUES

Today the Action Committees have to lie low, but in May and June they were the highest expression of our movement. They showed how simple it is to bypass the trade union and political bosses, how workers can spontaneously unite in action, without a 'vanguard' or a party.

Special mention should here be made of CLEOP (Committee for Student-Worker-Peasant Liaison) which saw to the provisioning of the strikers, above, all in the smaller factories. One of the first of these committees originated in the Agricultural School of Nantes, most of the others, too, were started in Brittany. They made contact with agricultural cooperatives and unions, and bought directly from the farmers and smallholders who were only too glad to cock a snook at the hated government. CLEOP also organized public discussions and published bulletins to fill in the gaps which were deliberately left in the official communiqués — in short, CLEOP played much the same part in the countryside that the Action Committees played in Paris. Meeting places sprang up, the committees became a network for disseminating information and ideas, and helped to cement solidarity between town and country workers in battles with the police and in organizing food transports.

At the end of the day, CLEOP, like the rest of the revolutionary student movement, became exhausted by fifty days of constant skirmishes with the police, and as the workers' struggle abated in its turn, the authorities moved in quickly to crush the last pockets of resistance.

But our temporary defeat is only the end of a chapter. When the movement takes the offensive again, its dynamism will return, and this time the battle will be on a field chosen by the students and workers themselves. The days of May and June will never be forgotten, and one day the barricades will surely be raised again. There is no better way to end this chapter than with the manifesto put out by one of that group of revolutionary students, known as the *Enragés de Caen*.

(1) The students have ushered in a university revolution. By their action they have made clear to one and all how basically repressive our educational institutions really are. They began by questioning the authority of their professors and the university administration and pretty soon they found themselves face to face with the CRS. They have proved that their Rector derives his powers from the Prefect of Police. Their action at the same time revealed the unity of interest of all the exploited and oppressed classes. It is in response to the movement born at Nanterre and continued at the Sorbonne in the face of police aggression, that the workers, the ordinary soldiers, the journalists, the research workers and the writers, have joined the battle.

(2) However, as soon as the workers came out on strike and the students tried to show their active solidarity with them, they came up against the CGT, which asked them not to interfere. While many students tell themselves that this is not the attitude of the majority of workers, they nevertheless feel rejected as 'middle class'. Quite a few students who were only too anxious to follow the lead of the working class are becoming disenchanted as the workers scorn them and refuse to take them seriously. Disenchantment is particularly strong among those students who were last to join the movement, and are really more interested in achieving a few concessions than in changing society as a whole.

The more progressive students, by contrast, realize that, unless the revolution finishes off capitalism and the old universities with it, there can be no real change for the better. Hence they persist, often without hope, in offering their services to the workers, beginning to feel ashamed of being students.

(3) Students must rid themselves of these false feelings of guilt. Although their action sprang from the university, it has a validity that far transcends the narrow academic walls.

First of all, and most important, students must realize that the problems of the university are not irrelevant to the problems of industry. True, in industry, the workers carry the main weight of exploitation, the ownership of the means of production is in the hands of a hostile class, and the decisive struggle is played out within the productive process. But a mere change of ownership, such as the transfer of economic power from private to State enterprise, will in no way put an end to exploitation. What characterizes the structure of modern industry is not only the division between capital and labour, but also the division between supervisors and supervised, the skilled and the unskilled. The workers are exploited economically but also they are reduced to the role of mere pawns, by having no say in the running of their factories, no part in decisions that affect their own fate.

The monopoly of capital invariably goes hand in hand with a monopoly of power and knowledge.

Now, this is precisely where the students can show the way. They attack the self-styled custodians of authority and of wisdom; those who, on the pretext of dispensing knowledge, preach obedience and conformism.

Rather than waste their time analyzing the connexion between the university and other social sectors, students must proclaim that the same repressive structures are weighing down on them and the workers alike, that the same mentality thwarts the creative intelligence of individuals and groups everywhere. It is in the universities that this mentality structure is elaborated and maintained, and to shake it, we must shake the entire society — even though we still do not know the quickest path to that goal.

That shaking will surely come: we can already see its signs in the protests which are rising now, not only from the working but also from the middle class, from the press, radio and television, from artists and writers, and from Catholic, Jewish and Protestant youth who have suddenly rebelled against an oppressive theology.

The struggle of the students has opened the floodgates; it matters little that this struggle was born in a petty bourgeois environment — its effects involve the whole of society.

Moreover, it is a far too literal and ill-digested Marxism that tries to explain everything in terms of the antagonism between the workers and the middle class. This antagonism itself springs from an economic, social and political basis. Every attack against this basis, no matter from what source, has a revolutionary bearing.

(4) Students must not fear to make themselves heard and instead of searching for leaders where none can be found, boldly proclaim their principles — principles that are valid for all industrial societies, and for all the oppressed of our time.

These principles are:

To take collective responsibility for one's own affairs, that is, self-government;

To destroy all hierarchies which merely serve to paralyze the initiative of groups and individuals;

To make all those in whom any authority is vested permanently responsible to the people;

To spread information and ideas throughout the movement;

To put an end to the division of labour and of knowledge, which only serves to isolate people one from the others;

To open the university to all who are at present excluded;

To defend maximum political and intellectual freedom as a basic democratic right.

In affirming these principles, the students are in no way opposing themselves to the workers. They do not pretend that theirs is a blueprint for the reconstruction of society, even less a political programme, in the conventional sense of the word. They do not set themselves up as teachers. They recognize that each group has the right to lay down its own claims and its own methods of struggle. The students speak in the universal language of revolution. They do not deny that they have learned much of it from the workers; but they can also make a contribution of their own.

2. The Workers

We have seen that the students' movement triggered off that of the workers. The students went into the streets and, by their courage, they brought out the people, took the universities, and attacked the Stock Exchange. Faced with the combined forces of the government, the educational authorities, the police, and the trade union bureaucracies, they showed their ability to provoke errors and to exploit them. Moreover, they proved that it is possible to occupy factories — would the workers but realize it — without running the slightest risks. The student movement developed its radical critique of the authorities to a fine point but, in the absence of mass support, it was bound to fail in the long run.

The students were deeply disappointed when, on the morning after the 'night of the barricades', the workers did not take to the streets, but limited their sympathy to going on a twenty-four-hour general strike, which had been called by the trade unions and was political only in its choice of date: 13 May — the day on which de Gaulle had assumed power in 1958. Then, on Tuesday, 14th, late in the evening, the students holding the Sorbonne learned that some workers had gone much further than their trade union bosses intended: they occupied the Sud-Aviation works in Nantes. This movement spread rapidly and spontaneously — from 14 to 17 May, a host of other factories fell to the workers.

In this wave of strikes, which were illegal because no advance notice was given, it was the young workers, most of whom were not members of the trade unions, who proved the most militant and tenacious. These strikes, unlike the official ones, were not for any precise wage claims, but simply, as several strikers put it, because 'we've had a bellyful'. A bellyful of low wages, true, but beyond that, a bellyful of futility and the boredom of the daily round, of a life that stamped them, like everyone else, a hollow replica of their fathers and grandfathers, perhaps slightly more comfortable, but no less vacuous. What they felt was something they had not learned from any books, something so primitive and deep that it did not give way before the power of the state or the threats of the bosses, or even before the cajoling of the unions.

To accuse the CGT of treachery in May and June is nonsense — it had shown its hand long before. The trade unions, in France as elsewhere in the West, play the part of the 'loyal opposition', and in May

1968, the workers simply turned down their thumbs not only on the contestants but also on the game itself.

Unfortunately most of them failed to take that final and decisive step beyond bourgeois legality: the actual running of the factories by and for themselves. The extraordinary scope of the movement is not any the less remarkable; it was both immense and spontaneous and it produced a degree of awareness and discussion that was often extremely high, and sometimes exemplary. The workers had no time for abstract theories; at the beginning especially they were groping their way, and would sometimes, particularly when frustrated, turn back to their old ways of thinking. They acted often for the sake of action alone, with no conscious goal, neither knowing nor caring where their actions would lead. Their feelings are hard to explain to anyone who has not, like them, been left to his own devices at a time of crisis, and found it necessary to act first and look for what theories can be deduced from the practice afterwards. But from their experiences perhaps we can learn something of the forces which are already constructing the future. Hence it is worth trying to understand, for example, the workers' feelings about the Grenelle Agreement and other industrial negotiations by the trade unions. Most of them realized, albeit dimly, that they were being sold down the river once again. It was this very feeling that one worker expressed to his astonished trade union leaders, when he said: 'It's not you who started the strike. It was the ones who were willing to use force. Afterwards you tried to take charge and fob us off with the usual claims. You threw a spanner in the works, and that's why we have washed our hands of you.' What had emerged at last, and had hitherto been no more than the pious hope of some of the extreme-left groups, was the explicit demand for responsibility and control over production, and it sprang from the sense of brotherhood that had developed in the struggle itself, and pointed towards a new and better society. It was this that made our movement so truly revolutionary, it is because of this that we can be sure it will spring up again. Moreover, in several cases strikers did, in fact, start running the factories on their own account. In this action can be seen the essence, the highest achievement, of the movement. Elsewhere the strikers organized their own food supplies with the help of students, small farmers and lorry drivers. Others again did try to apply radical solutions but grew more and more frightened as the general return to work speeded up and the traditional forces re-established their hold. The vision of the bolder among them acted as a leaven in the passive mass of the general consciousness, and deserves credit for that fact alone. Perhaps we had best look at some concrete examples.

The Case of the AGF

The AGF (Assurance Générale de France) is the second largest French insurance company, a nationalized industry and one which in four years has twice been amalgamated, first with six other companies into a new combine, and then with three more. This 'take-over' went hand in hand with the introduction of a high degree of automation and centralization. The trade unions never even raised the question of workers' participation in this 'great' State enterprise, and confined themselves to denouncing the arbitrary way in which the management (whom they accused of being a Gaullist clique) ignored the unions.

On Friday, 17 May, a small group of employees raised the question of management, bluntly and clearly, in a pamphlet distributed by students of the 22 March Movement:

Following the example of the students, we herewith submit a number of proposals to be debated in the general staff assembly of the AGF.

'(1) The AGF should be run by all those working in it.

'(2) The present management should be relieved of their posts. Every branch should appoint a delegate, chosen solely for his personal qualities and merits.

'(3) Those responsible for a particular branch will have a double function — to coordinate the running of the branch under the control of the employees, and to organize, with the delegates from other branches, a council which, again under the control of the employees, will run the enterprise as a whole.

'(4) Those responsible for their branch will at all times be accountable for their actions to the entire staff and can be dismissed at any moment by those who have appointed them.

'(5) The internal hierarchy is to be abolished. Every employee, no matter what his job, will receive the same pay, based provisionally on the mean wage bill for May (i.e. the sum of all wages divided by the number of workers).

'(6) The personal files of employees will be returned to them so that they can remove any item that is not of purely administrative interest.

'(7) All property and stock of the AGF will become the property of all, managed by all, and safeguarded by all at all times.

'(8) In the case of any outside threat, a voluntary guard under the control of the council will provide protection for the enterprise day and night.

On Monday, 20 May, a new pamphlet was distributed making the following points:

'As the fruits of social progress are in danger of being snatched back, we must:

– Beware of false friends and have confidence only in ourselves.

– Elect strike committees.

– Take over control on the lines of the earlier pamphlet.

'The strike has been won. Now we must start things up again by ourselves and for ourselves, without any authority other than the council we have elected. Who will then be the forces of disorder? Only those who seek to defend private property, their privilege and jobs as managers, and who stand for oppression, violence, misery and war ... Where you work is where the action is. There, with all the workers, you can choose to rebuild a new world, a world that will belong to all.

At the beginning, only a relatively small proportion of the employees (500 out of 3,000) participated in the occupation of the AGT Head Office, mainly because of the transport strike. The stay-in was started by a number of young workers, many of whom were not trade union members. Later, the trade unions took over, or rather tried to slow things down. The staff, however, was fully determined not to lose what had already been won. The list of original demands was impressive, and included four conditions, chief among them full strike pay, the right of the strike committee to introduce structural reforms, and worker participation in the decision-making machinery. When the administrative staff joined the strike on 22 May (130 voting in favour, 120 against, with 250 absent) the nature of the strike changed radically. The young technocrats and administrators and the trade union leaders were now in a dominant position on the strike committee. This 'take-over' did not pass unchallenged: among other incidents there was a violent row over the function of trade union officials, which led to the break-up of the so-called structural commission, charged with handling the question of workers' management. Some of the young technocrats on this commission, mostly members the CGC (Confederation of Administrative Staff) had tried to use their vote to force their own conception of management on the workers, to wit the modernization, and not the destruction, of the existing hierarchical structure. Other members of the commission, by contrast, put forward the principle of workers' direct participation in management, on Yugoslav lines.

The interest of these proposals is that they forced the workers to take a very hard look at the possible forms of direct participation in industry. Quite a few of them realized that the so-called co-management proposal of the technocrats was merely a blind that allowed them to strengthen their grip over the rest. In particular, by retaining the system of 'points' and promotion, confidential information, and by making profitability the chief criterion, 'co-management' must rapidly degenerate into the old system. By contrast, real workers' participation at the decision-making level is bound to weaken the power of the trade union bureaucrats and the technical experts. No wonder then, that the trade unions were so hostile to the following proposals submitted by the more radical members of the structural commission:

(1) Every decision, without exception, must be taken jointly by a rank and file committee consisting of twelve workers and the departmental chief.

(2) If they agree, the decision will be put into force immediately. If there is disagreement, the matter is brought before a works council, on which workers and management have equal representation. The workers' representatives are not permanent, but are appointed for a particular council meeting, and can be recalled at any time. The works council has no power to make decisions, its job is to re-examine the problem, suggest solutions, and refer them back for decision to the particular rank and file committee in which the conflict originated.

(3) If the conflict continues, the whole matter will be brought before a standing committee dealing with departmental affairs in general. This committee too has equal worker management representation and is elected for a maximum of one year, while subject to immediate dismissal. It decides the issue by a majority, with the head of the department having the casting vote. The decision is then enforced without right of appeal.

Two things are clear: that the experts are reduced to a technical rather than managerial function and that the trade union delegates have no say in departmental affairs. This explains the position of the management and trade unions quoted in *Le Monde* on 2/3 June, 1968: 'We must know exactly what, in practical terms, this involves for us. We are not yet ready for action, but we are keeping an open mind.'

In fact, the trade unions and technical staff made no attempt at all to apply these principles, but simply promised to enter into negotiation with the management once the strike was over. The habit of leaving decisions to the management dies hard! The principle of co-management was not even mentioned directly, only the creation of a commission to inquire into new methods of organization. It is evident that, at best, there would have emerged a consultative body, an unholy alliance between the trade unions, administrators, and bosses, who would share out the jobs between them, and agree to preserve the status quo.

This whole situation utterly disgusted the young workers who had thought all along that the strike was for greater things than that. They now had to listen to interminable discussions, to flatulent and hackneyed phrases instead of concrete proposals. And so the strike degenerated and the strike committee, whose 150 members had planned to work without a permanent secretariat, and to allocate their different tasks to a number of autonomous sub-committees, was suborned by the bureaucrats. The lesson is clear: once the workers stop fighting their own battles, they have lost the war.

The TSF Works at Brest

Another attempt to achieve workers' control was made during the general strike at the TSF (Wireless Telegraphy) works in Brest (Brittany).

Some years ago, the TSF opened a factory there as part of the State plan to develop the depressed areas. Technical and administrative experts were brought in from Paris and eleven hundred workers were recruited on the spot, mostly unskilled. The central board, no doubt in order to receive further State subsidies for the Brest factory, only gave it the most unprofitable contracts. As a result, they were able to oppose all wage claims on the grounds that the factory was running at a loss. This caused a great deal of anxiety, particularly among the technical staff who were afraid that the factory might close down and that they would be thrown out of work.

On 20 May, groups representing various branches of the factory (workshops, offices, laboratories) elected a strike committee and then set up 'workers' tribunals' which concluded that the administrative staff was incompetent, and insolent in its dealings with subordinates.

A report to that effect was sent out to the management board, and a pamphlet calling for the democratization of the factory was printed and widely distributed. It called for workers' control over training courses, a guaranteed promotions scheme, definition of jobs and responsibilities, and control over the finances of the factory.

On 18 June, after six days of fruitless discussion on various topics, including the setting up of worker-management councils, the workers decided to down tools by 607 to 357 against. The management continued in its refusal to admit workers' delegates to the board, and even the official CFTC representatives were unable to make them change their minds.

Work was restarted on Friday, 21 June (551 for and 152 against), after discussions between local trade union representatives and the Paris Board had led to the creation of a 'works council' consisting of five members appointed by the management and twelve appointed by the staff. This was charged with studying 'changes in structure' and improvement of working conditions. The works council had no more than an advisory capacity and was expected to submit its suggestions towards the end of the year.

This progressive nibbling away of the claims was very significant! At the beginning, the call was for direct workers' participation in management, then it was workers' councils and finally these became a mere study commission. Once again a real attempt to achieve a worker's democracy had been smartly outwitted.

The Atomic Energy Centre at Saclay

Let us now look at what happened at CEA (Atomic Energy Centre).

Of the 6 to 7,000 employees at the CEA (Saclay), some 4,500, including 25 per cent of the engineering staff, were covered by collective agreements. The rest were not members of the industry proper; they included charwomen, secretaries, draughtsmen, technicians and maintenance men brought in from outside. There were also a number of French and foreign students studying at the CEA.

During the strike, the CEA works were occupied: 83 per cent of the staff stayed in during the entire strike — and even over the Ascension and Whitsun week-ends at least 500 people remained in the Centre. During this time, long discussions were held on the subject of works reorganization and allied topics. The strike itself had been started by a small nucleus of research workers (practical and theoretical physicists) most of whom were extremely well paid. Not directly concerned with production, young, and in touch with the universities, these men acted in disregard, and often against the wishes, of the trade unions. The strike lasted for no more than fifteen days, and stopped when the administration promised to introduce a number of structural reforms and to make good all wages and salaries lost during the strike.

As a result of these reforms, a veritable pyramid of works councils was set up, with a consultative council, presided over by a chairman, right on top. In the constitution of the works councils, the trade union machinery was completely by-passed, groups of the workers electing one delegate each. All the delegates were subject to immediate dismissal and, at first, there was a demand that the chairman himself should be answerable to the whole staff. Needless to say, this demand was never met.

It is therefore true to say that, as far as giving the workers a say in management, the famous 'pyramid of committees' was completely irrelevant; its only usefulness was to keep the staff informed of what was happening at the top, but even here its work was severely restricted. The old strike committee, which had been formed spontaneously, was re-elected almost to a man, but it was now reduced to a kind of inferior intelligence service; and, moreover, was impeded at every point by the various committee chairmen.

The Rhône-Poulenc Works

It might also be interesting to examine the case of the Workers' Committees in the Rhône-Poulenc works in Vitry.

For years before the strike, the workers here had taken little interest in politics or in trade union activities. But once the student movement started, the young workers in particular suddenly turned militant, so much so that some of them even helped to man the barricades.

The big twenty-four hour strike of 13 May, with its 'parliamentary' aims, was joined by about 50 per cent of the workers. The staff grades did not take part and the foremen did so reluctantly. From 13 to 20 May, the factory kept running, but there was a growing sense of unrest among the workers.

On Friday, 17 May, the management decided to stop all assembly lines, probably with the intention of staging a lockout. On that evening, the trade union liaison committee called a general meeting (from 50 to 60 per cent attended). The majority of those present (60 per cent) voted for an immediate stay-in, but since the trade unions insisted on a clear two-thirds majority, the factory was not occupied that week-end.

On Saturday, the 18th, the trade union liaison committee decided to stage a stay-in strike on Monday, 20th. The CGT then proposed the formation of Shop Floor Committees, and this was accepted for various reasons by the CFDT and the FO.

This extraordinary proposal was probably a manoeuvre by the CGT to outwit the other two trade unions.

The stay-in strike began and, from the start, about 2,000 workers occupied the factory. At the end of the week, some fifteen staff-grades also decided to join the strike, after many votes and despite the opposition of their own trade union (the CTC).

The Shop Floor Committees

The Shop Floor Committees, as we saw, were formed at the suggestion of the trade unions, but were quickly swamped by non-union members.

There were thirty-nine Shop Floor Committees in all. They elected four delegates each to a central committee whose 156 members were subject to immediate recall. Meetings of the central committee were public and could be reported. Shop Floor Committees were organized in each building, so that while some combined various categories of workers — from unskilled to staff grades, others, for instance in the research buildings, were made up entirely of technicians.

On Sunday, 19 May, the CGT proposed the creation of an executive committee at a general meeting of all trade unionists, in which it held a majority. No member of this executive committee was allowed to serve on the central committee.

There were two ostensible reasons for forming a separate executive committee:

(1) The management was only prepared to discuss matters with trade union members;

(2) Trade union members were the only ones who were legally entitled to go on strike.

After a week of argument, the Shop Floor Committees finally succeeded in getting a non-trade union member into the executive committee.

During the fortnight preceding the Whitsun week-end, the Shop Floor Committees reached the highest peak of their activities. At the time, the workers all thought this was the obvious way to organize: all propositions were listened to and discussed while the better ones were put to the vote, for instance the entry of non-trade union members into the executive committee. During this entire period, the trade union members collaborated with the Shop Floor Committees without any trouble — all of them were simply comrades on strike. The executive committee limited itself to carrying out the decisions of the central committee.

The subject uppermost in all these discussions was direct control of the factory. At the same time, smaller committees of a dozen or so workers discussed such political subjects as the present strategy of the Communist Party, workers' rights, and the role of the trade unions.

By the beginning of the month, all the subjects had been talked out and a certain lassitude set in, although de Gaulle's speech on 30th gave the discussions a shot in the arm. Even so, on 1 June, there was a noisy meeting of the central committee devoted exclusively to the subject of allocating petrol for the Whitsun week-end!

When the factory was re-occupied after Whitsun, the spirit was no longer the same. Serious discussions gave way to card-playing, bowling and volley-ball. The trade unions began to peddle their wares again, sapping the strength of the movement.

It was during this second period that the trade unions started negotiations with the management, and needless to say, their first claims concerned the status of the trade unions in the works.

After the Grenelle Agreement, the CGT did not lose any time calling on everybody to go back to work ('the elections ...', 'we can obtain no more ...'), and despite very strong resistance from those occupying the factory, pulled out its own militants on Monday, 10th.

After this, a number of CGT membership cards were torn up, which did not stop the CFDT from associating itself with the CGT call for a general return to work on 12 May, nor did the fact that the vote for a continued stay-in was 580 against 470.

The Shop Floor Committees at Rhône-Poulenc-Vitry were set up, as we have seen, on a rather unusual work-unit basis, which, in some cases, tended to separate technicians and workers into separate committees. One fact sticks out: although there was some cooperation between the workers and technicians, there was no real fusion between the different committees. Clearly, the division of labour introduced by the capitalists is hard to kill.

Contact with outside strikers was maintained by a small group of radicals, whose example helped to start Workers' Committees in other factories, such as Hispano-Suiza, Thomson-Bagneux, etc. Most workers, however, tried to run their own private little semi-detached strike, just as they tried to lead their own private little semi-detached lives.

What happened at Rhône-Poulenc-Vitry shows clearly why workers as a whole are so apathetic and apolitical: when they took responsibility, they came alive and took an active part in making important decisions, when matters were taken out of their hands and delegated to the unions, they lost interest and went back to playing solo.

The Pattern for the Future

A society without exploitation is inconceivable where the management of production is controlled by one social class, in other words where the division of society into managers and workers is not totally abolished. Now, the workers are told day after day that they are incapable of managing their own factory, let alone society, and they have come to believe this fairy tale. This is precisely what leads to their alienation in a capitalist society, and this is precisely why socialists must do their utmost to restore the people's autonomy and not just doctor the economic ills of the West.

It is not by accident that liberals, Stalinist bureaucrats and reformists alike, all reduce the evils of capitalism to economic injustice, and exploitation to the unequal distribution of the national income. And when they extend their criticism of capitalism to other fields, they still imply that everything would be solved by a fairer distribution of wealth. The sexual problems of youth and the difficulties of family life are ignored — all that apparently needs to be solved is the problem of prostitution. Problems of culture come down to the material cost of dispensing it. Of course, this aspect is important, but a man is more than a mere consumer, he can not only get fed, he can get fed up as well. While most of man's problems are admittedly economic, man also demands the right to find fulfilment on every other possible level. If a social organization is repressive it will be so on the sexual and cultural no less than on the economic planes.

As our society becomes more highly industrialized, the workers' passive alienation turns into active hostility. To prevent this happening, there have been many attempts to 'adapt the workers', 'give them a stake in society', and quite a few technocrats now think this is the only hope of salvaging 'the democratic way of life'.

But however comfortable they may make the treadmill, they are determined never to give the worker control of the wheel. Hence many militants have come to ask themselves how they can teach the workers that their only hope lies in revolution. Now, this merely reintroduces the old concept of the vanguard of the proletariat, and so threatens to create a new division within society. The workers need no teachers; they will learn the correct tactics from the class struggle. And the class struggle is not an abstract conflict of ideas, it is people fighting in the street.

Direct control can only be gained through the struggle itself. Any form of class struggle, over wages, hours, holidays, retirement, if it is pushed through to the end, will lead to a general strike, which in turn introduces a host of new organizational and social problems. For instance, there cannot be a total stoppage of hospitals, transport, provisions, etcetera, and the responsibility for organizing these falls on the strikers. The longer the strike continues, the greater the number of factories that have to be got going again. Finally the strikers will find themselves running the entire country.

This gradual restoration of the economy is not without its dangers, for a new managerial class may emerge to take over the factories if the workers are not constantly on their guard. They must ensure that they retain control over their delegated authorities at all times. Every function of social life — planning, liaison and coordination — must be taken up by the producers themselves, as and when the need arises.

It is certain that the managerial class will do everything they can to prevent a real revolution. There will be intimidation and violent repression, prophets both new and old of every shape and form will be held up to bamboozle the workers. There will be election campaigns, referenda, changes in the cabinet, electoral reforms, red herrings, bomb plots and what have you. At the same time, the experts will preach about the dire threat to the national economy and international prestige of the country. And should the workers turn a deaf ear to them, and persist in restarting production under their direct control, the managerial class will end up, as always, by calling in the army and police. This is precisely what happened in France in 1968, and not for the first time either.

What of the future? We cannot produce a blueprint — the future alone can evolve that. What we must agree on, rather, are the general principles of the society we want to create. The politicians tell us we live in an age of technological miracles. But it is up to us to apply them to a new society, to use the new media so as to gain greater mastery over the environment. While people today simply watch television as a surrogate for the lives they have ceased to live, in the new society they will use it as a means of widening their experience, of mastering the environment and of keeping in touch with the real lives of other people. If television programmes were to be put on for their social value and not solely because they induce the maximum hypnosis in the greatest numbers, they would enable us to extend the real democracy to the entire population.

Just imagine the preliminary Grenelle talks transmitted as a whole; just imagine the 'dialogues' between the bosses and the professional trade union pundits transmitted straight to the workshops. The workers would just laugh themselves sick, and throw the lot out of office.

Or take the question of planning the economy. Clearly, even in the future, planning will have to be done, but not just for the sake of profit or balancing the books. Once the workers have learned to manage their own affairs, in full equality and collective effort, they will try quite naturally to place the whole system of production and distribution on an entirely new basis. As Vaneighem has put it: 'For my part, the only equality that really matters is that which gives free rein to my desires while recognizing me as a man among men.' *(Traité de savoir-vivre à l'usage des jeunes générations,* Paris, 1947.)

Contemporary history has shown that the abolition of the private ownership of the means of production, essential though it is, does not necessarily mean the end of exploitation. Under capitalism, wages and prices fluctuate more or less with the law of supply and demand. Hence we are led to believe that the amelioration of the workers' lot is a simple marketing (or planning) problem, and that all our pressing social questions can be solved by 'dialogues' between officials or parliamentary representatives.

Similarly the wage system hides the reality of exploitation by suggesting that pay is simply a matter of productive capacity — but how do you evaluate the productive capacity of, say, a schoolteacher?

In the capitalist system, the only standard of value is money, hence the worker himself has a price tag that fits him neatly into a social pigeon-hole and is set apart from the rest. He has become just another commodity, not a man but an economic abstraction, whose relationship with other men is governed by arbitrary laws over which he has no control. The time each worker spends on a particular job is expressed in working hours; it is only when the workers themselves take control, and appropriate the fruits, of their own production, that work will be determined by real needs and not by blind and arbitrary market forces. Social relationships will no longer be vertical — from top to bottom, from director to worker — but horizontal, between equal producers working in harmony. And the product of their toil will no longer be appropriated by parasitic organisms, but shared out fairly between one and all.

All this is doubtless a far cry from the general strike of May and June which, though it gave spontaneous expression to popular disgust at the present system and showed the workers their real power on a scale unprecedented in recent French history, failed precisely because the workers themselves failed to take the next logical step: to run the economy by themselves as free and equal partners. As Coudray puts it in *La brèche:* 'It should be said firmly and calmly: in May, 1968, in France, the industrial proletariat, far from being the revolutionary vanguard of society, was its dumb rearguard. In May, 1968, the most conservative, the most mystified stratum of society, the one most deeply ensnared in the traps of bureaucratic capitalism, was the working class, and more particularly that fraction of the working class which belongs to the Communist Party and the CGT.'

Now this failure cannot be explained simply in terms of treachery by the working-class organizations, for it is basically due to the erosion of initiative within the capitalist system. The ideological submissiveness and servility of the wage slaves must not be condemned, which serves no purpose, nor deplored, which helps to engender a moral superiority, nor accepted, which can only lead to complete inaction — it must be fought by an active and conscious assault, if necessary by a minority, on the system in every sphere of daily life.

The differences between the revolutionary students and the workers spring directly from their distinct social positions. Thus few students have had real experience of grinding poverty — their struggle is about the hierarchical structure of society, about oppression in comfort. They do not so much have to contend with a lack of material goods as with unfulfilled desires and aspirations. The workers on the other hand suffer from direct economic oppression and misery — earning wages of less than 500 francs per month, in poorly ventilated, dirty and noisy factories, where the foreman, the chief engineer and the manager all throw their weight about and conspire to keep those under them in their place.

French society in general, and Gaullist society in particular, is but the expression of modern bureaucratic capitalism, which must constantly expand or disintegrate. Hence the State must increasingly intervene to prevent stagnation. This in no way removes the inner contradictions of capitalism, or stops it from wasting resources on a gigantic scale. True, capitalism has been able to raise real wages, indeed it must do so if it is to foist its mass-produced rubbish on the working class, but it is quite incapable of harnessing the forces of production to rational goals — only socialism can do that.

Meanwhile, the increasing bureaucratization and automation of the economy is helping to split the producing class more and more into distinct strata: unskilled workers who serve as mere robots, skilled craftsmen, staff grades, technical experts, scientists and so on, each with special interests and grievances of their own. As a result, workers in the lowest and highest categories do not seem to have any common interests — other than unmasking the trickery of a system that robs Peter to pay Paul, and going on to see that the only solution to their individual problems is a joint one — revolution and a new society, in which objective logic and necessity will decide the claims of all.

This solution can only be reached by the association of all the non-exploitative categories of industry: manual workers as well as intellectuals, office workers and technicians. Every attempt to achieve workers' management by excluding any one category is bound to fail, and will merely help to re-introduce bureaucratic methods of control. Modern society has become 'proletarianized' to the extent that the old 'petty bourgeois' class is disappearing, that most people have been transformed into wage earners and have been subjected to the capitalist division of labour. However, this proletarianization in no way represents the classical Marxist image of a society moving towards two poles, a vast mass of increasingly impoverished workers and a handful of immensely rich and powerful capitalists. Rather has society been transformed into a pyramid, or, more correctly, into a complex set of bureaucratic pyramids. As a result, there are not the two poles of Marx but a whole Jacob's ladder, and there are no signs that this will be reversed. Hence the revolutionary movement must learn to translate the language of yesterday into the language of today. Just as it was difficult to explain collectivization to the peasantry in the unmechanized Russia at the time of the Revolution, so it is difficult in the modern world of increasingly specialized skills to put across to the workers the idea of direct control. Now this specialization is, in fact, just another aspect of the capitalist principle of divide and rule, since most skills can be taught much more widely than they are today, and there is no reason why the workers should not pool their information.

Capitalists, on the other hand, cannot do this because they work in competition. Moreover, few of them can even produce their own blueprints, and this applies equally well to all the ministers and permanent secretaries, who only endorse the reports of their experts. And even these work in separate groups, each concentrating on a special field and each using jargon appropriate to that field. The ruling class deliberately fosters this proliferation of tongues, and as long as they are allowed to have their way, the workers will continue to be kept in ignorance, and hence remain like sailors who dare not mutiny because the art of navigation is kept a secret from them.

The revolutionary students can play a very important part in changing this picture. Having been trained as future managers, they are in a position to make their knowledge available to all. To that end, the 'critical university' must be transformed into a people's university. If only a handful of 'technocrats' proclaim loudly enough that the monopoly of knowledge is a capitalist myth, the workers will not be long in realizing that they are being led by the nose, and that knowledge is theirs for the asking.

The events of May and June have demonstrated that when driven into a corner, the capitalists will use violence to defend their bureaucratic hold on society. Part of the hierarchy is concerned with maintaining political domination, another with administrative domination, a third with economic domination, but all are agreed to preserve the system. Or rather, all were agreed until the spontaneity and freedom released by the student movement blew like a breath of fresh air through all the petrified institutions, organizations and professional bodies of France, and forced many who had been among the staunchest defenders of the system to question its basis for the first time. A case in point is the action of schoolteachers, who came from far and wide to join in the deliberation of the far left militants of the Federation of National Education when, only two months earlier, the Federation had found it quite impossible to interest them in even the most tempting pedagogical debates. Now, teachers appeared in their thousands to discuss such fundamental problems as pupil participation, the dangers of a repressive environment, the fostering of the child's imagination, and allied topics.

It is difficult not to adopt a paternalistic tone when speaking of the struggle of high school boys and girls, whose refusal to be cowed often expressed itself in childish ways, all the more touching for that. As they occupied their schools, forced their teachers to enter into a dialogue with them, and joined the students on the barricades, often without fully appreciating what the struggle was about, they matured almost overnight. They had been spoon-fed on Rousseau and *Émile* for years, and at last they realized that it is not enough just to read about freedom in education.

Moreover, as they came home at night and were faced with utter lack of understanding by their parents, were threatened and locked up, they began to question the whole basis of French family life. Having once tasted freedom in action, they would not submit to the authority of those who had never dared to question the power of the State, and had meekly become conscripts at the age of eighteen, to be sent off to fight in the colonies. The liberty these parents refused to give to their children, the children now took for themselves.

The same kind of courage and determination was also shown by many technicians and staff of the ORTF (French Radio and Television). True, the majority of them were not 'revolutionaries' but they nevertheless challenged the authorities, if only by refusing to continue as slavish dispensers of State-doctored information. In so doing, they sabotaged the system at its moment of greatest danger, and robbed it of one of its chief ideological weapons. The ORTF strike highlighted how much can be achieved if just a handful of technicians begin to question society, and showed that what had previously passed as objectivity of information and liberty of expression was no more than a farce.

The 'premature' Revolution of 1968 has introduced an entirely new factor into the revolutionary process: the entry into the struggle of youth, often privileged, but in any case disgusted with present society and thus acting as rallying points for the toiling masses. The crisis of our culture, the break-up of all true values and the crushing of individuality will continue for as long as capitalism and its basic contradictions are allowed to persist. We have just lived through a major tremor, a 'cultural crisis' of capitalist 'life', a crisis in which the exploited themselves not only transformed society but also transformed themselves, so much so that when the struggle starts up again it is bound to be carried to a higher stage. The maturation of socialist thought can never be a purely objective process (because no social progress is possible without human activity, and because the idea that the revolution is preordained by the logic of events is no less ridiculous than trying to forecast it from the stars). Nor is it purely subjective in the psychological sense. It is a historical process which can only be realized in action, in the class struggle. It is not guaranteed by any law, and though probable, it is by no means inevitable. The bureaucratization of society explicitly poses the problem of management, by whom, for whom and by what means. As bureaucratic capitalism improves the general standard of living, it becomes possible to turn the workers' attention to the vacuity of their present lives (as seen, for instance, in their sexual, family, social and work relationships). Individuals find it increasingly difficult to solve this problem by applying the norms they have been taught, and even when they do conform they do so without any real conviction. Many will go on to invent new responses to their situation, and in so doing they assert their right to live as free men in a vital community. The real meaning of revolution is not a change in management, but a change in man. This change we must make in our own lifetime and not for our children's sake, for the revolution must be born of joy and not of sacrifice.

II

The Strategy of the State

1. Introduction

> *'The Empire, with the coup d'état for its certificate of birth, universal suffrage for its sanction, and the sword for its sceptre, professed to rest upon the peasantry, the large mass of producers not directly involved in the struggle of capital and labour. It professed to save the working class by breaking down Parliamentarism and, with it, the undisguised subserviency of Government to the propertied classes. It professed to save the propertied classes. It professed to save the propertied classes by upholding their economic supremacy over the working class; and, finally, it professed to unite all classes by reviving for all the chimera of national glory.'*

Karl Marx: The Civil War in France

All 'democratic' bourgeois authority is supposed to represent the interests of the nation as a whole. Since it ostensibly places itself above the conflicts within society, it can use the 'will of the majority' to remove the cause of these conflicts. It is in the name of this principle that it justifies its actions during periods of overt class struggle. At times of crisis, the machinery, strategy and true nature of authority are brought into the open. Indeed, to provoke this is one of the primary and fundamental tasks of the revolutionary movement. To make the workers accept the ideology of, and repression by, the State the bourgeoisie has brought in a whole system of control and enslavement — a system that becomes more and more complex with increased industrialization and automation. Now, this very complexity renders the State less and less capable of decisive action in an emergency. It must therefore do its utmost to stop such emergencies from arising in the first place.

The French crisis was, at first, a crisis within a single institution — the university. We shall therefore begin by looking at the strategy of the State, or rather its non-strategy, against the revolutionary student movement.

2. The State and the University

Nanterre is a college with a liberal administration, and its Dean, M. Grappin, wanted his institution to be 'one big, happy family'. But though Nanterre is anything but a barracks, it remains an institution whose authority derives from the State, an institution which is controlled by the State, and whose chief function is to serve the State. All the important decisions concerning Nanterre are taken at the Ministry of Education, and the Ministry suffers from a basic lack of historical understanding, or else they would have learned from Karl Marx that 'men make their own history, but they do not make it just as they please; they do not make it under circumstances chosen by themselves, but under circumstances directly found, given and transmitted from the past'. (*The Eighteenth Brumaire of Louis Bonaparte.*)

Thus, when the authorities claimed that at the core of the student demonstrations was a small number of militants, they were right in a way, but did not realize that this minority could only make itself felt because it expressed the feelings, and had the support, of the mass of students.

All institutions have the necessary machinery for dealing with claims for minor reforms within the framework of the system. But what can they do when faced with a movement that denies authority as such and refuses to enter into spurious dialogues? The power of the Head, the Dean in this case, rests ultimately on the power of the bureaucratic state. Now that state is only powerful if it is recognized; when it is ignored it can do nothing. If it is liberal, it cannot consistently oppose the wishes of the majority, and must instead try to get rid of the 'troublemakers'. And it is typical of Nanterre that it tried both courses, and failed.

'For the shoemaker there is nothing like leather', and the authorities were only able to understand opposition in terms of their own power structure. We know *we* are nice chaps, we know the *students* are nice chaps: hence the trouble must simply be their leaders. Once we have got rid of them, everything will be smooth sailing again. Here is Dean Grappin explaining the closure of Nanterre on 3 May:

'This exceptional measure is one whose extreme gravity I appreciate, but the excesses of a few have rendered it unavoidable. I appeal to all of you, and particularly to the students, to show by your work and by your attitude, that our college has not lost its true spirit.'

The technique is simple and, of course, underestimates the strength of the movement. As Professor Touraine explained in an interview, it was the worst possible solution. It relied largely on the fact that, at examination time, the students would be only too anxious to get back to their swotting. But in fact, the majority was ready to sacrifice a year of their time for the sake of hitting out at 'the true college spirit', and all the Dean's calculations misfired.

On 8 April, the administration stage-managed a meeting during which the 'good students' were given the opportunity to protest against the 'lunatic fringe'. Imagine the dismay of the authorities when they could drum up no more than 400 such paragons of student virtue!

The administration now began to panic, and decided to summon the 'leaders' to appear before a disciplinary council. This decision proved their downfall, for instead of isolating these 'leaders' it brought about a mass demonstration by the students.

'The Dean and the professorial body had tried to initiate a permanent dialogue at all levels, but this was not crowned by success. What were these daily agitations all about? In the name of a "university critique" the most stupid rhetoric was poured out in lecture theatres which, for the night, had been christened: Fidel Castro, Che Guevara, Mao Tse Tung, or Leon Trotsky.' (Peyrefitte in the National Assembly on 9 May.)

What precisely was this outburst about? We had, in fact, decided to set up a parallel 'critical university' to attack the ideological content of the lecture courses. Most of the academic staff were unwilling to have their authority and their ideas challenged in this way, particularly as the 'critical university' became the centre of political ferment, a strategical base for the anti-system. It was the critical university that gave a dissertation on Rimbaud and his love for the Commune, and forced a professor to cry out 'Gentlemen, we are writers and poets and not politicians. Art is above the sordid level of politics.'

Faced with the spread of a rival ideology, the university authorities reacted like any political power. That exceptional professor Touraine summed up the position in an interview he gave after the events of May: 'Politics has entered the university, never again to leave. The more modern and scientific a university becomes, the stronger grows its political and ideological commitment. The more young people are taught to think for themselves, the more they will challenge, criticize, and protest. The university continually creates its own opposition. The ferment is bound to develop. The movement of Nanterre was only the beginning. Personally I think that the problems of the professors have only just started ... But if politics must needs be thrown out of the university, then I myself will get out as well.'

3. The Authority of the State and the Vulnerability of Society

The State has an army, a police force, and judges, to fight its battles. The State is above the law because it makes the law, and it will not hesitate to use all its power to defend itself. This could be seen in its reactions to the demonstrations at the Place de la Concorde and l'Étoile — when pained incomprehension gave way to panic. The liberal mask was dropped, and overnight the State resorted to naked force. The authorities had no overall strategy but acted pragmatically from day to day, issuing order after contradictory order. And, of course, neither the police, universities nor judiciary could take any action without a decision at ministerial level — an ironic example of the split between the executive and administrative arms.

The initial strategy of the authorities was to try intimidation. Manipulating justice and the parliamentary machine, they went into business on a grand scale. There were sermons and sentences in the courts (and they even managed to stage a hearing on a Sunday!); the law played its part as obediently as any policeman. Those who were suspected of having participated in the demonstrations were held up to public ridicule, like so many drunkards in the stocks. But in fact the victims attracted more sympathy than disgust. It is generally agreed now that most of the police evidence was trumped up. Sentence did not depend on the part played by the accused, but on the violence of the general demonstration.

'At a time when Paris has been chosen as the site for negotiations on Vietnam, and is showing the whole world that it has no peer as a capital of peace, we cannot allow a handful of agitators to abuse the tradition of French hospitality, to commit acts of violence in the plain light of day, not even sparing passers-by. These acts call down severe punishment upon the heads of those responsible, the more so as all of us know that the great majority of young people have no desire to cause trouble.' (M. Caldaquès,

111

Chairman of the Paris Council.)

'What do they study, these young students? They would be more at home in gaol than in a university. It is disappointing to discover that a handful of young people in revolt can stop the entire university system.' (*Figaro*, 4 May.)

But hard though they tried to slander the movement, to put it outside of the law — they even went to the length of sentencing the noted Catholic student leader M. Clément (President of the Richelieu Student Centre) — their efforts all came to nothing. No one in his right senses paid the slightest attention to, for instance, such diatribes as the one mouthed by M. Peyrefitte on 6 May: 'What right does a union have to launch a strike which does not respect the legal formalities and, moreover, calls airily on teachers to abandon their mission, their students and their university tradition?' (Peyrefitte, 6 May.)

At this stage, as we saw, the authorities brought in the police and the army. It should be said in all fairness that the police were not ordered to shoot, but they nevertheless went into action with considerable relish. Their brutality is well documented: houses were broken into; young people rounded up at gunpoint; and afterwards in the cells, there were beatings and sadistic tortures. It should also be noted that the authorities called in the police well before the students had taken to the streets — as soon as the administration felt they had lost the argument — and that once unleashed the police behaved in a manner that disgusted even their masters. Thus Pompidou felt impelled to disavow their atrocities, and his speech on 11 May brought a sharp reaction from the police: on 13 May, the Federal Police Union issued a press communiqué, the last lines of which ran: 'The Union considers the declaration of the Prime Minister an endorsement of student violence and an attempt to disassociate himself from police actions the government itself had ordered. We find it astonishing that, in these circumstances, a dialogue with the students was not started before these regrettable riots occurred.'

On 14 May, a petition was circulated among the Paris Police Force: '. . . We may belong to the folk-lore of this great city but we will not allow ourselves to be turned into a laughing stock. ...' Rumour had it that the police (and particularly the mobile squads) were about to call a strike.

The police traditionally hate French students, whom they see as the pampered offspring of the bourgeoisie — indeed, in their own Fascist way, they live out their part of the class struggle. But this time the new tactics and extreme mobility of the demonstrators took them completely by surprise. Moreover, in their hunt for students, the police had cordoned off certain districts at night, and then carried out house-to-house searches that antagonized the local population. Indoctrinated, regimented, bribed with special privileges and bonuses, they had undeniably developed a certain 'flic' mentality. Usually, when called on, they respond with violence – but not always. In ordinary times, they are tolerated by the people, it is on this toleration that their power depends, and it only lasts so long as they are believed to be preserving the public peace. The Prime Minister's disavowal came when the country was in the throes of a crisis — the working class had entered the struggle. In these circumstances even the bulldogs in the police force began to wonder where their true loyalties lay. On 22 May, they issued what amounted to an ultimatum:

'We hope that the public authorities will bear in mind what we have said (wage claims for the whole force, a denunciation of the Prime Minister's speech, and expressions of regret that the police could not participate in the general protests), and that they will not try to use the police systematically to oppose the workers' demands for better conditions, lest the police find the performance of certain of their duties in conflict with their conscience.'

When the repressive measures were seen to be failing on all fronts, the authorities at long last decided to abandon the colleges to the students. Having done so, they tried to recover lost ground by again preaching about the importance of the impending examinations. All good children who knew where their real interest lay were called on to show up and overwhelm our little display of bad manners.

And so, while we in the 22 March Movement wanted to deal as quickly as possible with the purely internal issues and pass on to the more basic problems, the authorities tried to befog the issue and launched a large-scale press campaign on the subject of the examinations. Every interview with students was restricted to opinions on this problem. The movement was inveigled into grand debates on the necessity for new techniques of assessing progress, which in any case would only amount to a modified form of the old examination system. This debate went on for the entire second week of May, and I must say that it brought home to the more revolutionary among us how little can be achieved if the struggle is confined to university issues. But, many students became convinced that an improvement of the examination system was all we ought to be fighting about, and once again began to turn a deaf ear to our views on the enslavement of knowledge and the uselessness of the examination system as such.

The most radical of us thus found ourselves isolated. Nor could we have ever broken out, had not the occupation of the factories forced the government to turn away from the examination problem.

This new and aggressive move was made by the younger workers, trade union members or not, but in any case over the heads of the trade union leaders. They had watched the students, many of them had helped at the barricades, and now they were trying to stand up for themselves. The scope and vigour of the stay-in movement surprised even the workers' own leaders and the trade union bureaucracy. As for the authorities, they collapsed in the face of combined onslaughts by the students, young workers and apprentices who were now standing shoulder to shoulder before them.

They quickly promised the students all they had asked for, even participation in working out the reforms, but instead of splitting the movement, they merely encouraged the young workers to press their own claims with even greater vigour. And although these claims were economic, the movement itself was, political for it broke the bourgeois laws — the workers struck without giving notice, locked up some of their bosses, and turned a deaf ear to trade union appeals.

And so, because in its first phase the workers ignored the law, the government could not use its legal machine to stop them. Whom could they ask to sit opposite authority on arbitration boards, whom could they negotiate with?

The young workers had launched their first attack on the power of the State, and though some of their number lost their lives on the barricades in Paris, Caen, Redon and Rennes, they learned that the State has a soft belly. In fact, the State was completely impotent, it had been momentarily by-passed, and while it waited, it trembled.

It is physically impossible to crush a strike when there are ten million determined strikers. The authorities could neither muster enough men in uniform to storm the factories nor manipulate sufficient black-legs to do the job for them.

They ordered the arrest of all the well-known militants but these had gone to ground and their place was taken by active and capable men completely unknown to the secret police. The best strategy was therefore to sit and wait while the Communist leaders regained control of their trade union membership and meekly sued for peace.

Meanwhile, even the more conformist university students had a change of heart and took a critical look at the promised reforms. Thus while the strike extended to Rhodiaceta, Berliet, Renaults and to civil aviation, 300 students of the Ecole Polytechnique threatened to take over this bastion of French education. And so the government offered further concessions all around — with the same result. The Grenelle Agreement was signed and delivered to the trade unions, and the workers turned up their noses at it and stayed in their factories. At this point, the president of the CNPF (Federation of Industries) telephoned the CGT to make sure they would not be taking advantage of the situation. The capitalists had found their mouthpiece: responsible, serious trade union leaders, ready to listen to them, and to counsel moderation. Two days later Seguy was rebuffed by the workers of Renaults, and the employers began to tremble again. The unholy alliance of Grenelle represents the most treacherous piece of politics of this century. All the bureaucrats, Right, Left and Centre, sank their differences to save their own power. It was no longer a question of terminating a strike but of killing a movement which by its very growth had become a danger to them all — Pompidou saving the Communist party and the CGT, Seguy shoring up the government before it crumbled; that was the sordid deal fixed up that week-end at Grenelle. But its massive rejection by the workers pushed the authorities into what Coudray has called the 'void of incomprehension' and ushered in the third stage of the struggle. This phase, short though it was, showed up the political vacuum in French society and created a new historical phenomenon: a duality of non-authority. From 27 to 30 May nobody had any power in France. The government was breaking up, de Gaulle and Pompidou were isolated. The police, intimidated by the size of the strike, and exhausted by two weeks of fighting in the streets, were incapable of maintaining public order. The Army was out of sight, conscripts could not have been used for a cause in which few of them believed. There only remained the regulars, the veterans of Indo-China and Algeria, who were still smarting from the defeats the colonial liberation movement had inflicted on them.

The French Army, for all its technological hardware, has only a small force of foot-soldiers. The French Air Force, with its atom bomb, the Navy with its submarines, aircraft carriers and other Gaullist chimeras could not intervene in this conflict; all they could muster would be a scratch team. No stratum of the population was reliable enough, or strong enough, to oppose the strike. Pompidou's press statement on Friday, 24 May, is significant in this respect — it shows that the government was still trying to present itself as the supreme arbiter of all the various interests in society, while trying to keep private property, and the means of production, in the hands of the bourgeoisie. In his speeches, Pompidou attempted to reassure the workers, the peasants, the teachers, and students; he also tried to set one against the other, to break the solidarity they had forged in action. (see I : The Workers).

For a short time, the State had virtually 'withered away'. A vast new network was being built to exhange information (posters, tracts, visits, personal contacts) and goods. The new system had sprung up by the side, and independent of, the old. Above all, a new type of relationship between individuals and groups was begun, confounding the hierarchies and social divisions of work.

The way in which the trade union bureaucrats (those stalwart supporters of the old order) leapt into the open arms of the 'responsible authorities' shows both that they were unfit to represent the workers, and also that the government, deserted by its own supporters, was willing to grab any hand that was offered.

The long-term planning needed to run a modern economy necessarily involves a progressive attack on the old-fashioned relics of capitalism: small businesses, small tradesmen, and smallholdings. These victims of 'rationalization' are normally more conservative than the more dynamic and advanced captains of industry. They put forward their own specific claims, but cling to what small privileges they still enjoy, the more so as the government tries to protect them artificially against the full effects of competition from supermarkets and the like.

However, at a time of political crisis when stability can no longer be assured, the small businessman is the hardest hit of all, what with his lack of reserves and his absolute dependence on a continuous turnover. Moreover, while hitting him economically, the crisis also leads him to press his own claims more vigorously and to defend his own interests. An overt attack upon the system by the students and workers, therefore, widens the rift between the big and the small fry in the capitalist camp.

This leaves the authorities in a quandary: either they must yield to the pressure of the 'small fry' and act as the champion of all that is most backward in capitalism, or else they will drive the petty bourgeoisie into the workers' camp and so hasten a real change in society. True, the petty bourgeoisie might have been led to Fascism, but Salan was still kissing his wife after being let out of prison, Bidault was finishing his memoirs, and Tixier-Vignancourt was busy reciting the Gaullist credo of national unity. In short, there was no one to turn the petty bourgeoisie, filled though it was with nostalgia for the Empire, into Storm Troopers. Nor can you nowadays find the kind of illiterate peasants who marched with such enthusiasm against the Commune in 1871. In effect, before de Gaulle raised the spectre of Civil War, no one had even thought of this possibility: there was no counter revolutionary force strong enough to be mobilized for the job.

Unfortunately, the forces of the Left failed to exploit the existing power vacuum, to take full advantage of this novel, if not revolutionary, situation. The politicians of the FGDS (Social Democrats) and the CPF (Communists) never even thought of offering solutions which went beyond the old Parliamentary games.

It remains for us to explain why the workers themselves failed to realize and use their new-found strength. They rejected the agreement signed by their so-called representatives but for the most part made no move towards more positive action. The slogan of 'a popular government' acted like a damper for many, and their dreams and hopes escaped with their passion, into thin air. De Gaulle, with his promise of elections, gave all the politicians a new lease of life, and suddenly people began to fall for the old fairy tale that all their problems would be taken care of by the experts, in that enchanted castle — the Chamber of Deputies. The General's army rallied round him, after promises to free all the ex-generals of the OAS, and this was enough to squash what fighting spirit remained in the official Left. With the Communists in the bag, de Gaulle hastened to guarantee fair play, and as proof of his goodwill, he endorsed one of the chief Communist demands: the repeal of the hated social security restrictions. At this, everyone heaved a sigh of relief, all the politicians, all the admirers of the General, no less than the friends of Kosygin and Johnson. And what made it all possible was, we cannot stress it enough, that the organizations of the Left were unwilling for the masses to take power. In short, once the call for a general election was accepted, the revolutionary tide began to ebb.

To begin with, striking became increasingly hazardous, what with police intimidation of pickets, and threats and sanctions against the Leftists, endorsed by the Communist Party and the CGT. The drift back to work started, accompanied by sweet music from the radio, television and press (thank you, *Le Monde,* for those final howls that shattered your last pretence of objectivity!). A return to work in one sector favoured a return in the other sectors, while those who fought on (particularly in the automobile and electronics industries) had to face mounting pressure, not least from the CGT, which presented the meagre economic concessions it had obtained as a great victory. The full power of the State was restored, and industrial arguments returned from the streets and factories into the hands of the 'experts' — the professional trade union leaders. These could hardly wait to set up shop again, to barter in alliances and secret pacts, and to play the old manipulative games they know so well. Their role begins *where the struggle for workers' autonomy stops* — behind closed doors.

And once these men were back in business, the small shopkeepers and the small bureaucrats deserted the workers and crawled back to their old masters, while relishing the extra benefits they had gained by the struggle of the working class.

At the same time, all the political parties thankfully took to the hustings and restored politics to its exalted function in the rarefied atmosphere of ideologies, declarations of intent, programmes and promises. They again started monopolizing all discussion, excluding the masses, and speaking in order to dissemble. Politics being the business of the State and the government, the working class was told to get back to the factory bench and to put their corporate claims through the appropriate agency. Politics for the politicians and drudgery for the working class!

Then petty bourgeois, racist, nationalist, reactionary, Fascist, religious, Catholic, Protestant or Jewish, France gradually shook off the dust and marched sprucely down the Champs Elysées, shouting support for the old general.

Was this rebirth of hypocrisy inevitable? The clearest answer was given in St Nazaire. There, the local trade unions, far more Leftist than their national leaders, called for a counter demonstration against the Gaullists, and more than 150,000 workers, teachers, students and pupils made light work of the 300 to 400 reactionaries. By refusing to call for a similar counter-demonstration in the rest of the country, the trade unions allowed the bourgeoisie to settle back in peace and comfort and to begin unpacking the cash and valuables they had crammed into trunks and suitcases in readiness for retreat to the green hills of Switzerland. The blackmail of the CDR (the Gaullist strong-arm detachment) and other paramilitary organizations could only work in an atmosphere of working-class demobilization and apathy.

To sustain the power of a modern society therefore two things are necessary: the force of the police, and the apathy of the workers. The collapse of state power cannot be explained by the mere inadequacy of some Dean, Rector or Minister; it was due to the action of a determined group of people who challenged its very basis, who ignored the law in order to found a new order, based on common consent. When they did so the conscious or unconscious supporters of the system fell back, simply because they could not rise to the challenge. The students knew that they must bring politics down into the streets, fight for concrete objectives, and not for high-flown abstractions. They did, in the universities, what the workers failed to do in the factories: they ran them by and for themselves. We are not trying to sit in moral judgement on anybody, we are merely recording a fact revolutionaries would do well to remember in the future. If a relatively small number of students could succeed, it is doubly important to understand why the workers stopped dead in their tracks when they had the power to go on.

The structural reforms proposed by de Gaulle fit into the ideological attempts by all the authorities, from the State to the working-class bureaucracy, to render the masses more docile and easy to handle. 'Society must be made less rigid', is what a high State official declared, and this is precisely what the President of the Republic in his message of 7 June 1968 proclaimed he would do. De Gaulle implied that the law would grant every worker a share in the profits, that all would be kept adequately informed about progress in their industry and that all could, by means of their freely elected representatives, defend their own interests, their own points of view and their own (sic!) proposals. In a society guaranteeing workers' participation, in which everyone has a stake in the future, there is surely no good reason for objecting to commands from the top. 'Decisions can be arrived at by many, but must be implemented by one man alone.' And in fact, for almost a quarter of a century, the State has been setting up official bodies to look after the interests of the workers, to wit, the works committees, which have in most cases only two functions: to relieve the bosses of the trouble of managing welfare schemes, and of having to impart unwelcome news to the workers in person. As for the new bit about workers' participation, it was just another sop, as the workers themselves knew only too well. Even so, many employers, and most particularly those running small businesses, objected to the new proposals: they refused to countenance workers' participation in any shape or form. As for the big bosses, they argued that no new legislation was needed, since workers' participation was already a fact.

Our French system allows considerable participation on the national economic level, particularly in the planning commissions within the framework of the economic councils, where the different requirements of all sections of society are brought together, and most often harmonized, in accord with our principle of social partnership (sic!). Participation in business can only increase efficiency if it reinforces the existent structures. It must help to share out responsibilities but it must not sap authority (sic!). It is essential that the representatives of the staff grades and workers prove themselves trustworthy in this respect, that they do not forget the economic facts of life.' (General Assembly of the CNPF, as reported in *Le Monde,* 10 August 1968.)

What this means, when it is stripped of all the verbiage, is that the Employers' Federation expected their 'valuable go-betweens', the trade union leaders, to put economic 'growth' before the interests of the workers. This leads to a system of arbitration in which, although the workers have a say, the government has the last word. In short, de Gaulle's 'participation' is just another verbal fetish to take its place on the shelf beside *'La Patrie'* and 'the family virtues', and one that could be taken up by all the distinguished professors and retired dignitaries, all the earnest young Christian employers and the 'progressive' trade unionists.

Now all modern capitalist societies suffer from a fundamental contradiction which springs from the class struggle. The exploitation of the workers must continually aggravate the opposition of interests between the classes, and result in overt resistance or else the apathy and indifference of the working class. All industries, political parties, systems of government, and the very ideology of capitalism, are therefore shaken by crisis after crisis, conflict after conflict. The 'anti-social attitudes' of the workers and their famous 'blow you, Jack, I'm all right', are direct results of this situation, natural reactions against a system that turns the entire proletariat into 'outsiders'. Reduced to a passive consumer, isolated from his fellows, the worker builds a wall round his family and sets himself to defend it.

At the same time, capitalism must carry the working class with it, for its smooth running depends upon industrial 'peace'. Now, during its ten years in office, the Gaullist régime has changed France very little, with the result that we now have, existing side by side, an advanced technology and an archaic, nineteenth-century power structure. Overwhelmed by a constant stream of crises, e.g. the aftermath of the Algerian war, Gaullism has not even tried to deal with the permanent problems of the French economy.

Let us look more closely at the historical background. After a long period of sluggish progress in which it lagged behind the other industrial powers, French capitalism, after the Second World War, taking advantage of a boom in the world economy, suddenly took a gigantic leap forward. Despite the vacillations of its political leaders, internal conflicts, colonial adventures, and even the tremendous subsidies which the State was forced to pay to uncompetitive sectors of industry, French capitalism finally caught up with its competitors. To make good the losses she had suffered during the war, France was forced between 1948 and 1957 to increase industrial production by 75 per cent. From 1953 to the first quarter of 1958, the increase was 57 per cent as against 53 per cent in Western Germany, and 33 per cent in Western Europe as a whole. This fantastic development went hand in hand with a high degree of modernization which not only changed industrial techniques and productive relationships, but also the attitude of big business. More and more industries became amalgamated, and backward regions of the country were industrialized. The most 'advanced' sectors of French business adopted an American outlook: on the wages front they tried to avoid conflict with the workers by making unprecedented concessions.

But at every stage, the process of expansion, modernization, take-overs and nationalization came up against the 'other France', which saw in it a threat to its very existence. For rapid economic expansion tends to destroy whole sectors of industry (small farmers, small traders, and small industries).

This economic conflict is reflected on the political plane, and tends to render French capitalism politically unstable — the survival of these backward strata, and their exceptional numerical weight, has served to choke the parliamentary system. It has maintained and accentuated the fragmentation of the bourgeois political parties, each of which is clamouring for special privileges and protection on behalf of its particular electors. As a result, the government, far from being able, as it claims, to control individual groups for the good of all, is forced to grant special favours to special groups as the hour dictates.

4. The Gaullist Phenomenon

The views we have been presenting are those of P. Chaulieu *(Socialisme ou Barbarie,* 1958). We must now add an explanation of de Gaulle's rise to power in 1958, and the nature of the Gaullist régime. According to Claude Lefort, French society has undergone two major changes. The first is the extension of the activities of the State, which has come to control an immense sector of the economy, intervening ceaselessly in all its affairs and even playing a controlling part in private enterprise. The second is the new industrial revolution which has completely modernized and 'rationalized' the old methods of production and distribution. This process was not just quantitative, it also changed the very quality of capitalist exploitation — in France no less than in other industrial countries. The result has been a shift of emphasis from *laissez-faire* methods to scientific techniques for increasing productivity, and conveyor-belt methods call for a stable labour force and a more efficient negotiation machinery.

These two processes — greater productivity and better labour relations — demand a new political power structure and a re-alignment of the political, economic and social forces of capitalism. In other words, they call for a political and social system of the Anglo-Saxon type, in which cooperation between the political bureaucracy (the two-party system) and the trade union bureaucracy has reached a high degree of perfection.

A move towards this 'ideal' is characteristic of developments in post-war France. It was the very basis of the 'three-party system' (Communist, Socialist and Popular Republican), and underlay the policies of the RPF *(Rassemblement du Peuple Français),* the party founded by de Gaulle, after the war, and also of the party of Mendès-France. It was responsible for the growth and participation in the state apparatus of the Socialist Party and the MRP *(Mouvement Républicain Populaire).* The major parties between them shared a number of important posts not only in the government, but also in the provincial administration and the nationalized industries. They commanded the allegiance of a large part of the population, and turned themselves into highly bureaucratic and disciplined organizations.

However, this development was only the first stage — far from leading on to higher things, the process of political unification eventually collapsed. After the failure of the three-party system there came the resurrection of the Radical Party and the formation of a traditional Right, then the emergence of Poujadism and the split within the Radicals. The country returned to the old pre-war proliferation of parties, a state of affairs that was quite out of tune with the needs of modern capitalism: while the economic structure was tending towards increasing concentration, the political superstructure was becoming increasingly fragmented. Now whereas this state of affairs could be tolerated in the past, today it has more serious consequences — the major parties have become so important in running the administration that their disintegration paralyzes the state.

The old distinction between structure and superstructure has become increasingly blurred: the State now has a grip on every aspect of economic life and, conversely, its own steps are dogged by pressure groups of every shape and size. Every department of a Ministry, each parliamentary commission, is shadowed by one or more groups with their own organization, offices, research boards, public relations consultants, publications, and their own, often considerable, financial resources. The role of these organizations is often misunderstood, and some people still believe that they operate by cloak and dagger methods: spies in the Ministry and bribes of highly placed officials. But this is only a minor aspect of their activity. Much more important than those 'machinations of Capital' that were the subject of so many pre-war Left-wing thrillers is the overt and quite legal method of 'lobbying' Deputies.

Whom do these lobbies really represent? On the one hand, they speak for those unwieldy associations covering wide fields of interests, such as the General Confederation of Small Traders, and the National Federation of Agricultural Syndicates. On the other hand they are the mouthpieces of smaller groups which are the more effective in that their interests are more specific, for instance the Sugar-Beet Producers' Association, the Vineyard Owners, the Wheat Farmers, etc. At times they form such coalitions as the alcohol lobby, the road-planning lobby, etc. Again, when it comes to defending a group like the *colons*, coalitions of a dozen or more groups combine into such powerful pressure groups as the Indo-Chinese lobby, or the Algerian lobby.

All these groups try, by various means, to push the particular interests they represent and exercise a constant pressure on the centres of decision. Moreover, they are not simply content to leave it at that, but can rely on agents in all the major organizations, and often they even control deputies, whose election may depend on their support. With the help of these straw men, the pressure groups keep themselves informed of every plan and proposal of the State.

Before these groups, the State is reduced to helplessness. It hardly knows which agents are its own. Its everyday activity is inextricably tied up with these parasites, men who block its every step. This is reflected notably in the failure of every attempt to introduce fiscal reforms, or to control prices.

The result might be called a return to feudalism: a new kind of guild system seems to be developing hand in hand with greater economic concentration. In fact, this growth of pressure groups did not spring up by accident, but is the natural response to industrial 'rationalization'. These groups form what is essentially a defensive counterweight to the power of the bureaucrats, who would otherwise expropriate all the small traders and farmers. Now, these are the very people who, by their sheer number, are particularly important at election time. Neither the fact that they are scattered all over the country nor the nature of their work predisposes them to play an active social role — they only organize themselves in defence of their own small privileges.

Political fragmentation and private pressure groups reinforce each other in practice; the latter can operate more effectively the wider the range of parties competing for their favours. However, as we saw, this process completely undermines the authority of the State, and, in particular, hampers its every effort to introduce the kind of social reform French industry needs so badly.

But why do the leaders of French industry allow this unsatisfactory situation to continue? One reason, and perhaps the most difficult to understand, is the mentality of the French bourgeoisie. They tend to allow their ideology to override their self-interest. For instance, those among them who call themselves progressives or conservative often merely copy their parents instead of responding to the needs of the hour.

In particular, certain sections of big business have been unable to shed their outworn Malthusian attitudes, and deliberately encourage the most regressive tendencies of the most backward sections of the population.

Finally, and this is the crucial factor, the need to keep the Communist Party out of the government renders the authorities extremely vulnerable to every pressure from the Right, whose antics take on an inflated importance. But by keeping the Communists out, the State is deprived of support from those who would most readily accept its intervention in the economy. The anomalous position of the French Communist Party, which would be only too pleased to play the parliamentary game, is due to international rather than national considerations, and must therefore be seen against the background of the Cold War.

As a result of all the factors we have listed, the State cannot make any serious decisions at the national level, or upset the existing balance of parties. Hence the continued existence of the State itself is jeopardized.

The advent of Gaullism can only be understood as a response to the crisis of the State, in a specific situation. De Gaulle came to power to the acclaim of the *colons* and the Army. In fact, their choice of this particular leader showed up the weakness of those who talked of marching on Paris, their guns at the ready. Neither de Gaulle's record nor his speeches made him the kind of Fascist hero they needed, or, for that matter, a dedicated fighter against Communism.

Be that as it may, the white settlers in Algeria saw one side of Gaullism — the other side was turned towards the metropolis.

To the *colons,* or at least to the most militant and dynamic among them, de Gaulle alone seemed capable of creating a sufficiently strong government to silence the rival factions, while keeping a watchful eye on the interests of the ruling class.

The metropolis, on the other hand, saw in de Gaulle the man who could impose the social reforms recommended by Mendès-France — reforms that could only be introduced by an authoritarian régime that had the full support of the Right. This may seem paradoxical, but if the nature of Gaullism is ambivalent, it is only because the objective situation was ambivalent. There were, in fact, two crises to be overcome: a political one in Algeria and an economic one in metropolitan France. If one looks only at the events in Algeria: the insurrection of the Army and the *colons,* the advent of Gaullism appears as the first phase in an attempt to install a Fascist régime. But important as the insurrection in Algeria was, it was only one aspect of the situation. As soon as one looks at events in metropolitan France as well, the picture is changed, for here, the situation was not at all such as to call for a Fascist dictator.

In fact, as we have tried to show, the fundamental objectives of the employers had for years been not to repress the working class by Fascist methods, but rather to achieve economic expansion through social peace. These objectives have never changed. They grow even more necessary as foreign competition and the Common Market make it certain that any economic recession in France would be a major disaster.

Now, economic expansion entails full employment, and social peace means 'acceptable' wages — and in fact the standard of living has been kept sufficiently high to avoid conflicts. In short, the factors making for Fascism (widespread unemployment and poverty) were completely lacking at the time de Gaulle was called to power.

True, as we have shown, large sections of the petty bourgeoisie felt threatened by industrial expansion, and tried desperately to defend their privileges. Their resentment attracted them to the most reactionary political forces, but since no one had as yet deprived them of their place within the system of production and distribution and, indeed, since they still enjoyed (and continue to enjoy) special subsidies, they were not ready for civil war. They may have applauded Poujade at meetings, but they were by no means prepared to act as his shock troops. If Fascism means anything at all, it means at the very least: dictatorship based on a mass movement; forced exploitation of the working class; and putting the economy on a war footing. And France, as we have tried to show, was not moving in this direction. This was as true in 1958 as it was in June 1968, when de Gaulle was once again acclaimed as the saviour of France. On both occasions he tried to reform the State and to reorganize society, in the interests of the managerial classes. De Gaulle is a kind of economic Bonaparte — apparently above all classes he can manipulate the various political forces who would collapse without him. And once he has got the bureaucrats of the Right, Left and Centre to accept that all problems are political problems and cannot be solved on the Stock Exchange or in the trade union office, he can again appear as the champion of national unity.

And so, in June 1968, after promising new elections, de Gaulle once again got down to the business of re-establishing order. With the help of the CGT, he gave the workers to understand that their essential claims would be satisfied and that, for the rest, he would let them elect a popular government. The parliamentary Left for its part promised a splendid future for all: there would be new youth centres and palaces of culture, stadia, and swimming pools, cut-price cinemas and a democratic radio and television service, a democratic university and to top it all, for all the good little workers, a choice of skiing in the mountains or a holiday in the U.S.S.R.

While the demagogues promised joy and freedom in the future, the police moved in to guarantee the freedom of exploitation here and now. At Flins and at Sochaux they used grenades and left three dead behind.

In order to ease the work of the CRS, the CGT dismantled the defences at Renault and Billancourt, and at Mureaux reproved the militants who refused to give in. As for the students, the layabouts and foreigners who, more and more isolated, continued the struggle in the universities, supported the strike pickets, and denounced the elections as sheer treason, a single tactic was used — systematic repression. All meetings were roughly broken up, the 'leaders' were expelled, including some who were handed over to Franco and Salazar. Clearly, everyone benefits from the fruits of progress.

We know the results of the election: sweeping victory for de Gaulle, crushing defeat for the Communist Party. A lesson to be remembered — if the bourgeoisie is allowed to choose the arena, it will always cut the workers down to size.

And even if the Left had won the elections, we know perfectly well that different men would have promoted the same policies, plus or minus one or two nationalizations, plus or minus a few inflationary measures. Essentially, the capitalist system would have been preserved.

Today, the government must do its utmost to regain what ground it lost during the recent revolutionary upheavals. It has realized that the universities must be reformed if they are to help modernize and reform the economy, and turn out more organization men who know the art of compromise; it appreciates the value of associating students with progress within industry, of creating conditions which give more play to personal initiative and responsibility.

That is why the authorities now favour some system of student participation, greater freedom for lecturers, and even a measure of political life for the students.

If this new freedom can be contained within the university, the danger of widespread infection is contained. This no doubt will be the task of the more reactionary professors who are only too happy to preserve the monopoly of knowledge. They can count on the services of the Minister of the Interior and of his administrative staff to make sure that the faculties never again become the red bases of a new radical confrontation.

But next time we will understand that the enemy is only as strong as we are weak: when we can unmask him as the repressive agent of only one class of society, we bring the working class into the struggle.

Because they can only act within the limits of 'bourgeois democracy' neither the police, nor the Army, nor the law are powerful enough to contain the revolutionary process, once it takes the form of a multiplicity of autonomous groups.

In the police, only the 13,500 CRS and the 2,000 to 3,000 men of the special branches represent a really dangerous force. They live in barracks, are given special training and a highly developed form of brain-washing. As a result, they can be used as shock troops against almost any insurrection. Because of their uniform, their reputation and their SS tactics (at Charonne and the raids of May and June) they are detested by the population. All this helps to cement the solidarity between demonstrators, strikers, and even occasional witnesses of police brutality.

When there are only a few points of struggle, these shock troops are able to intervene in strength, as they did for example at Flins and in the Latin Quarter on the nights of 10 and 24 May. If we had dispersed at 10 p.m., if the struggle had spread to other suburbs and quarters of Paris and to the provincial towns, these troops would have been impotent to deal with us. For instance by our tactics during the afternoon and evening of 24 May, we completely outwitted the CRS — it took them twenty minutes to reach the Stock Exchange after the demonstrators had forced their way in.

These remarks apply equally to the *gendarmerie*. They are rarely stationed where they are needed, and to call them in poses a particularly delicate problem for the authorities. They are mostly the sons of poor peasants, they have few scruples about breaking the heads of 'privileged' students, or even of a few 'city slickers'. But at Flins we could see in their eyes that some of them were unhappy and ashamed to be fighting on the wrong side.

We have already mentioned that before calling in the Army, the government must apply a measure of blackmail and intimidation. In fact, so fearful were the authorities that they took considerable precautions in dealing with the Army. The conscripts (260,000 men) were kept on permanent stand-by, their camps were cordoned off and all access to newspapers and radios was stopped. All ex-students among them were, on various pretexts, either sent abroad or otherwise segregated. Action committees were formed spontaneously in the ranks to organize a break-out from these concentration camps run by the officers. The measures taken against them show clearly how much the authorities feared that the conscripts might join the student movement.

Massive intervention by all the armed forces is certainly a possibility to reckon with in the future, but this would involve turning the country into a Fascist state, and such things cannot be done overnight. Moreover, there are risks to the State itself in letting loose some of the special units (tanks, aviation, marines, commandos) who might very well start fighting for their own interests.

Furthermore, intervention on this scale would necessarily enlarge the struggle: it would bring out all the workers.

Admittedly if, during the power vacuum that existed in the months of May and June, Action Committees had started running the post offices, the social security centres, and other public services, it is possible that the Army might have been called in to intervene.

But in that case, an important fraction of the population would already have made up its mind to run its own affairs, and would have repelled violence with violence. The inevitability of this escalation acts as a strong deterrent upon those who would not otherwise scruple to crush the workers with all the weapons at their command. Moreover, while the special units of the Army can be used to drive the workers out of the factories, they cannot replace them at the bench or the office.

The legal apparatus ground to a halt during the months of May and June. What few measures were taken Pompidou immediately declared null and void, and in any case far from appeasing the revolutionaries, these measures merely served to swell their ranks. Only with the elections, when bourgeois legality was re-established, could Justice once again pick up her heavily weighted scales. 'The bureaucratic machine had seized up and began to disintegrate from within, so much so that it offered the gorgeous spectacle of a Minister responsible for maintaining public order unable to get through to his own department, because his own communication system had gone on strike.

'At last we could see clearly which were the useful cells within the State, and which were repressive or merely parasitic — all those who served a vital function deserted the moribund state to form the body of a new Society.' (A. Glucksmann: *Strategie et Révolution en France 1968.)*

III

Stalinist Bureaucracy and the Class Struggle in France

1. Introduction

The theoretical and practical exposure of Stalinism must be a basic function of all future revolutionary organizations.

De la misère en milieu étudiant

During these events ... the Communist Party appeared as the party of order and political wisdom.

Waldeck-Rochet,
Secretary of the French Communist Party

The rebirth of the revolutionary movement in France cannot be grasped without an analysis of the role of the French Communist Party, just as the revolutionary movement after the First World War cannot be understood without an analysis of the nature of the Social Democratic Party. Today, for the vast majority of workers, the role of the Social Democrats in France is clear: their participation in the various governments during the Fourth Republic, their overtly counter-revolutionary activities during the Algerian war, their permanent compromise with the bourgeoisie, for whom they acted as 'loyal stewards' (Léon Blum) — have utterly estranged them from the large mass of the exploited. If social democracy is not dead, this is largely due to Stalinism which has thrown so many workers into its arms.

If the workers were similarly aware of the true nature and role of the French Communist Party and of the CGT which it controls, they would break with it almost to a man, and this would be entirely to the good if only it led to the emergence of a truly revolutionary movement. As it is, the break which started many long years ago has been passive and predominantly negative in its results — the workers have voted with their feet. The May crisis did a great deal to change this picture: it not only helped to deplete the ranks of party members even further, but it also provided the more class-conscious among them with a new, revolutionary, platform. If this book contributes to this process it will not have been written in vain.

2. The French Communist Party and the CGT during May and June

If we examine the history of the French Communist Party, we shall find that the unsavoury role it played in 1968 was not a new one: it behaved in a very similar, if not identical, fashion (though in a different historical context) on two previous occasions: in 1936 and again in 1945. Nor is this a coincidence.

Now, though the French Communist Party generally speaks with two voices, combining Leninist ideological phrases with electoral and reformist practices, during May and June its practice and language became as one. This is perhaps best illustrated by its attitude to the three main facets of the revolutionary movement — the universities, the general stay-in strikes and the call for new elections — as reflected respectively in (a) Georges Marchais's article in *L'Humanité* of 3 May; (b) the reports by Seguy on 14 and 15 June; and (c) the electoral address by Waldeck-Rochet on television on 21 June.

The Communist Party and the Revolutionary Movement in the Universities

For some years past, the French Communist Party had been busily denouncing the activity of 'Leftist splinter groups' but without attaching any great importance to them. Thus, in January 1967, Georges Marchais, second in command of the French Communist Party, told the 28th Congress of the Communist Party that 'the press and other propaganda media keep referring to these splinter groups in an attempt to build them up, whereas in fact they represent nothing.'

From time to time the Communist press would publish articles on the numerical weakness of these groups. Then, on 3 May 1968, the tone suddenly changed, and this at a time when the revolutionary movement in the universities was still in its infancy.

'Despite their contradictions,' Marchais proclaimed, 'these splinter groups — some hundreds of students — have united in what they call the 22 March Movement ... led by the German anarchist Cohn-Bendit.'

Marchais had clearly become alive to the potential threat posed by the unanimity of the 22 March Movement, to the fact that its nature had undergone a qualitative transformation. Hence the smear that the movement was 'led' by 'a German anarchist', a line the authorities took up with gratitude. In fact, our movement holds the fundamental belief that the revolution needs no leaders, an assumption that is anathema to Marchais and all other bureaucrats. So not only does our movement have a leader foisted upon it, but one who, in contrast to the true Frenchmen of the Communist Party, is a foreigner. *Minute,* the journal of the extreme Right, would be more precise when it spoke of a 'German Jew'. In any case, the Communist Party bears part responsibility for the xenophobic witch hunt that culminated in the expulsion from France of all foreigners, intellectuals and workers alike — who had taken part in the revolutionary movement or were suspected of having done so.

Not satisfied with agitating the students — to the detriment of the interests of the mass of the students themselves and to the delight of Fascist provocateurs — these pseudo-revolutionaries now have the impertinence to think that they can give lessons to the working class. More and more of them have penetrated our factories or the hostels for foreign workers, distributing tracts and other propaganda material.

The true danger had been spotted, a danger against which the Communist Party and the CGT would now mobilize all their forces: an alliance between the revolutionary students and the working class. This alliance Marchais could only envisage in the form of 'lessons', because that is precisely the type of relationship the Communist Party has with the working class. The Party was grudgingly prepared to turn a blind eye to the activities of the revolutionary groups in the universities themselves, in any case it was unable to stop them. The UEC, the Communist Student Union, was moribund, its numbers dwindling and its influence over 'non-organized' students practically nil, and this despite continued Communist efforts to gain support. The revolutionary groups, for their part, had no wish to represent the mass of 'uncommitted' students — all those who slog away at their examinations simply in order to become economic, political and ideological leaders in the service of the State and of the bourgeoisie from which they have sprung and to whose ranks they are so anxious to return. The object of the revolutionary groups was rather to unmask the university as a bourgeois institution both in its composition and its function. Marchais uses much the same argument, but stands it on its head, by saying that 'the ideas and the activities of these "revolutionaries" are enough to make us laugh once we realize that most of them are the sons of captains of industry contemptuous of students of working-class origin — and that they will quickly snuff out their revolutionary flames to become directors in Papa's business, and then exploit the workers in the best traditions of capitalism'.

Marchais thus realizes that the university is a centre of privilege, and plays on the fact that its class structure necessarily produces a rift between workers and students. This does not, however, stop him and his Party from defending 'the mass of students' — i.e. those who will, in effect, be running 'Papa's businesses' — against the revolutionary students who have broken with their own class. Now, it is quite possible that a large number of revolutionary students will come to terms with the bourgeoisie, particularly if their revolutionary message goes unheard. This merely reflects the weakness of a revolutionary movement limited to the universities. In any case, the chief function of the modern university is to fit the student for a place in the social hierarchy, and only a radical transformation of society can alter this. This is fully realized by all revolutionary students and so is the importance of an alliance with the working class; what differences there are between us concern only the best ways of reaching that alliance.

'Nevertheless we must not underestimate their pernicious endeavour to spread dissension, doubt and scepticism among the workers, and particularly among the young workers.'

Marchais has realized that the workers and students are drawing closer together, and this, as we have stressed, as early as 3 May! So great in fact was the danger, that he went on to warn: 'These false revolutionaries must be unmasked completely, because, objectively, they serve the interests of the Gaullist authorities and the big capitalist monopolies; it is our duty to fight and isolate all those Leftist groups who are trying to harm the democratic movement while covering their tracks with revolutionary phrases.'

Yet try as they might, the Communist students were unable to isolate the Leftists; rather did they themselves become completely isolated in the universities. In the few cities where, on the eve of the uprising, the UNEF (National Union of French Students) was still controlled by the UEC (Communist Student Union) the UEC lost its hold over them almost overnight. At Rouen, for example, after the national committees of SNESUP (University Staff Association) and the UNEF called for a general strike, in answer to the closure of the Sorbonne, AGER, the local section of SNESUP, refused to endorse this decision. The revolutionary students (SCR, ESU, etc.), together with non-Communist lecturers, then called for the election of strike committees, which roundly attacked the Communists. After the occupation of the Renault factory in nearby Cléon, workers came across to attend lectures, and afterwards they loudly booed the officials of the CGT. In its attempt to isolate the revolutionary students, the French Communist Party thus suffered a resounding defeat. Its courtship of the 'mass of students' fell on deaf ears: the uncommitted either joined the revolutionaries in the course of the struggle, or else, as convinced reactionaries, went anywhere but to the Communist Party. The UEC acted as a repellent — for some because they were afraid of its revolutionary claims, for others because they knew it had none. All along, the UEC tried to divert the students from the struggle and to check their revolutionary tendencies. To that effect it joined the authorities in raising the spectre of the examinations — as a proven stick with which to beat the students.

The slander that the Leftists were playing into the hands of the Gaullists and Fascists by giving them cause for retaliation was one that was constantly repeated. Now, as every worker knows, all revolutionary movements meet resistance from the authorities, from the State, and from the employers, who may feel so threatened that in addition to the official organs of repression, they call in the Fascists as well. There is only one certain way of avoiding any possibility of a clash with the Fascists and that is not to attack the capitalist system in the first place. As for the lower middle classes whom the Communist Party graces with the name of the 'democratic forces', they will always take the stronger side. Though perhaps at first repelled by some of the revolutionaries' methods, they become revolutionary as soon as the revolution triumphs and counter revolutionary as soon as reaction wins the upper hand. In either case they will not play an active part — except during severe economic crises when desperation may drive them into the streets.

However, it should be remembered that economic crises never affect the lower middle classes alone but hit the working class even harder. And it is on the success or failure of the working-class uprising that the reaction of the lower middle classes invariably depends.

In Germany, where inconsistent policies by the Stalinists and Reformists alike led to the division and ultimate destruction of the working-class movement, and with it of any truly revolutionary alternative, the lower middle classes were thrown straight into the arms of Hitler.

In May 1968, in France, on the other hand, the revolutionary option was still open, and as the student revolt became more widespread, those workers who did not take their opinions straight from *L'Humanité* followed the events with attention and sympathy. They did not need the Communist Manifesto to tell them that 'finally, in times when the class struggle nears the decisive hour, the process of dissolution going on in the ruling class, in fact within the whole range of old society, assumes such a violent glaring character that a small section of the ruling class cuts itself adrift, and joins the revolutionary class, the class that holds the future in its hands'(Karl Marx).

The Communist analysis of the general strike

With the general strike of 13 May began the second phase of the movement: the entry of the working class into the struggle. The Communist answer was given by the CGT, whose general secretary Seguy is a member of the Politburo of the French Communist Party. It is his report to the National Executive of the CGT on 13 and 14 June which we shall be examining now.

Seguy's argument is interesting both in what it explicitly affirms and in what it glosses over. His report begins with a piece of information that came as no news to anyone, but from which few people would have drawn the same conclusion:

'We have just witnessed unprecedented events in the social history of France: a general stay-in strike by nearly ten million workers.'

Now the events were not, in fact, entirely without precedent, since a similar strike had taken place in May–June 1936 and again in August 1953, though it is true that never before had so many workers been involved. And lest the glaring discrepancy between the great strength of the movement and the puny results the Party was prepared to accept recoiled upon its head, Seguy decided, to cover up his tracks with the claim that: 'we foresaw it all' in that 'penetrating analysis we presented to the 36th Federal Congress on the subject of the economic and social situation in France'. Now that Congress merely repeated what all such congresses always say, namely that capitalism oppresses the working class: 'Their economic and social policy arouses increasing discontent and hence increasing opposition. As a result, the workers become more and more conscious of their common interests, coordinate their struggle and so open up wider perspectives.' Krasucki, secretary of the CGT, had told the 34th Federal Congress some years earlier much the same thing: 'The growth of the opposition and the progress of the union have created a new situation and have opened up favourable and encouraging perspectives for all workers and democrats.' Thus every Congress sees 'the opening of greater perspectives for a greater struggle', not so much against the bourgeoisie and the capitalist State, as against 'monopolies' and 'personal power'. In short, Seguy may well have 'foreseen it all' all, that is, except the general strike (that great anarchosyndicalist myth which as 'everyone knows' died a long time ago). Seguy recalls the wave of twenty-four hour strikes against the arbitrary laws promulgated by the government, and the more 'vigorous' actions at the Dassault Aviation Factory in Bordeaux, at Rhodiaceta in Lyons, and at the Atlantique works in Saint-Nazaire — 'all evidence of the general unrest and clear indications of what was to follow'. He conveniently forgets to mention that during each one of these actions, Leftist voices were raised to demand that it be extended into a general strike, to proclaim that the working class was ready to do battle against the authorities. The official Communist answer was always the same: you take your wishes for facts; the working class is utterly unprepared. The basic strategy of the CGT was to oppose any call for a general strike, and to keep the struggle at the local level. Hence when any political novice could have 'foreseen' that a general strike was in the air, the CGT did all it could to 'foresee' that it did not take place. Nor was that the first time they had acted in this way. In 1953, for instance, when the miners struck for more than a month (from 1 March to 4 April) and workers throughout France declared their solidarity with them, all the CGT did was to steer the struggle from the political into the purely financial plane, once again on the grounds that the workers were unprepared for battle. And so the workers went back to work, loudly protesting at turbulent meeting after turbulent meeting that their leaders had sold them down the river. Delfosse, secretary of the Miners' Section of the CGT, rounded on them with: 'You are an ungrateful lot of fools. We have stood by you all along.' Berthelin, of the FO (Force Ouvrière), also added his voice: 'Quite a few of those disturbing the meetings are in the pay of the UNR' (the Gaullists). Sauty of the CFTC told the men: 'Even if everyone stops work tomorrow, the day after tomorrow the numbers will dwindle, and the day after that there won't be anyone left.' However, the prize must surely go to Berthelin for his further comment: 'The malcontents include a lot of young people who have never been in a strike and who imagine that by striking they can get everything they want.' In other words, the militancy of the young workers was nothing but ignorance and inexperience — small wonder they turned their backs on the trade union movement!

For years, union leaders had done nothing but use the workers' struggle for their own bureaucratic advantage. 'There was nothing spontaneous about the events,' Seguy boasted in his 1968 report, and spontaneity is the chief enemy of all bureaucrats — it challenges their very existence. True, no one has ever pretended that a particular struggle has no links with previous struggles, and to that extent no movement has ever been spontaneous, i.e. unhistorical. By the spontaneity of the working class we simply refer to its ability to take direct action and to develop its own methods of struggle irrespective of, or even against, the wishes of all those great or petty 'vanguards' who proclaim themselves leaders of the proletariat. 'The reason why spontaneity is so important in the struggle of the Russian masses is not that the Russian proletariat is "uneducated", but rather that revolutions cannot be run by schoolmasters' (Rosa Luxemburg: *The General Strike).*

By 'spontaneous' we do not, therefore, mean 'without precedent', but simply 'without official blessing' and in this sense the recent French strike wave was completely spontaneous. It spread like wildfire without the trade unions being able to stop it. As for the 'official' strike which the trade unions themselves called on 13 May, Seguy explained its real purpose when he declared: 'At the same time, 13 May delivered a serious blow to the anarchist groups, those provocateurs who entertained the mistaken hope of being able to lead the movement.' The shoe was in fact on the other foot, for the CGT, unable to beat the movement, tried instead to head it, or rather to head it off. 'Two days later [15 May], fully conscious of the newly created possibilities of entering into a more decisive phase of the battle' (opened up by the students whom he conveniently forgot to mention), 'we sent recommendations to our (his) militants, to assume full responsibility for the organization of the struggle, thus ensuring its coordination and effectiveness.' These vague phrases did not deceive anyone, for only a day earlier, on 14 May, when the workers occupied Sud-Aviation in Nantes and confined the manager to his office, Seguy had publicly denounced the real militants over the radio (Europe No. 1). In fact, the idea of a stay-in strike did not come from the CGT itself, and so, of course, they opposed it bitterly.

The stay-in strike did, however, have the blessing of the local FO* branch, which had for years been renowned for its opposition to the Reformist leaders. It was therefore not by chance that Sud-Aviation in Nantes was the first factory to hold a stay-in strike. The CGT did not call a meeting of its Federal Committee until 17 May, but by the 15th, the Renault factory in Cléon had been occupied, by the 16th it was the turn of Renault at Flins and Boulogne-Billancourt, and by the 17th Rhodiaceta had joined in as well — all of them without the encouragement of the CGT. The only one of these strikes Seguy mentioned in his report was the one in Billancourt, and this is what he had to say about it: 'Those of Boulogne-Billancourt, under the experienced leadership of their CGT officials, have just given us an excellent example of the effective application of the CGT recommendations.'

This was, of course, sheer fabrication: all the workers in the factory and all outside observers are agreed that the young workers struck spontaneously. Seguy knew this perfectly well, the more so as many of his own stalwarts did not hide their surprise at being swept up into the front line, with never an order for a general attack.

'The Trade Unions were overrun from below. This is what various observers have claimed, manifestly ignorant of what has really happened, or else enraged by the success of our tactics (sic!) and filled with envy (sic!).' Now, 'envy of the success of the CGT tactics' is the last thing anyone in his right senses could have felt, and nobody is deceived by Seguy's laborious reconstruction after the event. The facts, and I think I have demonstrated this at some length, are that the CGT never

* *Force Ouvrière,* third most powerful trade union; split off from CGT when latter fell under Communist control.

foresaw, let alone helped to launch, the workers' movement, that the tail never wagged the dog. In the universities, the Communist Party tried to stop all direct action and paid the price of destroying its own student organization; when the CGT used the same tactics in the factories, it signed its own death warrant as well, for thousands of CGT members began to ask themselves what was the good of having permanent officials who keep in the background whenever they are most needed.

But Seguy had not yet done; he still had to explain why a general strike was called over the head of the Party: 'As the class struggle has entered a more critical phase, certain doubtful elements, most of them renegades, have felt free to insult us by suggesting that we let the hour pass when the working class could have assumed power.' Thus, even Seguy was forced to recognize that the class struggle had become more acute, though it was, of course, unfortunate for him that his detractors should have posed the question of the revolutionary potentialities of that situation. Workers everywhere were, in fact, asking themselves what, precisely, they were waiting for, when students and lecturers everywhere were successfully challenging the power of the State — they knew that the students and the lecturers, and not some ministerial commission, had reformed the universities and had created new centres of decision-making. The State representatives in the universities, that is the administrators, had been swept away; the Rectors no longer enjoyed the support of anyone other than the police.

The State was thus reduced to what it essentially is, a police job, but Seguy refused to see even that:

> 'To tell the truth, the question of whether the hour of insurrection had struck or not has never even been posed, neither in the Federal Committee nor in the Administrative Committee which, as everyone knows, consists of serious and highly responsible militants, men who are not in the habit of permitting themselves to mistake their desires for reality.'

Now reality is the very last thing these 'serious and highly responsible militants' desired. The whole problem had, in fact, greatly taxed the ingenuity of the Federal Committee, and Seguy was hard put to it to convince them that, revolutionary though it may have been, the situation was not propitious for a general insurrection: 'No, the ten million strikers did not seek power, all they wanted was better conditions of life and of work.'

But then, no revolution — neither the French nor the Russian — began with a call for power or a radical transformation of society. All the Russian workers demanded in February 1917 was bread and peace. However, at the same time they set up workers' councils which, for more than eight months, coexisted with the machinery of the State and the capitalist class. The insurrectional phase did not really begin until October 1917, that is, eight months after the beginning of the Revolution. But, for the CGT, there are apparently no intermediate steps between wage claims and the full assumption of power. We do not deny that the problem of power would have had to be raised (socialism is not built in a day), but what we do insist on is that the creation of workers' committees on the shop floor, committees that made decisions on the spot instead of waiting for trade unions or employers to approve them, was the first step on a road that might have led to workers' control of the entire economy.

In any case, renouncing a revolutionary policy under the pretext that there is an army and a police force is to renounce any attempt at a radical transformation of society, even by legal and parliamentary means, for clearly the bosses will call on the Army to defend them even against defeat in the polling booths. Was it not because they feared a military putsch in 1958 that a Chamber with a Leftist majority called in de Gaulle? If the Army is ready to fire at millions of striking workers, we do not think it would hesitate to fire at some four hundred heroic deputies of the Left (and when we say four hundred that is the very maximum).

'If, to make an absurd assumption, we had abandoned our Trade Union role and had dropped what our detractors so disdainfully call our "alimentary claims" and had become the generals of a revolution, we should at one stroke have lost the precious confidence of the workers.'

The only disdain we feel is for the CGT in their role of generals of a counter-revolution; the only absurd assumption is that the CGT has retained the 'precious confidence of the workers'. There was never any question of our despising the 'alimentary claims' of the workers, only of deciding whether the time was ripe for attacking its causes, the capitalist system itself, or only its effects — whether our movement could lead to the abolition of wage-slavery, or whether that abolition must continue to be one of the pious phrases dished up at every May Day celebration. Let Seguy read the following quotation: 'Trade Unions work well as centres of resistance against the encroachments of capital. They fail partially from an injudicious use of their power. They fail generally from limiting themselves to a guerilla war against the effects of the existent system, instead of simultaneously trying to change it, instead of using their organized forces as a lever for the final emancipation of the working class, that is to say, the ultimate abolition of the wages system. Instead of the conservative motto : "A fair day's wage for a fair day's work!" they ought to inscribe on their banner the *revolutionary* watchword: "Abolition of the wages system!"' (Marx: *Value, Price and Profit.)* Yet another detractor who despises the workers' 'alimentary claims'!

Not only did the CGT fail to go beyond its 'alimentary claims', but it went back even on these, for the Grenelle agreement they signed compromised on the original claim for a forty-hour week, retirement at sixty, and a change in the labour laws. And this was the agreement that Seguy fully expected the strikers to greet with enthusiasm — or so his speeches in the Renault works suggested. These speeches were, however, greeted with catcalls — the workers were almost unanimous in rejecting what the bureaucrats had so readily accepted. And so the strike continued — as Thorez has pointed out in 1936, 'you have to know how to stop a strike'. To that end, the bureaucrats now tried to take the political heat out of the movement which from the very start had been political in the sense that it challenged the entire system, both by its spontaneity and also by its scope; they called for new general elections. The strikes, they proclaimed loudly at a demonstration held by the CGT and the Communist Party on 29 May, had always been about wage claims and not about the overthrow of capitalist society, as the workers' desire for a peaceful parliamentary decision clearly proved. The bourgeoisie very happily accepted this double package, signed the Grenelle agreement and dissolved the Chamber. But the workers themselves continued to strike, and no elections could be held under these conditions. And so the CGT got down to the business of breaking the strike.

'Since the elections open up concrete perspectives in our perennial struggle for democracy it is in the workers' own interests that we lead them to victory by first settling their claims so that the elections can take place normally. In that spirit the Federal Committee has included a paragraph of the utmost importance in its declaration of 5 June, namely: "Wherever the essential claims have been satisfied it is in the workers' interest to pronounce themselves overwhelmingly in favour of a return to work.'" Since the CGT had gone back on even the original claims, i.e. the reduction of the working week, the lowering of the age of retirement, the change in the labour laws, the new policy of the CGT amounted, in fact, to a call for a return to work at any price. And as, in these conditions, it was extremely difficult to persuade ten million strikers to heed the call *en masse,* the CGT decided to demoralize each industry in turn.

'The others have left us in the lurch,' said those who continued. 'I am ashamed to have gone back while my mates are still fighting,' said thousands of others. The 'massive pronouncement in favour of a return to work' was nowhere forthcoming; in many factories the vote was just over 50 per cent. The following passage is revealing:

"'Well, let me tell you — and I am no student — how they got us to go back to work." The speaker wore the uniform of the *RATP (Régie Autonome des Transports Parisiens).* "I was working in the Lebrun Depot, in the Thirteenth *Arrondissement;* it was the twentieth day of the strike, 4 June, when the CGT leaders gave the order to go back to work. None of our claims had been met and even if they had we, on Paris Transport, ought not to have gone back before the rest. It was only right we should have stood by them. Seeing that we were 90 per cent for the strike — as a vote showed — do you know what the CGT leadership did? They went to see the boys one by one, telling them that all the other depots had gone back. They invented voting results when nobody had voted, and they did this in every depot, telling each one that the others were in favour of going back. Some of us went up to the office to ask for an explanation; unfortunately we weren't enough, so the officials pitched into us. On the 5th, we posted pickets as usual, but, as if by chance, six big police vans had drawn up outside early in the morning, Paris police and the *Garde Mobile,* bristling with guns. We were prepared to stick it out all the same, what with the local people and the students behind us, but the CGT officials told us another pack of lies, made false promises, and the lot. After having divided the movement, they got the other depots to pack it in and they demoralized us as well. And so we, too, went back — with tears in our eyes. So if some of the boys turn in their cards, who can really blame them? But I've kept mine, and not for nothing either.

There are quite a few accounts I'd like to settle with RATP.'"
(L'Evénement, July–August 1968.)

And still the struggle continued. Entire sectors of, for instance, the metal industry remained on strike. But all the CGT now had to do was to sit back and wait for the isolated pockets to grow tired of going it alone. The government, too, now had a chance to show that it still existed — it had been forgotten for such a long time! ... What it had been unable to do for weeks to send the hated CRS against the factories — it could now do almost with impunity. True, it did not try it at Billancourt, so near Paris, with its 30,000 workers, but at remote little Flins, and at Sochaux. 'Leftist groups, often complete strangers to the workers, pretending that the struggle for wage claims was of no importance, violently opposed the wishes of those workers whose claims had been satisfied, and who wanted to return to work' (CGT).

The truth is altogether different. For as soon as they heard what was happening, the students rushed to Flins, not to oppose the wishes of the workers, but to express their solidarity with them and to do battle with the CRS. One of the students was killed. There was also a fight at Sochaux where two people died. To prevent a spontaneous new flare-up of the struggle, the CGT felt impelled to call for a one-hour strike, no more, against this triple assassination. 'How many dead do we need for a twenty-four hour strike?' the Leftist press asked. The CGT itself published the following communiqué: 'When the government had ordered the CRS into the [Flins] factory and while the workers were peacefully assembled, strangers to the working class, led by Geismar, who is increasingly proving himself an expert on provocation, insinuated themselves into the meeting and incited the workers to re-occupy the factory. These groups, drawn up in para-military fashion, had previously appeared during similar operations in Paris, and were quite blatantly acting in the service of the worst enemies of the working class.' And the CGT, as a fair reward for all the strike-breaking services it had rendered to that true friend of the working class, the Gaullist government, now demanded that all groups of the extreme left be outlawed.

After Daniel Cohn-Bendit's residence permit had already been withdrawn, Seguy still saw fit to declare: 'It would seem that the warnings we issued, even before the Prime Minister hinted that this individual was a member of an international organization, are about to be confirmed.' For the first time, the CGT had, in fact, foreseen something, indeed done something about its forecasts. In his report, Seguy does not bother to hide the role of the CGT in the government ban of all extreme left-wing groups: 'But by exposing the government as an accomplice of these provocateurs ... we forced them to make a show of their innocence and to remove the troublemakers on the eve of the elections.'

A far cry, this, from Lenin's: 'The government has thrown down the gauntlet to anyone with the least shred of honour, by describing as troublemakers the students who protested against arbitrary forces. ... Just cast your eye over the government proclamation; it is full of such words as disorder, commotion, excess, effrontery, licence. On the one hand, they speak of criminal political aims, of political protests, and on the other they treat students as simple troublemakers who need to be taught a lesson in discipline. ... The government needs an answer, and not from the students alone. ... It addresses itself to public opinion, boasting of its repressive energy, mocking at all liberal aspirations. All thinking people ought to take up this challenge. ... The working class constantly suffers oppression and outrages on an infinitely greater scale from the same arbitrary forces which are now embattled with the students. The working class has already begun the struggle for its liberation; let it remember that this great battle imposes great obligations, that it cannot liberate itself from despotism without liberating all the people. ... No worker is worthy of the title of socialist, if he can look on indifferently while the government sends its troops against young students. The students have helped the workers; let the workers now come to the aid of the students' (Lenin: *Complete Works,* Vol. IV*).*

What, we wonder, would Lenin have made of those trade union bureaucrats who not only looked on indifferently while revolutionary students were being shot, but even called for repressive measures against them? In any case, the bourgeoisie was quick to applaud these honourable gentlemen:

> 'The CGT has thus definitely taken a stand against the insurrectionary student movement, and yesterday's declarations by M. Seguy also represent the opinion of the Communist Party. The tone has changed: for the class diatribes of yesteryear, the CGT of M. Georges Seguy has substituted the cold and firm language of men of authority who know their business ... Sang-froid and

responsibility are words that recur constantly in his statement ... The strikes will be extended and will probably reach their height at the beginning of next week. It is by paying this price that the Trade Unions hope to deflate the insurrectionist student movement and the irresponsible groups behind it' (Hamelet in *Le Figaro*).

And there is little doubt that when Seguy went on to speak of 'public opinion' it was, in fact, the bourgeois press he had in mind: 'Public opinion, deeply upset by all the trouble and violence, confused by the equivocal position and the free and easy attitude of the State, has come to look upon the CGT as a great force for peace and order.'

The bourgeois order, let it be understood!

The Communist Party in search of voters

Let us now leave the CGT, and go on to the French Communist Party, or rather its spokesman Waldeck-Rochet. He is on record as 'vigorously protesting against the substitution of police repression for peaceful negotiation'. For the party, as for the CGT, the whole struggle was apparently aimed at nothing more than negotiation with the State, with the bourgeoisie, and it was within the framework of the capitalist system that it had to remain confined:

'In the impressive movement we have just witnessed, the attitude of the Communist Party has been perfectly clear: it has defended and continues unreservedly to defend the claims of thinking and working France.' The terminology is revealing, it is glorious France that the Communist Party is defending — not the exploited masses. True, France also includes the workers, and the Communist Party 'has done its utmost to obtain the legitimate satisfaction of claims that have been neglected for far too long. It [the Communist Party] has proved to be a great party of progress.' The term 'legitimate' in this passage should be underlined — the legitimate struggle for satisfaction within the legitimate framework of the system, that is, of capitalism.

In other words, the Communist Party is fighting for claims that are compatible with the continued existence of the bourgeoisie — only in this sense is it 'progressive', much as the 'Centrists' call themselves a 'Party of Progress and Democracy'. And on the very day that Waldeck-

Rochet made his speech, the Centrist leader, Duhamel, declared that 'economic progress is hampered by social injustice'.

To make it doubly clear that the Communist Party is a stickler for legality and has never looked beyond it, Waldeck-Rochet continued:

'The Communist Party has appeared as a party of order and political wisdom, appealing to working-class discipline, freely accepted (*sic*).' Now we have seen just how freely the working class accepts the discipline imposed upon it by political and industrial leaders. Yet no one will challenge his claim that the Communist Party is 'a party of order', and that it, together with the CGT, which it controls, has been instrumental in re-establishing order in France — bourgeois order, to be sure. To that end it waged a bitter fight, first against the Leftists, that 'group of troublemakers', and then against thousands of workers. 'Communist militants, as befits men of experience and good sense, have done their utmost to avoid every provocation.'

Now, this fight against the Left was in fact the only one the Party ever engaged in — the better to compromise with the bosses and the state.

'By denouncing provocation no matter from what quarter, we have acted with great discernment.' What wonderful discernment, that can lump the students together with the CRS! Still, there is no doubt that the Party was alive to the real issues, and that it did its utmost to sow confusion among the ranks of the working class. To what extent it succeeded only the future can tell. As for the 'men of experience and good sense' they deserve credit, not for seizing the creaking machinery of the state, not for fighting the authorities and the bourgeoisie, not for organizing the defence of the working class against police brutality, not for exploding the myth of parliamentarianism, of legality and of partial concessions that the authorities can retract at will, but for fighting the Leftists. In this field, in effect, the Communist Party has a long and unenviable record of successes.

'The ultra-Leftist groups attack and insult us because, from the very start, we have refused to have recourse to provocation and ugly violence.'

I have tried to explain at some length the nature of the Leftist 'provocation': all the student movement tried to do was unmask the true nature of the State, in practice rather than by means of theoretical analyses the State can safely ignore.

To provoke the bourgeois State means forcing it to show its claws; to disprove its claim that it is essentially different from Franco or the Eastern bureaucracies. Now these claws exist no matter what the majority in Parliament, and this is what the Communist Party is trying to disguise. Hence it blames all the violence on those who are incapable of it, because they lack the means. But there is little point in unleashing the tigers only to run away when they pounce: self-defence is a major task of any revolutionary movement. The Communist Party, on the other hand, argues that 'we have acted and continue to act with a sense of responsibility when we guard against giving the government any excuse to smash the workers'.

Now, the government has its own means — the television and also the police — of obstructing the workers, and will use them no matter whether the Communist Party is on its guard or not. The only thing the Communist Party can do and does do is divert the workers' movement by giving it the kind of objectives that threaten neither the government nor the bourgeoisie. The strategy of the Communist Party, which, according to Waldeck-Rochet, was to 'bar the path to bloody adventurism, to prevent a military dictatorship' — is one that could be invoked to frustrate all revolutions, for it tacitly grants that the State alone can lay down when and at what point it may be challenged. The revolutionary is far more concerned about what forces he has to overcome, to what extent the State can really rely on the army, for example. Now this is the analysis the Party 'militants' forgot to make; they never asked whether de Gaulle could, in fact, have called in the army to mow down French workers. We shall return to this problem in the chapter on the strategy of the State. Suffice it to say at this point that de Gaulle and the Communist Party both made use of this argument; de Gaulle uttering it by way of a threat and the Communist Party accepting it at face value and without discussion. The mere hint of a putsch should the electoral alternative be rejected had the Communists hopping with ballot fever, just as the dissolution of the Chamber of Deputies set the CGT itching to call off the strike.

'The Gaullists keep waving the Tricolour, but the Tricolour is not the exclusive property of anyone, least of all those who have sacrificed the interests of the mass of Frenchmen on the altar of a handful of multimillionaires.' Now to describe the Gaullists as representatives of 'a handful of multimillionaires' is to mask the reality of contemporary capitalism, utterly to mistake the real nature of the modern state.

And so the mass of Frenchmen — workers, peasants, bourgeois (not multimillionaires but perhaps all those who have not yet gone beyond their first million), soldiers, policemen and clergymen, are enjoined by the Communist Party to rally against the multimillionaires, behind — of all things — the Tricolour.

'In all our demonstrations, we Communists scorn the black flag of anarchy, but march firmly under the tricolour banner of the nation and the red flag of socialism.'

Apparently, some Communist leaders must have thought that there were far too many of the latter, for in their later demonstrations only the Tricolour appeared; had not Lamartine, that well-known theorist of revolutionary socialism, said that 'while the Tricolour was borne through the whole world, the Red Flag went no further than the Champs de Mars'? True, nowadays the Red Flag flies over many ministries and embassies and it, too, has become a highly respectable patriotic emblem. There was a time when the Communist Party, even under Stalin, used rather to look down on all forms of nationalism and patriotism. But that was before 1936, the year the Soviet Union became the Soviet Fatherland ...

Just listen to Waldeck-Rochet: 'We Communists have always fought and shall continue to fight remorselessly the lack of national feeling that certain anarchist elements vaunt as a sign of their revolutionary ardour. We, for our part, are proud to have restored to the working class what Aragon so nobly called THE COLOURS OF FRANCE!' (10 June 1968.)

Nobly indeed! For what Aragon had done was to consign the 'colours of France' to the rubbish dump, and to extol the Red Flag:

> *'Les trois couleurs à la voirie!*
> *Le drapeau rouge est le meilleur!'* (1932)

Or compare Waldeck-Rochet's: 'The Communists love their country passionately ... and because they love it, they want to see it free, prosperous and peaceful ... a good place for all the people ... who are the living reality of France' (10 June 1968), with Aragon's: 'I detest my country; the more French things are, the more they revolt me. A

Frenchman! You take me for a Frenchman ... but I have resolutely turned away from a country that has produced nothing but a bit of bad verse and assassins in blue uniforms ...' (18 April 1925).

Or, finally, compare Waldeck-Rochet's: 'That is why we have denounced and fought demagogy, the lies and provocations of the "ultra-Leftists", supported as they are by the PSU, vaunting their Maoism, their anarchism, their Trotskyism. By their methods, their recourse to ugly violence and to hysterical declamations, these groups have done their utmost to besmirch and discredit that great popular movement which is now drawn up before the Gaullist threat' (10 June 1968), with Aragon's

Comrades
Lay low the cops ...
Fire on Léon Blum ...
Fire on the pontiffs of social democracy ...
Fire, I say, under the leadership of the Communist Party.'
(Quoted by *L' Enragé*, 17 June 1968.)

And after declaring that the Communist Party is the most serious opponent of Gaullist rule (a highly questionable claim) Waldeck-Rochet goes on to say: 'However, the choice today is not between Gaullist rule and the establishment of Communism in France, but between personal power that can only lead to military dictatorship and a democratic régime founded on the union of all democratic forces.' Thus, having first characterized Gaullism economically as the régime of a handful of multimillionaires, the Communist Party now goes on to characterize it politically as a party of personal power — so that once again Waldeck-Rochet has opened his mouth and said nothing at all. As for the threat of a military dictatorship, it could apparently be averted by holding elections, and no doubt, even more surely, if the Gaullists won at the polls. In any case, even if they did not, the Communist Party, and the rest of the official Left, was not prepared to offer the electors a socialist alternative — small wonder that so many of them voted as they did.

General Analysis

To sum up, during the months of May and June, the Communist Party and the CGT played the game of the State and the bourgeoisie in theory no less than in practice. When we speak of the Communist Party and the CGT we are, of course, referring to the bureaucrats running them both, and not to the membership — there is a wide gulf and a clash of interests between the rank and file and their leaders. The rank and file has, in fact, problems that are quite distinct from those of the bureaucracy. Thus during the period immediately prior to the May events, the Communist bureaucrats did their utmost to prevent the workers from calling a general strike. In the universities, the Party opposed every radical challenge to the authorities even on the theoretical plane, let alone in practice, and had only this complaint: the universities were crammed and understaffed and did not admit enough working-class children — there was no attempt at an analysis of the real function of a university in a hierarchic society, namely its support of the hierarchy. Now such an analysis would have shown precisely why there are so few working-class children in the universities — the men at the top try to ensure the best places for their own sons and daughters. It is only to the extent that the privileged classes themselves cannot supply all the needs of the hierarchy that they are forced to draw on other strata of society — their idea of the 'democratization' of education. Now, the Party is not opposed to a social hierarchy as such; it simply wants to change its composition, and that is precisely why it objects to the Leftist analysis. As it was, the mass of students was not deceived, with the result that our movement greatly increased in strength, particularly from 3 to 13 May. During this, the first period of the struggle, the role of the Communist Party was simply to prevent workers and students alike from issuing a radical challenge to their common exploiters.

During the second phase, when this confrontation nevertheless took place — in the form of the general strike which the CGT so strongly opposed and which it tried to sabotage, initially by failing to issue directives — the Party did its utmost to steer the struggle into the 'safe' channels of industrial claims so as to prevent the workers from questioning private property as such or bureaucratic meddling with nationalized enterprises. And in the end it was even prepared to compromise on its industrial claims, settling for less than a forty-hour week and forgetting the pension at the age of sixty. This package, the CGT rightly felt, could only be sold to the workers if they were strictly segregated from the 'violent' and 'irresponsible' students, and this the bureaucrats tried to achieve by hook or by crook.

During the third phase, the Party did its utmost to bring the strikes to an end by getting the workers to accept the terms of the Grenelle agreement. However, when the workers refused and continued to strike, the Party tried to divert the struggle into the parliamentary field by offering them new elections. De Gaulle readily accepted this view and dissolved the Chamber. The bureaucracy now redoubled its efforts to stop the strike, sector by sector. And to prevent any militant opposition or renewed strike action, the Party intensified its campaign against Leftism, a campaign that culminated in the government ban on all extreme left-wing organizations. Only then did the Party feel free to enter the election campaign, which it fought in the name of order, legality and bourgeois democracy, all symbolized by the Tricolour.

3. The Nature of the Communist Bureaucracy

The behaviour of the Communist Party throughout these critical months can only be understood in the context of international politics and the historical background. The present phase of capitalism is characterized by the concentration of economic and political power in the hands of the State, and by the parallel growth of a 'workers' bureaucracy in the industrial and political field. Now this bureaucracy, far from trying to represent the workers, endeavours to persuade them of the general benefits of capitalist production, while staking its own claim to a managerial say in the running of industry and the State. Internally, it is organized very much as is the capitalist system: it has a hierarchical structure in which the top becomes increasingly remote from the bottom. And as industries are becoming ever more complex and gigantic, the bourgeoisie and the capitalist State have discovered that they are quite unable to manage the vast problem of labour relations, and more than welcome the help of the new bureaucracy. In particular, they are quite willing to grant these bureaucrats privileges, to consult them during moments of crisis, or even to charge them with the conduct of public affairs, for only in that way are they able to find willing helpers in imposing their vital demands — greater productivity, wage freezes, no strikes — on the mass of the workers, who would otherwise turn a deaf ear to them. But not content with this subservient role, the 'workers' bureaucracy has been trying to wrest a seat in the very centres of economic power, on the boards of the increasingly important State industries, the latest offspring of the capitalist system. As a result, the workers' bureaucracy now consists of two strata: trade unionists and managers of industry. Their short-term interests do not always coincide: the trade unionists, unlike the managers, must preserve a semblance of concern with the proletariat, for it is only inasmuch as they can claim to be 'representative' of the workers that they have any power. However, their model of society — State, property, planning, specialist control of the economy, a social hierarchy based on ability, the subordination of man to the industrial machine, the improvement of living conditions through the production of more consumer goods, State control of all social and cultural activities — does not differ essentially from that of the economic bureaucracy. And that is precisely why both branches of the bureaucracy, in France no less than abroad, have the same long-term interests as the bourgeoisie, and why the Communist Party of France is so concerned with what it chooses to call the 'national interest'.

This explains why the Communist Party is unable to come out with a real analysis of modern French capitalism, why it disguises the real issue with such red herrings as 'personal power', 'a handful of multimillionaires' and other twaddle which only serves to disguise their community of interest with their so-called adversaries. In point of fact, there is nothing to distinguish the theses of the Communist Party from, say, those of the Gaullist Left, albeit the Party dismisses them as utopian and confused. It does not fight them as such, but simply argues that the Gaullist movement is incapable of implementing them, since it is the Gaullists' right and not the left wing that has the greatest electoral appeal and hence the major say.

But this is only part of the picture. The Communist Party, which once represented the revolutionary consciousness of the proletariat, has been subject to yet another process of degeneration: it has become a mere appendage of the Soviet bureaucracy. In that role it often comes into open conflict with the Social Democratic or Gaullist bureaucracies. Thus when the interests of the Soviet bureaucrats clash with those of their capitalist counterparts, the Communist Party will invariably mobilize the workers against the latter. Conversely, once the Soviet bureaucracy has come to terms with the capitalists, the Party will go out of its way to cement this agreement, and stop any working-class activity that might jeopardize it. During periods of conflict the Communist bureaucrats bandy about revolutionary phrases; during lulls they invariably adopt a patriotic and reactionary tone. It is only by grasping these two aspects of the Communist bureaucracy self-interest and subservience to the Soviet bureaucracy — that we can hope to understand the political vagaries of the French Communist Party from its beginnings to our day.

It is its attachment to the Soviet bureaucracy that causes the Communist Party of France to adopt an ultra-nationalist stance every so often, to be more patriotic than the patriots, more flag-waving than even the Gaullists, the better to deflect the working class from its true objective — the struggle against the bourgeoisie and all forms of authority — and to mobilize them against the Soviet bugbear of the moment, be it 'Revanchist' Germany, American Imperialism, or 'personal power'. It is this double role that dictates their day-to-day attitudes and language, and not some temporary aberration or treachery, as so many good socialists still like to believe. The Communist Party of France defends its own interests and only betrays those who fail to understand that these interests are not so much unpatriotic — and who could blame them for that when the workers have no country? — as unsocialist.

Unfortunately, the Party's links with the Soviet bureaucracy have yet another untoward result: they play directly into the hands of bourgeois propagandists. When dealing with Stalinist Russia, the capitalists do not have to resort to lies or slander — they need only describe the 'socialist paradise' as it really was: a country of purges, concentration camps, forced collectivization and police terror (Cheka, OGPU, NKVD, or whatever the successive names of this permanent institution may be). There is not a Gaullist candidate, particularly if he is on the left of the Party or even an ex-Trotskyist militant like David Rousset, who does not labour this point. As a result, the bourgeoisie has an easy time in dismissing all working-class demands as so many attempts to set up a totalitarian dictatorship. This is precisely what the Gaullists tried to do throughout the electoral campaign. The Communist Party therefore allied itself with the authorities in two ways, firstly by preventing the struggle from assuming revolutionary dimensions, and secondly by permitting the capitalists to raise the bugbear of Stalinism.

It is only because of its authentic revolutionary origins, because of memories of what the Russian Revolution was before it became transformed into a hideous bureaucracy, that the Communist Party of France has been able to keep its hold on the French working class. Even today the Party continues to publish the works of Marx and of Lenin and of other revolutionaries, even though these writings have ceased to have any bearing on the Party's practical policies. It behaves like all reformist bodies, plays the electoral game, adopts the practices of bourgeois democracy, is deeply involved in the system, and makes pacts of all sorts with capitalists. It participates in local government while obeying the laws and principles of its class enemies; during elections, it speaks with a thousand voices, defending small holdings when it addresses the peasants, petty trade when it speaks to the shopkeepers, and calling for better conditions in the army when it speaks to the soldiers. In short, the

Party has a theory for purely internal consumption, and an electoral policy for external use, and the two cannot possibly be reconciled. Now, while the electoral policy has turned the Party into a 'big party', the theory helps to provide Party activists with an ideology — this is important to them, for in that way alone can they feel superior to the Social Democrats who differ from them only in overtly rejecting the Marxist-Leninist line. In short, this unsavoury mixture of theoretical rectitude and electoral compromise provides the Party itself with millions of voters, and its militants with a sense of purpose. This is the entire difference between Stalinist and Reformist organizations, and explains why Communist militants can defend the same policies as the Social Democrats, but with the added conviction that they alone are working for the revolution. This fact alone explains why the Party was so violently hostile to the student movement, because the May events brought the profound contradictions between the conviction of the militants and the policy of the bureaucrats into the open. During relatively peaceful periods deliberately fostered by the Party — reformist practices can be justified by pointing to the impossibility of a truly revolutionary alternative, but how can this be done during revolutionary periods? That is why the Party does its utmost to ensure that no such situation arises, for only thus can it prevent its own militants from becoming 'infected' with the Leftist virus. During peaceful periods, the Party bureaucrats can afford to dismiss Leftist propaganda as the ravings of splinter groups with no influence over the masses of workers. In other words they can claim that the workers will not heed the revolutionary message and that the Party therefore has every right to disguise its 'true' revolutionary intentions. But this argument no longer holds during general strikes, when the Leftist message begins to 'bite' and rank-and-file Party militants begin to realize that the workers are responding to the very truths the Party has been at such pains to conceal from them. No wonder then, that, in May 1968 for instance, the Party leaders were so bitter in their denunciations of Leftism! It also explains their peculiar tactics against the Left; ostensibly still members of a revolutionary and Leninist Party, they could not attack Leftism for what it was, and so had perforce to resort to lies and calumny.

In fact, these calumnies were but weak echoes of what they used to be only a few years ago. Indeed, the language of Marchais was so 'mild' that we wonder why Léon Mauvais, that great expert on Left-wing deviationism, did not demand his expulsion from the Party, just as he did in the case of André Marty, in 1952. One of the complaints he voiced on that occasion was that 'André Marty's attitude to the Party may be gauged from the fact that, in the last report he sent to the Politburo, he referred to Trotskyites not as "Trotskyite rabble" or as "Trotskyite police spies", which is our habitual and natural manner of referring to these individuals, but as the "Trotskyist International" or even as a "Trotskyist party".' In other words, the Communist Party 'habitually' smears Leftists (here Trotskyists) as enemies of the working class. This smear would never stick were it not that the Communist rank and file, accustomed as they are to follow orders from the top, have gradually been robbed of their critical faculties. Let us see how this happens in practice, particularly in the Communist trade unions.

The Communist trade union bureacracy cannot, of course, afford to use open violence against the workers whom, after all, they are supposed to represent, but must wheedle them into acting against their own interests, for instance in calling off a strike.

There are, admittedly, occasions when the trade union bosses throw their normal caution to the wind and try to impose their will by force, but these are the exception: such methods invariably recoil and lose them the support of large numbers of militants. Hence the bureaucrats prefer to save their violence for individuals whom they first isolate from the mass of workers. For the rest they try to cow all opposition with a whole armoury of tricks and ruses. These they can play the more easily, as the workers are kept in complete ignorance of what is happening at the top.

Not that the workers themselves fully accept this situation. In periods of industrial peace, they simply stay away from union meetings and take no interest in a policy that is obviously not tailored to their needs, but during crises, they come up directly against the will of the bureaucracy. In fact, the class struggle continues at all times and expresses itself in a variety of forms ranging from passive resistance to wildcat strikes either against a particular employer or in solidarity with other workers. Now, once a group of workers wants to go on strike they are expected to pass through the normal trade union channels, and if the trade union does not approve — and it rarely approves of any strike that it has not called itself — it will try to put up every possible obstacle, with the result that, unless millions of workers are determined to strike at one time, the struggle remains purely local and generally fizzles out.

To frustrate a strike, all the bureaucracy need normally do is to refuse to issue directives, and then sit back and watch it die. In a factory, the shop-steward faced with a demand for strike action will accordingly do nothing at all, hoping for the pressure to subside. If it does not, he will eventually call a meeting and adopt a completely passive attitude. This takes the workers, who are accustomed to instructions from above, completely by surprise and helps to shake those who are still undecided. ('The shop-steward is obviously not interested, so we are bound to fail.') If the 'rabid' elements still persist, a secret vote is called for, and such votes invariably favour the most conservative elements. True, in a police state, the secret vote is a guarantee of democracy, but among comrades all it guarantees is anonymity for the weaklings.

Generally, at this stage, the bureaucracy carries the day — the workers do not feel strong enough to start a strike without the support of their union. But if even this tactic fails, the bureaucrats have yet another card up their sleeve: they preach defeatism and try to undermine the workers' morale.

To begin with, they will try the trusted old policy of divide and rule: 'You may go on strike, but the rest won't follow you, despite all their promises. They are sure to leave you in the lurch.' Or: 'It's easy for you to go on strike, but then you don't have any children to feed. ...' Or again: 'If you're so keen on this strike, why weren't you in the last one?' One group of workers is told that the rest have already gone back to work when, in fact, they have not — a tactic that, as we saw, proved most effective in breaking the strike of the Paris transport workers in June 1968. And what real chance have the workers of catching them out in time, when only the officials have the right to enter other factories, to see for themselves?

Financial pressure is brought to bear on the workers as well — everyone knows that, just when they are most needed, the solidarity funds are invariably at their lowest.

And once the workers have been brought to their knees by all these manoeuvres, the blame is thrown on them.

In fact, their demoralization is maintained by the bureaucrats who have a vested interest in relegating the workers to the role of mere puppets, a flock of trained sheep who bleat when they are told to do so, and at no other time. Under no circumstances must they be allowed to have any say in the affairs of 'their' trade unions.

The shop-stewards, for example, who, in principle, are supposed to be links not only between workers and management but also between workers and their trade unions, are, in fact, so many mouthpieces for the bureaucracy. In their dealings with their workers or the management, the shop-stewards never take their orders directly from the workers but from their trade union bosses. They are not chosen freely by the workers from the most militant among their own ranks, but from a list of names submitted by the union. It goes without saying that those on the list are never put there for their revolutionary ardour or for the trust their fellow-workers have in them. Nor do the candidates necessarily come from the shop floor they are supposed to represent; some shops may have several shop-stewards while others have complete strangers or none at all. This situation gives the trade union the strictest control over the shop-stewards, and prevents the workers from pressing their own claims. In effect, the shop-stewards represent their union rather than the workers.

Since he does not represent them, and does not have to be their spokesman, the shop-steward does not have to tell them what has been agreed in the manager's office, let alone ask their opinion before he goes up.

And should he be foolish enough to go against the wishes of the bureaucrats and consult the workers all the same, his name is certain to be absent from the list of candidates at the next election.

The trade union bureaucrats take a similarly high-handed attitude when it comes to the publication of factory magazines. Most of the articles are general propaganda for the current policies of the CGT; for the rest they consist of titbits, inter-union disputes, and personal recriminations. These papers in no way represent the interests or reflect the pre-occupations of the workers; at best they reflect the quarrels of their self-appointed leaders. Thus, whenever the workers take independent action, for example by striking, holding spontaneous meetings, or by electing action committees, the factory press passes over the matter in complete silence. That is why a revolutionary movement must do everything it can to encourage the workers to express their own views on their own struggle and their own problems. We must create a workers' press that will be something more than a mouthpiece of the trade union bureaucracy.

It is during shop and factory meetings that the workers make their wishes known most clearly, especially when such meetings are called for the purpose of taking concrete action. Now since such meetings often arrive at conclusions that are opposed to trade union policy, and since the shop-stewards can rarely prevent them from being called, the leaders keep in reserve for such occasions a whole battery of outside speakers and demagogues, trade union specialists. Some of these men are well-known public figures (which did not prevent the Renault workers from booing Seguy), others are skilled politicians who know how to 'handle the masses', that is, to browbeat them. In the presence of such men, the workers generally refuse to say anything; the meeting turns from a discussion into a monologue, the more so as the hall is generally arranged in such a way as to make it more difficult for anyone but the official speaker to make himself heard. The other 'officials' on the platform can add their bit whenever they feel like it, but the worker in the body of the hall must first get up and move conspicuously and laboriously across the floor, before he can have his say — if the chairman lets him, that is. If he is known as a 'trouble-maker' he will generally be called right at the end or right at the beginning of the meeting, only to be cut down by the professionals, and this in such scathing terms that few others will care to carry on where he left off. And at the earliest opportunity, the platform will generally see to it that the original purpose of the meeting is forgotten and treat the audience to a homily on general trade union policy.

But it may happen that the speaker, eloquent though he is, fails to carry the men with him. In that case, the bureaucrats will call for another meeting, this time at Union headquarters. Now if the workers find it difficult enough to make themselves heard on the shop floor, they get no chance at all when faced with a whole bevy of yes-men, loudly applauding the official view, and shouting down any opposition. These meetings, moreover, take place after working hours, and many workers who live far away, or have families, cannot attend.

With such tactics it is not very difficult to engineer majorities, so it is imperative that the workers insist on holding all meetings at their place of work and preferably during working hours. Here the workers must feel free to speak their minds, and the time allocated to outsiders must be strictly limited. As it is, at the least sign of trouble, trade union pontiffs invade the factory and monopolize the time by mouthing the same old platitudes, with the result that the workers get utterly bored and stay away — they have heard it all before. To preserve a semblance of democracy, the workers are often asked to vote on motions hastily read out after the meeting. Now this they should never permit; they must insist that every vote be preceded by a debate and that sufficient advance notice be given to allow them to discuss it between themselves. Moreover, they must be at liberty to scrutinize the results, and also see to it that resolutions running counter to the bureaucrats' wishes do not get conveniently forgotten, as happens only too often. Thus, in April 1953, when the 4CV assembly shop at Renault's went on strike, and all the other branches wanted to come out in sympathy, the bureaucrats held a referendum but kept the results to themselves. The inference is obvious.

In short, the trade unions have become completely alienated from the workers. As a result, the workers have also lost faith not only in the trade unions, which they are fully justified to do, but have grown sceptical of all working-class movements.

Now this situation will continue until such time as the workers decide to take charge of their own destiny, until they refuse to delegate their powers to any set of bureaucrats. The workers' struggle against the exploiters is automatically a struggle against the trade union bureaucracy, since the two invariably work hand in glove — this, as I have tried to show, became particularly obvious during May and June 1968. Inasmuch as the struggle against capitalism and the State is a struggle for freedom and self-government, its objectives can clearly not be achieved with the help of organizations whose very structure is designed to thwart them. Hence, if the workers want to run society, they must first learn to fight their own battles.

What happens if they do not is best shown by the role of the French Communist Party and the CGT during these past thirty years.

A particularly good illustration is the Popular Front, an alliance between Communists, Social Democrats and Radicals in the name of anti-Fascism. It was under the Popular Front that the Tricolour first made its appearance at Communist demonstrations. In 1934, the Soviet bureaucracy suddenly realized that its sectarian disdain of 'other progressives' over the past six years had been a serious error. Hitler's rise to power posed a direct threat to the Soviet Union, and to avert it, Stalin decided to ally himself with the Western democracies. Accordingly, men who had been described as 'social traitors', worse enemies of the working class than even the Fascists, overnight became comrades, true friends who must not be criticized under any circumstances. And in fact, so successful was this policy that the 'Left' won the French elections of 3 May 1936. Trade union unity was also achieved in that year: at the Congress of Toulouse held in March. Hence all the conditions the Communist Party thinks necessary for revolutionary action even today were realized in 1936: political unity of the Left, unity of the trade unions, electoral victory.

Simultaneously strikes broke out all over the country, and it was once again an aeroplane factory that the workers first occupied: Bréguet in Le Havre. This particular stay-in was in protest against the dismissal of workers who had participated in the May Day demonstration. The strikes spread rapidly to Toulouse and Paris, and on 28 May, the entire car industry came out. The strength of the movement may be gathered from the fact that, on Whit-Sunday, 600,000 people marched to the Mur des Fédérés, to pay homage to the heroes of the 1871 Commune. More and more workers now joined the strike movement. On 4 June, the Left formed a new government under Léon Blum, leader of the Socialists. The Communist Party itself did not join the government but gave it full support. As for their attitude to the strikes, we can do no better than quote Montreuil: 'Direct observation enables me to define the part played by the trade unions in this strike. Most of them neither desired nor called this strike, in full accord with the decisions taken at the recent Congress of Toulouse. It would seem that the leading militants misjudged the strength of the rising tide. This movement was born in the mysterious depths of the labouring masses.'

'Mysterious' only to the Social Democratic historian Lefranc, alias Montreuil. In any case, there was no mystery as to the manner in which the trade unions once again tried to steer the strike into safer channels.

'We have seen,' wrote Marchais, 'how the trade union leaders, more prudent than their men, were able to restrain them during the turbulent days of 1936.' And Lefranc once more: 'The Trade Union Movement was a powerful force for order.' How right he was is borne out by the fact that the largest number of workers came out in those industries where trade union membership was lowest: foundries, 4 per cent membership; textiles, 5 per cent; food industry, 3 per cent. By contrast, the railways, with a 22 per cent trade union membership; the Post Office, with 44 per cent; the civil service, with 36 per cent; and the teachers, with 44 per cent, played a very small part in the strikes. On 7 June, the employers, the government and the trade unions met and signed the Matignon agreement. It provided for (1) wage increases of from 7 per cent to 15 per cent; (2) collective bargaining; (3) trade union representation in all factories; (4) the election of shop-stewards.

The government added two weeks of holiday with pay and a forty-hour week.

But, as in 1968, the strikes did not stop, and the CGT began to cajole the workers. 'The CGT representatives explained to Richemond, representing the employers: "We promise to do all we can, but faced with a tide like the present, the best thing we can do is to give it time to subside. Perhaps now you will realize your mistake in ridding your factories of trade union militants during the years of depression and unemployment. There is no one left with enough authority to get the comrades to take orders." And I can still see Richemond, who was sitting on my left, lower his head and say: "I agree, we've made a terrible mistake"' (Léon Blum).

From the beginning of the 1936 strike wave, the Trotskyists, the Anarchists, the Revolutionary Syndicalists, and Marceau-Pivert's Social Revolutionaries, grasped the revolutionary potential of the situation. 'Everything is possible,' Marceau-Pivert wrote on 24 May. 'What the collective consciousness of millions and millions of men and women cries out for is a radical and speedy transformation of the political and economic situation ... The masses are much more advanced than people think ... They expect a great deal; they are not content with the insipid brew as of camomile tea which is being dished up to them ... No, what they want is deep surgery, for they know that capitalist society is mortally sick ...' No wonder that the Communists denounced the Left as the worst enemy of the working class, and that the government, with the full support of the Party, banned the Trotskyist *Lutte communiste*.

On 11 June, Maurice Thorez told a meeting in the Jean Jaurès High School: 'You have to know how to stop a strike once all the claims have been met. You must even know how to compromise over some of the less essential claims which have not yet been met. You can't always have your cake and eat it.'

And from the moment they entered the Popular Front, the Communists even discouraged all attempts to broach the subject of nationalization; indeed they opposed Léon Blum's SFIO, which included nationalization in its election programme, on the grounds that the conditions were not yet ripe. Frachon had this to say in *L'Humanité* of 17 January 1936: 'To claim that it [nationalization] is a simple matter, a basic demand that must be met, is merely to raise false hopes among the workers.' In fact, the only concern of the Communist Party was not to annoy the bourgeoisie, lest it jeopardize the Laval-Stalin pact of 1935. The interests of the Soviet bureaucracy come before the interests of the workers at all times. Hence the address sent by the Central Committee of the Party to President Daladier on the eve of the Radical Congress at Biarritz in October 1936: 'Your great party, which has played so important a role in the history of the Third Republic, can rightly pride itself on its close links with the French middle classes ... The workers, so proud of their skills and so magnificent in their professional dignity, have every desire to make common cause with the peasants, whose rude labour has done so much to make France the great country she is, and with the middle classes, which embody the magnificent qualities of labour and thrift. Like you, we think that public order is indispensable ... Public order demands respect for the law, and that is why we are all agreed in insisting that the laws be respected by all, no less than private property, the fruit of labour and of thrift ... All we desire for our country is order and prosperity ... We want a future inspired by the glorious traditions of the past and we are in no way upset when we are reproached for ... having restored the Marseillaise to its old popularity.'

The same insistence on order, respect for private property and nationalism was persistently sounded in *L'Humanité*, which kept congratulating itself on its part in cementing national unity. Thus Paul Vaillant-Couturier wrote in the issue of 11 July 1936: 'Our party has not fallen from the sky, but stands firmly rooted in the soil of France. The names of our leading fighters have strong and deep links with our land; we follow in the footsteps of history. The reason why our message is so well received by the people ... is because it calls to something deep within them, something specifically French ... In a country so strongly, and sometimes so dangerously, individualistic as ours, a sense of discipline and love of order are badly needed to restore balance and proportion. Our party, by its deep attachment to moral and cultural values ... by its good sense, its exaltation of labour, and its love of clarity, has earned its rightful place in the eternal life of France.'

No journal of the Right, or even of the extreme Right, could have said it better. And this is the kind of prose a 'proletarian' Party sees fit to hurl at the working class, this is the Leninism of Stalin and Thorez!

And what was the upshot of all their collaboration with the class enemy? In June 1937, Blum resigned. On 1 January 1938, prices went up by 50 per cent (index based on 13 household articles) or 48 per cent (index based on 29 food products).

Moreover, by its policy of non-intervention, the French Popular Front had allowed the Spanish Revolution to be crushed. Strikes broke out almost everywhere, once again against the wishes of the CGT, but this time without their old defiant spirit. As an observer, J. P. Maxence, put it: 'They no longer had the same drive [as in 1936], no longer the same sense of purpose. Gone was the old unanimity, the old élan, the good humour, the readiness to brave all legal sanctions. In a space of six months, the spirit of the working class had been weakened, and crushed!'

And so the Chamber, which still had a Leftist majority of thirty-six, went on to approve of the Munich agreement and, in 1940, meekly handed itself over to Marshal Pétain. That is what happens when the working class is diverted from its true path, when it is forced to make 'reasonable' compromises, when it is misled into thinking that capitalism is a reliable ally against, and not the mainspring of, Fascism and war. In 1936, before the strikes, the Metal Workers' Union had a membership of only 50,000 and the strike was general. Afterwards, the membership rose to 775,000, but four years later, in May 1940, it dropped to a mere 30,000. This reflects the rise and fall of just one working-class organization under the tutelage of Social Democratic and Communist bureaucrats.

As for the Communists, their policies, or rather their technique of blowing hot and cold by turns, continue to this day.

Much as the Popular Front policy was determined by the Laval-Stalin pact, and the consequent rapprochement between the Soviet and the Western bourgeois democracies, so Communist policy in 1939–41 was determined by the Hitler-Stalin pact which came like a thunderbolt from out of the blue. For years, the Party had inveighed against Germany with chauvinistic ardour; now the declared enemy was once again the French bourgeoisie and Anglo-Saxon imperialism. The war which had been brewing for years was no longer the battle of democracy against Fascism, but an imperialist war in which the workers had no stake. If this had been the language in 1936, at a time when the workers held the factories, then, yes, it would have been revolutionary, and the whole history, not only of France, but of Europe, might have taken a different course. But coming when it did, it was merely a cheap means of whitewashing the Hitler pact, and anything but revolutionary.

Not surprisingly, the very nationalism the Party had preached so enthusiastically now rebounded on its own head. In 1939, the CGT, or rather what was left of it, once again split into two, one section rallying to the support of the bourgeoisie as it had done in 1914, the other to the support of the Soviet bureaucracy. Then, after the collapse of France, when the bourgeoisie itself split into two factions, one behind Pétain and Germany, and the other behind General de Gaulle and French nationalism, the Communists concentrated all their fire on de Gaulle, that 'agent of the London Bankers'. According to a Party proclamation: 'The nation does not wish to see France a slave of British Imperialism.' In January 1941, de Gaulle was still 'the ally of the reactionary English government of lords and bankers'. I do not quote these attacks on de Gaulle with indignation, because they were perfectly correct in themselves, but simply to show that, instead of directing its venom at the bourgeoisie as a whole, i.e. against Pétain *and* de Gaulle, the Party singled out one and conveniently forgot the other and, incidentally, the horrors of German Fascism. Indeed, such was the logic of their position that they felt entitled to petition the German authorities for permission to re-publish *L'Humanité*. And it was not until after June 1941, i.e. after Hitler attacked the U.S.S.R., that the Communists joined the French Resistance. Then, suddenly, de Gaulle was no longer an agent of Anglo-Saxon imperialism, but an ally in the great struggle of Democracy (with a capital D) against Fascism (with a capital F). Once again chauvinism was the order of the day, with such slogans as 'Kill yourself a Boche today'. This was a time when the Party denounced, even delivered over to the Gestapo, a host of Leftists who refused to be drawn into the struggle. This was also the epoch when numerous French intellectuals joined the Communist Party, and when thousands of workers who refused to do labour service in Germany joined the Communist Resistance, so that the Party recovered part of the strength it had lost in 1939–41. Moreover, the prestige of the Communist Resistance, the title of 'Party of Martyrs', the renown of the 'glorious Soviet armies' brought the Communists hundreds of thousands of new sympathizers, who hoped not only to see the end of the war but also a radical change in society. The strength of the Party was reflected by the slogan 'Towards the Millionth Member'. In 1945, the Party received five million votes and could send 161 deputies to the Chamber; the bourgeoisie, compromised by its collaboration with the enemy, was weak as never before. Moreover, the workers were armed, and ready to impose their will. But nothing at all happened, nothing changed, except that the Communist Party was in the government, that Thorez was Vice-Premier, Croizat Minister of Labour, Tillon Minister of Aviation. A coalition government with the SFIO, the MRP, and General de Gaulle! The explanation of this new bit of class collaboration was found in the Yalta and Potsdam agreements by which the world had been shared out between the Americans, now the dominant capitalist country, and the Stalinist bureaucracy. All Communist parties in the West were expected to ensure that nothing happened to upset the new apple cart. Thorez disarmed the workers' militia and told the Ivry Central Committee on 21 January 1945 that the Party favoured 'one state, one army, one police'. This was the time when the notorious CRS first saw the light of day, fathered by a Socialist Minister, blessed by a Communist Vice-Premier, and hugged to the bosom of General de Gaulle. The reconstruction of the national (read capitalist) economy became the chief plank in the new Communist platform, and the call for socialism was whittled down into a call for the nationalization of isolated sectors of the economy. 'Productivity, higher productivity and still higher productivity, that is your highest class duty,' Thorez told a miners' meeting in Waziers on 21 July 1945. In the same speech he also said: 'It is quite true that we alone, we Communists, had the authority to end the strikes in June 1936, that we alone had the authority to say five months ago: "Let us put an end to the silly civil-war game!"' It was a Communist Minister who introduced all sorts of incentives to force the workers to increase production. And Comrade Duguet told the 1946 CGT Congress that strikes were of benefit only to the trusts — the latest theoretical discovery of Marxism-Leninism-Stalinism! Fraternally united with the Social Democrats, the Communists put all the pressure they could on the proletariat.

The year 1945 also saw the beginning of the colonial struggle. On the subject of the uprising in Sétif (Algeria) Léon Faix, the great Party specialist on colonial questions, came out with the following pronouncement: 'It is highly significant that the chief tools of the colonial oppressors should be the MTLD (Movement for the Triumph of Democratic Liberties) and the PPA (Algerian Popular Party) under Messali Hadj and his thugs, who now clamour so loudly for independence but did nothing and said nothing when France was under the heel of the Nazis. These troublemakers ought to be taught a lesson they will not forget' *(L'Humanité,* 12 May 1945). Faix's voice was heard: 40,000 Algerians died under the bombs of the French Air Force on the orders of the Communist Charles Tillon.

But even while the Communists were able to teach the Algerian workers a lesson, the French workers, exhausted by their productive effort and lack of food, and disillusioned by the whole post-war political scene, drifted away in increasing numbers, not only from the Party but also from the CGT. The year 1947 hastened this process even further. In April, a strike broke out in the very bastion of the United Metal Workers, in Renault-Billancourt, and hard though the Stalinist bureaucracy tried to break the strike by calumnies and violence, the workers stood firm. Then, on the night of 30 April, the Party bosses did one of their perennial quick change acts: unable to smash the strike from without, they decided to lead it and exhaust it from within. They were even prepared to pay a high price: they left the government and called for an end to the wage freeze. But their basic purpose was still to end the strike and, above all, to stop it from spreading further. On 26 November, while the Cold War had already begun, *La Vie Ouvrière,* the organ of the CGT, still saw fit to proclaim: 'It is a fact that for the past two and a half years, France has been the capitalist country with the least number of strikes. The reason is quite simple. The workers don't strike for fun. When their claims are met, they are quite content to go on working. That is precisely what happened in 1945–1946, when Croizat and other Communists were Ministers.'

And since the capitalist system is able to meet all the claims of the working class (another great Marxist-Leninist discovery, this!), provided only a handful of Communists are in the Cabinet, why bother about socialism? And what was it but sheer ingratitude that could have made the Renault workers go on strike under these circumstances? Clearly they had been egged on by Left adventurists, the same people who were causing so much trouble in Algeria, no doubt on the orders of the white reactionaries, the *colons.*

But it was once again a change in the international situation, and not the discontent of the workers, that caused the Communist Party to change its strategy. On 12 March 1947, President Truman presented the U.S. Congress with the famous doctrine that bears his name. The United States would help all countries threatened by and anxious to resist armed minorities. On 5 June 1947, General Marshall, speaking at Harvard, put forward his plan for the rehabilitation of war-shattered Europe. On 27 June, Bevin, Bidot and Molotov met in Paris to decide what precisely Europe was in need of. Molotov warned — as Bevin duly reported to the House of Commons while Bidot said nothing at all — that if American aid were accepted there would be a complete split between East and West. In September of that year, Communist parties from all over Europe assembled in Warsaw, founded the Cominform, a bastardized substitute for the Third International which had been dissolved by Moscow during the war. Zhdanov used the opportunity to present the assembled delegates with a new Tables of the Law, appropriate to a world divided into two blocs. He rounded on the French Communist Party for its participation in the government when in fact it had done no more than apply the old Moscow line. On their return home, the French delegates immediately tried to repair the damage. They not only produced a new ideology but, what was far more difficult, withdrew from the government, national and provincial, and from their cushy jobs in the nationalized industries, which they had enjoyed since 1945. In this, they were greatly helped by the new wave of strikes that swept France in November–December 1947. On 10 November, the Marseilles branch of the Communist Party organized a demonstration against the rise in tram fares. Five demonstrators were arrested, and sentenced to twelve months' imprisonment each. The enraged workers massed outside the court, smashed through the barriers, and were plainly in an ugly mood. The CRS was called in but refused to march against the demonstrators (present-day members of the CRS please note).

The Mayor, a member of the RPF (a precursor of the Gaullist Party), was wounded. Throughout the night there were fights between RPF supporters and the workers, in the course of which one young Communist was killed. Clearly, when it comes to acting in the interests of the Soviet bureaucracy, the Communist Party fears neither violence nor 'provocation'. By next morning Marseilles was in the throes of a general strike.

Working-class resentment was also intense in the Northern collieries. Driven like slaves by the Germans and their French henchmen throughout the war, the miners had hoped that after the Liberation, conditions would greatly improve and, in particular, that they would be allowed to return to their old custom of working collectively and sharing their pay. Their tradition was one of mutual aid, social justice and solidarity. But not only had the French slave drivers been kept on, but Thorez himself had come to address the miners on the advantages of 'individual work', and of competing with one another in separate seams in the mines. All this had delighted the former managers, who had been shaking in their boots, certain that the day of retribution was near. Hence the managers went out of their way to please their new masters: trade unionists and politicians who had jumped up from nowhere after the nationalization of the mines. Now it was only when one of these newcomers, the Communist boss of the Mineworkers' Union, Delfosse, was dismissed by Pierre Lacoste, the new Minister of Production, from his post in the Mine Board — to which he had been appointed by the former Minister — that the Communist Party saw fit to do what it had not done on behalf of the sorely oppressed miners — it called for a strike. By 17 November one-third of the workers was out.

In Paris, some hundred-thousand metal-workers came out on 19 November. In the CGT, Communists and Reformists were at loggerheads. The latter fought against the 'politicization' of the trade unions, i.e. against their being made instruments of Communist policy, and when the Communists used the twenty trade unions under their control to form a national strike committee, led by Frachon, the Social Democrats thought it was high time to break away.

From 29 November to 9 December, the strikes became more and more violent. During the night of 2 December, the Paris-Arras train was derailed — the rails had been torn up over a distance of some twenty-five yards, and sixteen people were killed. 'Fascist provocation', *L'Humanité* wrote; 'Communist sabotage', replied the Right. The government prepared to clear the miners out of the northern collieries, and the workers put up a bitter resistance. Then, quite suddenly, on 9 December, the National Strike Committee ordered the strike to end. Why had they called it in the first instance? Some have alleged that it was part of a serious attempt to seize power, but one who ought to know best, Jules Moch, the then Minister of the Interior, told British and American journalists on 18 February: 'Were the strikes a sign of an insurrectionist movement? I, for one, do not think so. The documents in our possession show that the Communist tactics were much more subtle than that. They had orders to cause trouble in all areas benefiting from American aid, but not to prepare for a Revolution.' In effect, as Frachon declared in *L'Humanité* on 7 December, 'the CGT never gave the order for a general strike'. And, indeed, they pitched their demands very low. In short, they did not so much want to embarrass the government, as simply to show that no government could function without them. At the same time they tried to tip off the American senators, who had come to study conditions on the spot, that they were about to waste their precious aid on a country that was in danger of becoming Communist. The Social Democrats, for their part, stepped up repressive measures against the workers to show the Americans that no such danger existed, and there was, in fact, a powerful 'third force' — neither Communist nor Gaullist. In the event, Jules Moch and the Atlantic alliance triumphed. As for the workers, they had once again been pawns in a power struggle between East and West — nobody gave a damn for their real interests. And when, in 1948, the trade-union movement split up into the pro-American FO and the pro-Soviet CGT, the workers withdrew from both in increasing numbers.

On the international scene, the years 1947 and 1948 saw the consolidation of capitalist power in the West and of bureaucratic power in the East. Much as the Communists were thrown out of the French government, so the Social Democrats were kicked out of Prague (in March 1948). At about the same time the Greek partisans were subdued with American help. The rift between the two blocs was practically complete, and although the Soviet bureaucracy had powerful allies in the Communist parties of the West, it was harassed by divisions and splits among its own satellites, which culminated in Stalin's open break with Tito. After Germany Korea was cut right through the middle. The Cold War had begun to heat up. From 1947 to 1952, the French Communist Party led the nation into a host of anti-American battles, but since it tried to carry all sections of the population with it and fought under the banner of 'national independence', it avoided causing any embarrassment to the patriotic bosses. In other words, the Communist Party took a very hard line on international politics and a very soft one when it came to the demands of the working class. As a result, its numbers dwindled even further, so much so that when Duclos was arrested during demonstrations against U.S. intervention in Korea, the workers barely raised a voice in protest.

Yet as the Cold War continued, both sides realized that the workers would not stand for another world war and the increased exploitation it would have entailed, and accordingly tried to arrive at some sort of settlement. The 'thaw' began with the end of the Korean conflict. The year 1953 brought the uprising of the workers in East Berlin, and a new, almost general, wave of strikes in France — workers in the East and in the West alike were affirming their independence. In France, the 1953 strikes were quite spontaneous and, once again, had the trade-union bureaucrats hopping mad. And once again they succeeded in squashing them. But what they failed to squash was the workers' growing consciousness of their own strength, a consciousness that culminated in the explosive events of May/June 1968.

In 1956, the rift between the workers and the Party bureaucracy was widened still further. The year had begun with the election victory of the Left, which had promised to put an end to the Algerian war. But the war not only continued; it was intensified. Guy Mollet was greeted with a shower of tomatoes in Algeria and capitulated to the *colons*. The Communist Party nevertheless saw fit to vote him special powers, in order to strengthen his hand against — the Right (sic!). As a result, opposition to the war, rife throughout France, had to be organized by the people themselves, and came to a head when a group of conscripts about to be packed off to Algeria barricaded themselves in, and later stopped the trains by constantly pulling the communication cords. The Communist Party washed its hands of the whole issue. On the one hand it did not want to break with the Social Democrats and so was prepared to sacrifice the Algerians together with the rebellious conscripts; on the other hand it was still opposed to the independence of Algeria and called for a 'true partnership with France' as a means of preventing Algeria from failing into the hands of the American Imperialists. Needless to say, all this did was to strengthen the hand of *French* imperialism, so much so that even the 'old guard' Communists began to grumble. Communist students, teachers, and workers embraced the cause of Algerian freedom — and not just the sham peace propagated by the Party leadership — in increasing numbers.

The war in Algeria was thus not only a factor in increasing political consciousness in general, but it also convinced the militant Left that it could not rely on either the Communist or the Social Democrat bureaucracy. This point was driven further home to them by the Suez adventure and the Hungarian uprising — both in 1956. At this, yet another crisis gripped the French Communist Party, and a new wave of militants broke away. The Party sank to a new low in other ways as well; a case in point was André Still's editorial in *L'Humanité* entitled 'Budapest smiles'.

The revolutionary Left was greatly strengthened by these events; their attacks on Stalinism helped to 'resuscitate' Trotsky, so much so that French publishers suddenly fell over themselves to publish his writings.

From 1956 to 1968, these Leftist groups continuously grew in strength and, in particular, succeeded in capturing the imagination of university students. For some years the Communist Student Union (UEC) had been torn by bitter struggles between those toeing the official Party line, the pro-Italians, the pro-Chinese and the Trotskyists. The Central Executive of the Party realized that if these arguments were allowed to go on, the general membership might become contaminated, and so kicked out all opposition in the UEC, reducing it to a corpse. As a result, the Leftists grew considerably in strength. This trend was reflected within the Party itself, which lost a great deal of its national influence to the Leftist opposition. In fact, both the students and the workers benefited in equal measure, for the waning of bureaucratic control is a necessary (though not a sufficient) condition for all revolutionary activity. The influence and power of the Communist Party are inversely proportional to the influence and force of a truly revolutionary movement. The Party itself, of course, refused to admit all this, the more so as it could still rely on millions of votes at the polls. It forgot that these votes were only on paper, and that it no longer enjoyed the active support of the workers. They had ceased to believe that anyone the Party described as an Anarcho-Hitlero-Trotskyite was an enemy of the working class, and no longer hounded him as they had done in 1945. Nor did they any longer assemble in their thousands as soon as some Fascist smashed a window of *L'Humanité*.

Today the workers feel free to challenge the bureaucracy openly in their factories, and though they may meet violent resistance from the bureaucrats themselves, they need no longer fear that their own comrades will cold-shoulder them. They now realize that there is little to choose between the Communists and the Social Democrats or the

Gaullists — which is why they were so apathetic when General de Gaulle took power in 1958. Aware that the leaders in whom they had trusted for so long had led them up the garden path, the workers had no wish to defend a sham Republic that had served them so badly. Hence they left it to the bureaucrats to bemoan the death of 'true parliamentary democracy'.

For the next ten years, from 1958 to 1968, the Gaullist and Communist bureaucracies put up a pretence of being opposed to each other; the May events forced them to drop even that. True, in their joint efforts to stop the strike and to hold elections, they again tried to present themselves as real alternatives to the voters. At the time they succeeded, but how much longer will the masses allow the wool to be pulled over their eyes?

In May, the French workers briefly defeated the authorities, by-passing their political and trade-union bureaucracies, much as the Russian workers by-passed the Mensheviks in 1917. This took the Russians six months, from February to October, during all of which time they had their own soviets and, unlike the French, were not held back by Party and trade-union bosses. The enemy today is much stronger, not because of his tanks and guns, but because he has powerful allies in the workers' own camp. This was proved in Paris in 1968 no less clearly than in Budapest in 1956.

The realization that hundreds of thousands of others have had identical experiences may help to overcome the apathy of the many workers who have begun to see through their bureaucratic 'leaders', but, feeling isolated, dare not oppose them. Moreover, many who have felt it beyond their power to do battle against the bourgeoisie as well as against their own bureaucrats, now realize that they are stronger than they thought.

Channelling the new-found strength into a truly revolutionary movement calls for a re-examination of the fundamental goals of socialism and for a re-alignment of the forces capable of achieving them.

IV

The Strategy and Nature of Bolshevism

1. Introduction

Of the many characteristic features of the events of May and June, one, I think, deserves particular attention: the structure of the revolutionary student and workers' organizations, or rather organisms. From the very start, the 22 March Movement made no distinction between leaders and led — all decisions were taken in general assembly, and all reports by the various study commissions had to be referred back to it as well. This not only set a valuable example for the rank and file committees in the factories and Action Committees in the streets, but pointed the way to the future, showing how society can be run by all and for the benefit of all. In particular, the end of the division between leaders and led in our movement reflected the wish to abolish this division in the process of production. Direct democracy implies direct management. Hence, though the 22 March Movement at first included a number of convinced Bolsheviks, Trotskyists and Maoists, its very structure was opposed to the Bolshevik conception of a proletarian vanguard. Small wonder then that quite a few Trotskyist groups such as the FER, eventually left the movement, while those who stayed behind did so as an expedient, in the hope of using the movement to strengthen their own organization. In May and June, there were several attempts to establish the 'true revolutionary party', which the working class 'so sadly lacked', and when all of them came to nothing the inevitable cry went up from the far-left press that the workers' struggle was doomed to failure — only an authentic Bolshevik party could lead it to victory. Thus the *Lutte ouvrière* drew this lesson in its special August issue: 'Everyone knows it, and the revolutionaries among us say so confidently to the Gaullists: despite your electoral victory, May and June were only a beginning.

'But it is not enough simply to proclaim our determination to continue the struggle; to bring it to a successful conclusion, we must draw the lessons of the past, and one of the chief lessons this spring has taught us is the need for a revolutionary party. Now this is no new discovery, and revolutionaries who have remained faithful to the Bolshevik tradition have been proclaiming it for decades. But during the past few months, this problem has been posed in an infinitely more urgent and concrete manner.'

Now since these good Bolsheviks also realized that the behaviour of the French Communist Party has caused many good revolutionaries to turn their backs on every type of centralized and disciplined organization, they went on to declare: 'The Communist Party of France is a centralized and disciplinary party. Its centralism and discipline are precisely what makes it so efficient. Young revolutionaries are gravely mistaken in thinking that, because the Communist Party is centralized, it must necessarily play a counter-revolutionary role.' And further on: 'Because the main movement has been spontaneous and because its principal adversary has been a centralized party, one must not draw any rash conclusions, throwing out the baby with the bath-water, and claim that spontaneity alone is capable of advancing the workers' movement.' And after an analysis of all the possibilities that the events of May and June opened up, *La Lutte ouvrière* continued: 'Two factors would have permitted the accomplishment of our task. The first is a higher degree of spontaneous class consciousness ... the second is a revolutionary party ... The role of the party ... is to guide the struggle of the workers not only by defining their correct objectives but also, and above all, by showing at each stage of the struggle, at each new step forward, the path that leads straight to that objective. The need for a revolutionary party is not a new lesson we have to learn. The entire history of the workers' movement, of its victories and defeats, from the Paris Commune to the October Revolution, bear witness to this need.' Now this has been the constant theme of all Bolshevik writers. Thus Trotsky in his preface to a history of the 1871 Commune wrote: 'Once in power, the Commune should have completely reorganized the National Guard, put reliable men in charge and imposed strict discipline. The Commune failed to do so because it was itself in need of a strong revolutionary leadership. Hence it was crushed. In fact, as we page through the history of the Commune, one conclusion is inescapable: the party needed a firm command. Those who fought in 1871 did not lack heroism; what they lacked was singleness of purpose and a centralized leadership — and that is precisely why they were beaten.' The same attitude was adopted by Trotsky's disciples after the Hungarian Revolution of 1956 and, as we shall see, also in connexion with the events of May–June 1968.

Conversely, they argue that the Russian Revolution succeeded because it had a strong Bolshevik party.

Hence any attempt to understand the present strategy of the Communists and Trotskyists and to prescribe the necessary antidote must necessarily involve an analysis of the Russian Revolution, the major attempt to translate their ideology into practice.

Now, in what follows we shall try to show that, far from leading the Russian Revolution forwards, the Bolsheviks were responsible for holding back the struggle of the masses between February and October 1917, and later for turning the revolution into a bureaucratic counter-revolution — in both cases because of the party's very nature, structure and ideology.

For the role of the Bolsheviks during the Russian Revolution, I shall largely rely on Yvon Bourdet's excellent analysis: 'The Revolutionary Party and the Spontaneity of the Masses' as published in the journal *Noir et rouge;* for its role during 1917–1921, I shall refer to the notes compiled by the British Solidarity Movement and accompanying their translation of Alexandra Kollontai's *The Roots of the Workers' Opposition.**

*Published by Solidarity, c/o H. Russell, 53a Westmoreland Road Bromley, Kent.

2. The Role of the Bolshevik Party during the Russian Revolution

On reading Trotsky's *History* of *the Russian Revolution* we are struck by a fundamental contradiction: as an honest historian he shows us just how much the Party lagged behind the masses, and as a Bolshevik theorist he must reaffirm that the Party was necessary for the success of the revolution. Thus he writes: 'The soldiers lagged behind the shop committees. The committees lagged behind the masses ... The party also lagged behind the revolutionary dynamic — an organization which had the least right to lag, especially in a time of revolution ... The most revolutionary party which human history until this time had ever known was nevertheless caught unawares by the events of history. It reconstructed itself in the fires, and straightened out its ranks under the onslaught of events. The masses at the turning point were a hundred times to the left of the extreme left party.' *(History* of *the Russian Revolution,* * Volume 1, 403f.)

This passage alone should suffice to destroy the myth of the Bolshevik Party as the revolutionary vanguard of the proletariat. Its 'lagging behind' was patent even during the first days of February 1917 — the overthrow of the Czar and the creation of workers' councils, were the work of the masses themselves. In this connexion Trotsky quotes Mstislavsky (a leader of the left wing of the Social Revolutionaries who subsequently went over to the Bolsheviks) as saying: 'The revolution caught us napping, the party people of those days, like the foolish virgins of the Bible.' To which Trotsky himself adds: 'It does not matter how much they resembled the virgins, but it is true they were all fast asleep.' *(op. cit.* Volume I, 147.)

This was as true of the Bolshevik Party as of all other left wing organizations. In effect: 'Up to the very last hour, these leaders thought it was a question of a revolutionary manifestation, one among many, and

* Gollancz and Sphere Books, London. All page references are to the Sphere edition.

not at all an armed insurrection ... The Central Committee was unable to give any directives for the coming day.' (*op. cit.* Volume I, 147.) In short, the Bolsheviks were anything but leaders of the masses in February, and subsequently they lagged behind both the action of the masses and also their revolutionary spirit. Thus in July 1917, when 'about 10,000 men assembled, to shouts of encouragement, the machine-gunners told how they had received an order to go to the Front on 4 July, but they had decided not to go to the German Front against the German proletariat but against their own capitalist ministers. Feeling ran high. "Let's get moving!" cried the workers. The secretary of the factory committee, a Bolshevik, objected, suggesting that they ask instructions from the party. Protests from all sides: "Down with it. Again you want to postpone things. We can't live that way any longer." Towards six o'clock came representatives from the Executive Committee, but they succeeded still less with the workers.'(*op. cit.* Volume II, 127.)

The Bolsheviks not only played no part in this struggle but tried to squash it; they wanted to refer the whole matter back to Party Headquarters, and when their leaders arrived these were. shouted down. A wide gulf had opened up between the Party and the 'masses' who had a dynamic of their own and, from the start, set up their own soldiers' and workers' soviets. It was here and nowhere else that the real decisions were taken. In the workers' soviets, each member, Bolshevik or not, could make his voice heard and hence influence events. No political group as such had the right to decide any issues, even though the delegates were originally chosen from among Party militants (Mensheviks first, and then Bolsheviks). However, these men were picked not for their political orthodoxy but because of their active participation in the workers' struggle, and when they tried to act as dampers they were generally dismissed very quickly — at least while Soviet democracy still existed. Trotsky has described the role of the Bolsheviks in July 1917, as follows: 'The Bolsheviks were caught up by the movement and dragged into it, looking around the while for some justification for an action which flatly contravened the official decision of the party. (*op. cit.* Volume II, 30.) And, so as not to lose face, rank and file Bolsheviks were forced to go flatly against the decisions of their leaders: 'Their Central Committee addressed an appeal to the workers and soldiers: "Unknown persons ... are summoning you into the streets under arms, and that proves that the summons does not come from any of the Soviet parties..." Thus the Central Committee — both of the Party and the Soviet — proposed, but the masses disposed.' (*op. cit.* Volume II, 33.)

Here we are not so much interested in whether or not the Bolsheviks had good reasons for opposing these demonstrations as in the fact that they had no sway over the masses. Clearly, five months after the Revolution and three months after the October uprising, the masses were still governing themselves, and the Bolshevik vanguard simply had to toe the line. 'Popular Bolsheviks — Nevsky, Lashevich, Padvoisky — speaking from the balcony, tried to send the regiments home. They were answered from below: "Go to hell! Go to hell!" Such cries the Bolshevik balcony had never yet heard from the soldiers, it was an alarming sign ... What was to be done? Could the Bolsheviks possibly stand aside? The members of the Petrograd Committee together with the delegates of the Conference and representatives from the regiments and factories, passed a resolution: To end all fruitless attempts to restrain the masses and guide the developing movement in such a way that the government crisis may be decided in the interests of the people (sic!)...'(*op.cit.* Volume II, 33 f.)The fiction of the proletarian vanguard had to be maintained at any price!

Trotsky himself added: 'The members of the Central Committee who were present sanctioned this change of tactics.' (*op. cit.* Volume II, 34.) As if they had had any choice in the matter! (At least before 1921, by which date the secret police and the army could be mustered against the masses.)

But the Party could not just sit by with folded arms. Speaking for the Party leadership, Kamenev said:

'"We did not summon the manifestation, the popular masses themselves came into the street ... but once the masses have come out, our place is among them ... Our present task is to give the movement an organized character."' (*op. cit.* Volume II, 37.) Kamenev therefore admitted that the Party was no longer at the head, that it was no longer directing anything, that all it could do was to organize *post facto*. And how? 'The afternoon summons from the Central Committee to stop the demonstration was torn from the presses — but too late to replace it with a new text.' (*op. cit.* Volume II, 42.)

Pravda accordingly appeared with a blank page, and this is what the Bolsheviks call organizing a movement! And despite all their efforts, the demonstration did take place, and attracted 'at least 500,000 persons'.

The conclusion is obvious: 'The movement had begun from below irrespective of the Bolsheviks — to a certain extent against their will.'(*op. cit.* Volume II, 71.)

Trotsky, moreover, declared in a speech at about that time: 'They accuse us of creating the mood of the masses; that is wrong, we only try to formulate it.' (*op. cit.* Volume II, 7A.)

In short, the great vanguard was reduced to the role of mere mouthpiece, and failed even in this. Still, it might be argued that though the Party was sleeping in February, and though it lagged behind the masses in July, it nevertheless has the October Revolution to its credit. Nothing could be further from the truth.

From April to October, Lenin had to fight a constant battle to keep the Party leadership in tune with the masses: 'Even the victory of the insurrection in Petrograd was far from breaking everywhere the inertia of the waiting policy and the direct resistance of the right wing. The wavering of the leaders subsequently almost shipwrecked the insurrection in Moscow. In Kiev, the committee, headed by Piatakov, which had been conducting a purely defensive policy, turned over the initiative in the long run — and also the power — to the Rada ... The actual overturn in Voronezh ... was carried out not by a committee of the party but by its active minority ... In a whole series of provincial cities, the Bolsheviks formed in October a bloc with the Compromisers "against the counter-revolution" ... In spite of the vast work that has been done in recent years towards concealing these facts ... plenty of testimony has been preserved in the newspapers, memoirs and historic journals of the time, to prove that on the eve of the overturn of the official machine even the most revolutionary party put up a big resistance.' (*op. cit.* Volume III, 145 f.)

Early in October, Lenin could only impose his view by going over the head of his Central Committee: 'His letter to the Central Committee he not only sent to the Petrograd and Moscow Committees, but he also saw to it that copies fell into the hands of the more reliable party workers of the district locals.' (*op. cit.* Volume III, 1931.)

And again: 'Lenin appealed to a Petrograd party conference to speak a firm word in favour of insurrection. Upon his initiative, the conference insistently requested the Central Committee to take all measures for the leadership of the inevitable insurrection of the workers, soldiers, and peasants.' (*op. cit.* Volume II, 132.)

Thus Lenin, aware that the glorious vanguard was again lagging behind the masses, tried desperately to preserve its prophetic role and, in so doing, had to break the very rules of democratic centralism he himself had formulated.

'In the upper circles of the party,' he wrote, 'a wavering is to be observed, a sort of dread of the struggle for power, an inclination to replace the struggle with resolutions, protests and conferences.' And this is what Trotsky had to say about it: 'This is already almost a direct pitting of the party against the Central Committee. Lenin did not decide lightly upon such steps, but it was a question of the fate of the revolution and all other considerations fell away.' (*op. cit.* Volume III, 132 f.)

In short, the success of the revolution called for action against the 'highest circles of the party', who, from February to October, utterly failed to play the revolutionary role they ought to have taken in theory. The masses themselves made the revolution, with or even against the party — this much at least was clear to Trotsky the historian. But far from drawing the correct conclusion, Trotsky the theorist continued to argue that the masses are incapable of making a revolution without a leader. To begin with he admits that 'Tugan-Baranovsky is right when he says that the February revolution was accomplished by workers and peasants — the latter in the person of the soldiers. But there still remains the great question: who led the revolution, who led the workers to their feet? ... It was solved most simply by the universal formula: nobody led the revolution, it happened of itself.' (*op. cit.* Volume I, 145.)

Trotsky not only put the question very well but also gave a clear answer: the Revolution was the spontaneous expression of the will of the masses — not just in theory but in actual practice. But Trotsky the theorist could not accept the obvious answer: he had to refute it since the idea of a centralized leadership is the crux of his dogma and must be upheld at all costs. Hence he quoted with approval Zavadsky's dictum that, spontaneous conception is still more out of place in sociology than in natural science. Owing to the fact that none of the revolutionary leaders with a name was able to hang his label on the movement, it becomes not impersonal but merely nameless.' (*op. cit.* Volume I, 151.)

We wish to say no more. Anonymity is precisely what characterizes a spontaneous movement, i.e. one that disdains the tutelage of official organizations, that will have no official name. Trotsky's argument is quite different: there can be no revolution without leadership and if no leaders can be pointed out, it is simply because the leaders are anonymous. Thus, after recalling that the 'Union of Officers of February 27', formed just after the revolution, tried to determine with a questionnaire who first led out the Volynsky Regiment, Trotsky explains: "They received seven answers naming seven initiators of this decisive action. It is very likely, we may add, that a part of the initiative really did belong to several soldiers.' (*op. cit.* Volume I, 150.) Why then will he not admit that the soldiers took more than 'part' of the initiative? Because Trotsky prefers another explanation: 'It is not impossible that the chief initiator fell in the street fighting carrying his name with him into oblivion.' Thus Trotsky, the historian, doctors the historical evidence to introduce a mythical leader, whose existence cannot be verified because he is dead! Another example quoted by Trotsky highlights the absurdity of this line of argument: 'On Friday, 24 February, nobody in the upper circles as yet expected a revolution ... a tram car in which a senator was riding turned off quite unexpectedly with such a jar that the windows rattled and one was broken ... Its conductor told everybody to get off: "The car isn't going any further" ... The movement of the tramways stopped everywhere as far as the eye could see.' (*op. cit.* Volume I, 151.)

Trotsky makes the following comment: 'That resolute conductor, in whom the liberal officials could already catch a glimpse of the "wolf-look" must have been dominated by a high sense of duty in order all by himself to stop a car containing officials on the streets of imperial Petersburg in time of war. It was just such conductors who stopped the car of the monarchy and with practically the same words — This car does not go any further! . .. The conductor on the Liteiny boulevard was a conscious factor of history. It had been necessary to educate him in advance.' (*op. cit.* Volume I, 151 f.)

And a few lines further down he repeats the same refrain: 'Those nameless, austere statesmen of the factory and street did not fall out of the sky: they had to be educated.' (*op. cit.* Volume I, 152.)

The Party as such played no role in these decisive days, but those who were the real actors, 'the conscious instruments of history', had needs to be educated, and by whom if not by the Party? In short, the past actions of the Party justify its present inactivity. There are but two alternatives for Trotsky: either people have fallen out of the sky or else they must have been educated by the Party. The first hypothesis being absurd, the second is the only possible answer. But as the Jewish father said to his son: 'My boy, whenever there are two alternatives, choose the third.' Now that alternative is simply that the workers could have managed without a Party, just as they do in their everyday life. Let us see what Trotsky himself has to say on this subject: 'The anaemic and pretentious intelligentsia ... was burning with desire to teach the popular masses ... but was absolutely incapable of understanding them and of learning anything from them. Now, failing this, there can be no revolutionary politics.' This judgement applies equally well to Trotsky himself, who was responsible for the regimentation of labour and for shooting the Kronstadt rebels. But Trotsky is not aware of this fact, and his *History* is so valuable precisely because he is honest, or stupid, enough to list the facts that contradict his every conclusion. Forgetting what he has written on page 151, he notes that 'one of the factories carried this placard: "The Right to Life is Higher than the Rights of Private Property". This slogan had not been suggested by the party.' (*op. cit.* Volume I, 419.)

No one would wish to challenge his claim that 'the thought of the worker has become more scientific ... because it was fertilized to a large extent by the methods of Marxism.' True, the use of the term 'scientific thought' is questionable, but there is no doubt that scientific Marxism has played a large part in the education of both Mensheviks and Bolsheviks. It should be added that other trends — anarcho-syndicalist, anarchist, social revolutionary — made their contribution too. And as Trotsky himself admits when discussing working class thought, its development was chiefly due to 'the living experience of the masses'.

It was this living experience which went into the creation of the soviets in 1905, soviets which the Bolshevik Party largely ignored, a fact for which Trotsky himself severely criticized the Party at the time. But as soon as he himself turned Bolshevik theorist, he had perforce to dismiss the whole idea of workers' spontaneity. Thus while he says in Volume II, page 72, that the masses were complaining that 'even the Bolsheviks are dawdling and holding us back,' he goes on to say on page 88: 'What they (the German Spartacists) lacked was a Bolshevik party.'

The absurdity of his hypotheses — all due to the fact that he cannot admit the idea of a spontaneous revolution — becomes even clearer in the following passage: 'A careful study of the materials characterizing the party life during the war and the beginning of the revolution ... reveals more clearly every day the immense intellectual backsliding of the upper stratum of the Bolsheviks during the war when the proper life of the party practically came to an end. The cause of this backsliding is twofold: isolation from the masses and isolation from those abroad, that is primarily from Lenin.' (*op. cit.* Volume III, 134.) This 'twofold backsliding' is nothing less than an indictment of the Bolshevik Party: by stressing the importance of Lenin in the way he does, Trotsky is, in fact, depreciating the value of the Party. And Lenin, far from being the infallible revolutionary Trotsky makes him out to be, between February and October 1917, went back on a good many positions he had earlier defended. Thus while he had stressed the importance of soviets in 1905, in January 1917, when he gave a lecture to Swiss workers, he merely mentioned the soviets in passing. This did not prevent him, a few months later, to the dismay of the majority of the Party, from once again adopting the anarchist slogan: All power to the soviets! The Party, faithful and disciplined though it was, could not perform these gyrations with the same speed. The break between Lenin and the Party may prove Lenin's genius when it comes to changing the political line, but it also proves how ill-fitted a Party of the Bolshevik type is to deal with a revolutionary situation. Hence Trotsky's claim that 'the March leadership of Kamenev and Stalin lagged behind the gigantic historic tasks.' (*op. cit.* Volume I, 403.)

However, Trotsky was quick to refute this line of reasoning when it was dished up to explain the failure of the White Guards. Thus he had this to say about the abortive Kornilov putsch: 'The sums of money set aside for organization were, according to Vinberg, appropriated by the principal participants and squandered on dinner parties ... One of the secret contributors, who was to deliver to some officers a considerable sum of money, upon arrival at the designated place found the conspirators in such a state of inebriation that he could not deliver the goods. Vinberg himself thinks that if it had not been for these truly vexatious "accidents", the plan might have been crowned with complete success. But the question remains: Why was a patriotic enterprise entered into and surrounded, for the most part, by drunkards, spendthrifts and traitors? Is it not because every historic task mobilizes the cadres that are adequate to it?' (*op. cit.* Volume II, 219 f.)

Now if every historical task indeed mobilizes the necessary cadres, it will do this for the revolution no less than for the counter-revolution. Hence Trotsky should not really blame the Bolshevik leaders for the failure of the Party to rise to its 'historic task'. The reason Stalin and Kamenev found themselves at the head of the Party was because they were elected by the whole of that Party, and it is therefore the Party as such that is to blame and not X or Y. Again, if the presence or absence of Lenin explains the success or failure of the Party, the Party reduces to Lenin and becomes superfluous.

As for the gap between the Party and the masses, it can have two causes: either the masses are too apathetic for revolution or else, as happened in 1917, the masses are only too anxious to carry the revolution a step further, and the Party itself is apathetic. In the second case it is not the masses who cannot 'rise' to its historic task but the Party. This rupture between the Party and the masses is due to the Party's very nature: a small, closed group of professional revolutionaries, sure of being the repository of truth and incapable of adapting themselves to any independent initiative of the masses. A case in point was their attitude to the soviets, or workers' councils, which gave the atomized masses their own centres for action and collective decisions. The soviets sprang up quite spontaneously in 1905 and did not figure in any party programme. It was only in retrospect that they were analyzed by various writers of the Left. Some of these — particularly the anarchists, the extreme left Social Revolutionaries and minority groups within the Social Democratic Party, were frankly in favour of the soviets — and so, in 1905, was Leon Trotsky. Anton Pannekoek was another and his movement for workers' control was attacked by Lenin in *'Left-wing' Communism: An Infantile Disorder*. All the Bolsheviks were frankly hostile. Those in St Petersburg were convinced that 'only a party based on class conceptions can direct the political movement of the proletariat and preserve the purity of its intentions, whereas the workers' councils are so many heterogeneous and indecisive bodies'. (Quoted by Oscar Auweiler in *The Workers' Councils in Russia 1905–1929.*) At the same time, P. Mendeleev declared in the name of the Bolsheviks: 'The council of workers' deputies is a political organization and Social Democrats (Bolsheviks and Mensheviks) must leave it because its very existence impedes the development of the social democratic movement. The workers' council may exist as a trade union or not at all.' Whence Mendeleev concluded that the Bolsheviks should use the following strategy: 'First of all we must try to get the workers' council to limit itself to its trade union tasks, and secondly, in case this attempt fails, the workers' council must be made to acknowledge the leadership of the Social

Democratic Party, and thirdly, this having been done, it must be dissolved as quickly as possible, seeing that its parallel existence with other social democratic organizations serves no purpose.' And this at a time when workers were beginning to form workers' councils in all the factories, and workers' 'parliaments' in all the major towns! The Social Democrats did not even think fit to invite the workers to participate in their party's august deliberations, but expected them to carry out blindly what the proletarian vanguard ordered from on high, and then to declare themselves redundant. That the workers' councils 'impeded' this sort of development is a truism — they challenged the wisdom of the Party leaders in practice and not simply in theory. This was more than our professional revolutionaries were prepared to swallow. In 1907, Lenin got the Fifth Congress of the Social Democratic Workers' Party to pass a resolution whose subject was highly revealing: 'On the independent workers' organization and the anarcho-syndicalist currents within the proletariat.' He condemned all these 'currents', and declared: 'The participation of Social Democratic organizations in councils composed of delegates and workers' deputies without distinction of party ... or the creation of such councils, cannot be countenanced unless we can be sure that the party can benefit and that its interests are fully protected.' (Quoted by Oscar Auweiler, page 103.)

In dealing with workers' organizations, the Bolsheviks had but one major concern: to strengthen their own organization. Since the Party was the sole guardian of the proletariat and the revolution, any attempt by the workers to make a revolution without the Party must clearly be wrong or indeed impossible, as Trotsky argues in his *History of the Russian Revolution*. When the workers disavow the Party in practice, the Party simply disavows the practice of the workers.

This disdain for the working class and its capacity for self-emancipation can be heard most clearly in Lenin's *What is to be done?*, a theoretical justification of the leadership principle. In it, Lenin simply repeats the words of Karl Kautsky, whom he still admired at the time: 'The workers, we have said, still lacked a Social-Democratic consciousness; it could only come to them from the outside. History in all countries attests that, on its own, the working class cannot go beyond the level of trade union consciousness, the realization that they must combine into trade unions, fight against the employers, force the government to pass such laws as benefit the condition of the workers ... As for the Socialist doctrine, it was constructed out of philosophical, historical and economic theories elaborated by educated members of the ruling class, by intellectuals. Thus Marx and Engels, the founders of modern scientific socialism, were bourgeois intellectuals. Similarly in Russia, the social democratic doctrine sprang up almost independently of the spontaneous development of the working class movement ...'

Lenin summed it all up by saying: 'The workers can acquire class political consciousness *only from without,* that is, only outside of the economic struggle, outside of the sphere of the relation between workers and employers.'

Now this claim that class political consciousness can only reach the working class from the outside, has been refuted in practice, and ought to cease being part of any socialist's stock of ideas. The history of French trade unionism before 1914 in itself is sufficient proof that the workers can transcend what Lenin calls their 'trade union consciousness'. The Charter of Amiens adopted in 1906 makes this quite explicit: 'The CGT is affiliated to no political party, but is a union of class-conscious workers fighting for the abolition of wage-slaves and employers. The Congress pledges itself to support the workers in their class struggle against all forms of capitalist exploitation and oppression, both material and moral. Accordingly the Congress sets itself the following tasks: in the short term, trade unionists will try to improve the workers' lot by calling for such immediate reforms as increases in wages, a shorter working week, etc. But this is only one aspect of our work. The trade unions also pave the way for the complete emancipation of the working class, which cannot be achieved except by expropriation of the capitalists. To that end, they will call general strikes, so that those resisting capitalism on the wages front today may tomorrow take charge of production and distribution and so usher in a completely new era ...'

This text shows clearly that the working class can rise a great deal beyond the 'trade union consciousness', and precisely in a country where the influence of the Social Democrats was extremely tenuous. Conversely it was when Social Democrats started to gain influence in France that the trade unions reverted to their role of economic intermediaries, and changed into the bureaucratic machines of today, machines that form an integral part of capitalist society. The Leninist ideology, in postulating the 'incapacity of the working class to make a revolution, or, as we shall see, to manage production in post-revolutionary society, is in direct conflict with the inaugural declaration of the First International: 'The emancipation of the workers must be brought about by the workers themselves'. The fact that 'scientific socialism' was the creation of bourgeois intellectuals is undeniable, and, indeed, it bears the unmistakable marks of this: it is alien to the proletariat and perhaps it ought not to be quite so proud of this alienation as it obviously is. Moreover, Bolshevik organizations were born in an industrially backward country (which explains rather than justifies their own backward nature). This type of organization, and the ideology that went hand in hand with it, would, after 1917, seize upon the backwardness of Russia and also on the lack of revolutionary spirit among the workers outside, as a pretext for bringing to fruit the counter-revolutionary germs it contained from the very beginning.

The Leninist belief that the workers cannot spontaneously go beyond the level of trade union consciousness is tantamount to beheading the proletariat, and then insinuating the Party as the head. The original aims of French trade unionism, and the creation of soviets show that Lenin was wrong, and, in fact, in Russia the Party was forced to decapitate the workers' movement with the help of the political police and the Red Army under the brilliant leadership of Trotsky and Lenin. Moreover, the decapitation was not enough, the body, too, had to be destroyed, and since this task required less finesse and revolutionary education, the honour of finishing the work so brilliantly begun by Lenin and Trotsky, fell to the uncultured Stalin.

However, in fairness to Trotsky, it must be said that, in 1902, when Lenin wrote *What is to be done?*, Trotsky not only opposed it violently but had the wit to foresee its worst dangers: that the Party would substitute itself for the working class, the Central Committee for the party, the Politburo for the Central Committee, and finally the General Secretary for the Politburo. It is to be hoped that Trotsky's critique may one day be published in full, for it, better than anything else, would provide us with a critique of modern Trotskyism. Lenin's views were also challenged by Rosa Luxemburg, representing the far-left wing of the German Social Democratic Movement. While she shared Lenin's disgust with the reformist and parliamentary German Social Democratic Party, she also attacked his own centralism and his ideas of discipline.

In his 'One step forward and two steps back', Lenin glorified the educational effect of factory life which 'accustoms the proletariat to discipline and organization'. To this Rosa Luxemburg replied: 'The discipline which Lenin has in mind is driven home to the proletariat not only in the factory but also in the barracks and by all sorts of bureaucrats, in short by the whole power machine of the centralized bourgeois state ... It is an abuse of words to apply the same term "discipline" to two such unrelated concepts as the mindless reflex motions of a body with a thousand hands and a thousand legs, and the spontaneous coordination of the conscious political acts of a group of men. What can the well-ordered docility of the former have in common with the aspirations of a class struggling for its total emancipation?' *(The Organization of the Social Democratic Party in Russia.)*

In fact, it was Lenin's own consciousness which failed to transcend the organizational level of the bourgeoisie. Speaking of the revolutionary movement that, at the turn of the century, shook the autocratic Russian Empire and later culminated in the Russian Revolution of 1905, Rosa Luxemburg wrote (in 1904): 'Our cause (i.e. Socialism) has made immense progress. However, in this, the initiative and conscious direction of the Social Democratic organization played no more than an insignificant part. This fact cannot be explained away by arguing that our organization was not prepared for such great events (although this was true), and even less by the absence of the all powerful central apparatus Lenin has recommended. On the contrary, it is more than likely that such an apparatus would simply have increased the confusion of the local committees, stressing the gulf between the impetuous masses and the cautious attitude of the Social Democratic Party.' *(The Organization of the Social Democratic Party in Russia.)*

'The ultra-centralization advocated by Lenin,' Rosa Luxemburg continued, 'is filled, not with a positive and creative spirit, but with the sterile spirit of the night watchman.' Prophetic words these, for within a few months the Party became incapable of understanding, and even fought, the establishment of workers' councils. Prophetic also for what happened in 1917, when the Party proved quite incapable of playing the leading part for which it had been prepared so long, and left the entire job to a Lenin *(quod Jovi licet non bovi licet)*. Rosa Luxemburg had clearly foreseen all this, and had accordingly advocated the 'tearing down of that barbed wire fence which prevents the Party from accomplishing the formidable task of the hour'. In fact, far from dismantling the fence, the Party eventually put the entire Russian proletariat behind it.

Rosa Luxemburg's conclusions are no less relevant today than they were at the time they were written: 'Finally we saw the birth of a far more legitimate offspring of the historical process: the Russian workers' movement, which, for the first time, gave expression to the real will of the popular masses. Then the leadership of the Russian revolution leapt up to balance on their shoulders, and once more appointed itself the all-powerful director of history, this time in the person of His Highness the Central Committee of the Social Democratic Workers' Party. This skilful acrobat did not even realize that the only one capable of playing the part of director is the "collective" ego of the working class, which has a sovereign right to make mistakes and to learn the dialectics of history by itself. Let us put it quite bluntly: the errors committed by a truly revolutionary workers' movement are historically far more fruitful and valuable than the infallibility of even the best Central Committee.' *(Organization of Social Democratic Party in Russia.)*

The value of these remarks is in no way diminished by the fact that, today, we have dozens of Central Committees each insisting on its own infallibility, and all alike unable to learn the lessons of the Russian Revolution on which they base most of their self-justifications.

In February 1917, we have said, the Party line and dynamic was opposed to that of the masses organized in soviets. Lenin had to labour hard, not to convince the masses of the need to seize power in the factories and towns, but to convince his own party that the masses were ready for this step. It was the party that had to rise to the level of the masses, not the other way round. Lenin had to turn 'anarchist', and to carry an incredulous party with him. October thus represents the point where the action and aspiration of the masses coincided with those of the temporarily de-Bolshevized Bolshevik Party, and this happy state persisted until the spring of 1918. The Bolshevik Party could not, moreover, behave otherwise, because it was still trying to win the support of the workers. The previous eight months (i.e. February to October 1917) had brought on an extraordinary proliferation of factory and workshop committees. In April 1917 a conference of factory committees at Petrograd had declared: 'All decisions affecting the internal management of factories, such as the length of the working day, wages, hiring and dismissing of workers, etc. must come from the factory committee.' Another conference of factory committees held in June 1917 demanded 'the organization of complete control by the workers of production and distribution' and 'a proletarian majority in all institutions wielding executive power'. Still another congress, after the seizure of power, declared: 'The workers' control commissions must not merely be used to check production ... but must prepare for the transfer of production into the hands of the workers.'

The January 1918 issue of *Vestnik Metalista* (Metalworkers' News) contained an article by the worker N. Filipov which said, *inter alia*: 'The working class, by its very nature, must hold a central place in the productive process. In the future, all production must reflect the spirit and the will of the proletariat.'

In this truly revolutionary period, Lenin told the Third Congress of Soviets held at the beginning of 1918: 'Anarchist ideas have assumed virulent forms.'

A. Pantakrava, wrote: 'On the morrow of the October Revolution, these anarchist tendencies have become prevalent, precisely because the capitalists have increased their resistance to the application of the Decree on Workers' Control and continue to oppose the workers' management of production.'

We shall see that from the spring of 1918 it was the Bolshevist-Leninists themselves who opposed workers' management. Before that happened, the anarchosyndicalist Maximov could still write: 'The Bolsheviks have abandoned not only their theory of the withering away of the state, but Marxist ideology as a whole. They have become anarchists of a sort.'

However, the anarchist Voline, writing in *Golos Truda* (The Voice of Labour) at the end of 1917, had this to say: 'Once their power has been consolidated and legalized, the Bolsheviks, as state socialists, that is as men who believe in centralized and authoritarian leadership — will start running the life of the country and of the people from the top. Your soviets ... will gradually become simple tools of the central government ... You will soon see the inauguration of an authoritarian political and state apparatus that will crush all opposition with an iron fist... "All power to the soviets" will become "all power to the leaders of the party".'

And this is precisely what happened in 1918. To achieve their ends, the Bolsheviks had to smash all opposition and the anarchists in particular. This political repression went hand in hand with the repression of the workers in the factory.

Thus Captain Jacques Sadaul wrote: 'The anarchist party is the most active and militant and probably the most popular opposition group of all ... The Bolsheviks are greatly disturbed.'

Voline confirmed this account: 'To tolerate anarchist propaganda would have been suicide for Lenin. It (the Bolshevik authority) did everything possible to impede and then forbid and repress by brute force, all manifestations of libertarian ideas.'

This repression began with a change of attitude on the question of workers' management. From 1918 onwards, opposition was kept within the Bolshevik party — outside all criticism was suppressed. Hence it is by looking at developments inside the Bolshevik Party that we can best follow the process of repression, which culminated in the silencing, even within the party, of anyone who spoke up for the crushed proletariat. The Tenth Congress of the Bolshevik Party, in March 1921 dissolved all Party fractions, while outside, the Party was busy firing on the workers and sailors at Kronstadt, and on what pockets of resistance there still were in the rest of the country. In particular, the Ukrainian Makhno Movement was a force the Bolsheviks had to destroy at all costs.

3. The Makhno Movement and the Opposition within the Party

The Makhnovchina, better perhaps than any other movement, shows that the Russian Revolution could have become a great liberating force. It was inspired by Makhno, a young Ukrainian anarchist, and has been almost totally ignored by bourgeois historians no less than by Stalinist and Trotskyist apologists — and for good reason. It shows the Bolsheviks stifling workers and peasants with lies and calumnies, and then crushing them in a bloody massacre.

Geographically, the Makhno movement covered a region inhabited by seven million people and measuring some 150 miles in diameter. Its centre was the small Ukrainian town of Gulye Polye with 30,000 inhabitants.

The movement flourished from 1918 until the summer of 1921, when it was finally crushed by the Red Army.

From 1918 to 1921, armed Makhnovite groups fought the White Guards and later the Red Army without respite. They were responsible for holding the Ukrainian front against the White general Denikin, whose armies Makhno defeated in 1919, and then against General Wrangel. The best way of showing who they were and what they stood for is to quote from the manifesto published by the Cultural and Educational Section of the Insurrectional Makhnovite Army. It was widely distributed among the peasants and workers.

'(i) *Who are the Makhnovites and what are they fighting for?*

'The Makhnovites are peasants and workers who in 1918 rose up against the brutality of the German, Hungarian and Austrian interventionists and against the Hetman of the Ukraine.

'The Makhnovites are workers who have carried the battle-standard against Denikin and against every form of oppression and violence, who have rejected lies from whatever source.

'The Makhnovites are the workers who by their life's labour have enriched and fattened the bourgeoisie in the past, and are today enriching new masters.

'(ii) *Why are they called Makhnovites?*

'Because during the greatest and most painful days of reactionary intervention in the Ukraine, they had within their ranks the staunch friend and comrade, Makhno, whose voice was heard across the entire Ukraine, challenging every act of violence against the workers, calling for struggle against the oppressors, the thieves, the usurpers and those charlatans who were deceiving the workers. That voice still rings among us today, and unwaveringly calls for the liberation and emancipation of the workers from all oppression.

'(iii) *How do you think you will obtain this liberation?*

'By overthrowing the coalition of monarchists, republicans, social democrats, communists and Bolsheviks. In its place we call for the free election of workers' councils which will not rule by arbitrary laws because no true soviet system can be authoritarian. Ours is the purest form of socialism, anti-authoritarian and anti-government, it calls for the free organization of the social life of the workers, independent of authority, a life in which each worker, in a free association with his brothers, can build his own happiness and well-being in accordance with the principles of solidarity, amity and equality.

'(iv) *What do the Makhnovites think of the Soviet régime?*

'The workers themselves must choose their own councils (soviets), to express the will and carry out the orders of these self-same workers. The soviets will be executive organs of, and not authorities over, the workers. The land, the factories, the businesses, the mines, transport, etc. must belong to those who work in them. All that the people inherit must be socialized.

'(v) *What are the paths that will lead to the final goals of the Makhnovites?*

'A consistent and implacable revolutionary battle against all false theories, against all arbitrary power and violence, no matter from what quarter, a struggle to the death. Free speech, justice, honest battle with guns in our hands.

'Only by overthrowing all governments, every representative of authority, by destroying all political, economic and authoritarian lies, wherever they are found, by destroying the state, by a social revolution, can we introduce a true system of workers' and peasants' soviets and advance towards socialism.

Trotsky was one of Makhno's bitterest adversaries among the Bolsheviks, and never forgave Makhno for refusing to serve under his supreme command in the Red Army. On 4 June 1919, Trotsky began his first campaign of calumny and military intimidation, by publishing the notorious order No. 1824. It forbade the holding of a congress in the Ukraine, and accused Makhno of delivering this front over to the enemy. 'The Makhno brigade has constantly retreated before the White Guards, owing to the incapacity, criminal tendencies, and the treachery of its leaders.'

Trotsky's order stipulated, *inter alia:*

'(1) It is forbidden to hold this congress, which must not take place under any circumstances;

'(2) Participation in the congress by any worker or peasant will be deemed to constitute an act of high treason;

'(3) All delegates to the said congress must be apprehended and brought before the revolutionary tribunal of the Fourteenth Army of the Ukraine.

So much for Trotsky's respect for the workers' right of free assembly!

The accusation that Makhno had retreated before the White Guards, when in fact he defeated them, was repeated by the entire Soviet press. But for the time being, continued attacks by the White Guards prevented Trotsky from implementing his Order 1824 — he shelved it but did not forget it. In November 1920, the Soviet authorities invited several officers of Makhno's army to a military council meeting, and shot them. The ensuing battle raged for nine long months. At the end, Trotsky's troops, who were superior in number and in arms and had constant replacements, won the day. It was in the course of the last battle that the Makhnovites issued the following appeal to their brethren in the Red Army:

'STOP, READ AND THINK!'

'Comrades of the Red Army!

'You have been sent out by your commissars to fight the re-volutionary Makhnovites.

'On the orders of your commander you ruin peaceful villages, you will raid, arrest, and kill men and women whom you do not know but who have been presented to you as enemies of the people, bandits and counter-revolutionary. You will be told to kill us, you will not be asked. You will be made to march like slaves. You will arrest and you will murder. Why? For what cause?

'Think, comrades of the Red Army; think, workers, peasants suffering under the lash of new masters who bear the high-sounding name of "worker-peasant authorities"! We are revolu-tionary Makhnovites. The same peasants and workers as you, our brethren in the Red Army. We have risen up against oppression and slavery, we fight for a better life and a more enlightened one. Our ideal is to build a community of workers without authori-ties, without parasites, and without commissars. Our immediate aim is to establish a free Soviet régime, not controlled by the Bolsheviks, without the pressure of any party.

'The government of the Bolsheviks and Communists has sent you out on a punitive expedition. It hastens to make peace with Denikin and with the rich Poles and other rabble of the White Army, the better to suppress the popular movement of the revo-lutionary insurgents, of the oppressed, of the rebels against the yoke of all authority.

'But the threats of the White and Red commanders do not frighten us. We shall reply to violence with violence. If necessary, we, a small handful of people shall put to flight the divisions of the Red Army because we are free and love our liberty. We are revolutionaries who have risen up in a just cause.

'Comrades, think for whom you are fighting and against whom! Throw off your shackles, you are free men!

'The Revolutionary Makhnovites.'

Let us hope that one day some publisher will see fit to translate Arshinov's *History of the Makhno Movement* which is unobtainable today but is fundamental to any true understanding of the history of the Russian Revolution. Makhno's defeat spelled the defeat of the

Revolution; Trotsky's victory, the victory of the bureaucratic counter-revolution.

Even while the struggle for Soviet democracy was still being carried on under a black banner in the Ukraine, elsewhere the Bolsheviks had succeeded in crushing every form of resistance. Inside the party, a bitter controversy on the question of 'one-man management' was started in the spring of 1918. The deliberate policy of the Bolshevik leaders to run all factories by State-appointed managers was not only a flagrant breach of Bolshevik promises but also led to the demoralization of the most advanced sectors of the Russian proletariat. This development was a strong contributive factor to the bureaucratic degeneration of the Bolshevik party. Lenin's 'The immediate tasks of the Soviet Government', published in *Izvestia* on 28 April 1918, explained the stand of the Party leadership in quite unambiguous terms: it emphasized discipline, obedience and the need for individual rather than collective management. 'Discipline is a prerequisite of economic renewal ... Greater output is essential ... The class-conscious vanguard of the Russian proletariat has already tackled the task of enforcing discipline at work, for example, the Central Committee of the Metal Workers Union and the Central Council of the Trade Unions, have begun to draft the necessary measures and decrees.'

These 'measures and decrees' whereby 'labour discipline' was to be enforced make tragic reading in the light of subsequent events. They start by bemoaning the 'absence of all industrial discipline'. They then prescribe measures 'for the purpose of improving labour discipline such as: the introduction of a card system for registering the productivity of each worker, the introduction of factory regulations in every enterprise, the establishment of rate of output bureaux for the purpose of fixing the output of each worker and the payment of bonuses for increased productivity.' (Lenin: *Selected Works*, Vol. VII, page 504.)

It requires no great imagination to see in the pen-pushers recording the 'productivity of each worker' and in the clerks manning 'the rate of output bureaux' the as yet amorphous elements of the new bureaucracy.

But Lenin went much further. He quite explicitly came out, as early as 1918, in favour of the individual management of industrial enterprises. 'The struggle that is developing around the recent decree on the management of the railways, *the decree which grants individual leaders dictatorial powers* (or "unlimited powers") is characteristic,' he wrote. Only the 'conscious representatives of petty-bourgeois laxity' could see 'in this granting of unlimited (i.e. dictatorial) powers to individual persons a departure from the collegium principle, a departure from democracy and from other principles of Soviet government'. 'Large scale machine industry,' he went on, '– which is the material productive source and foundation of socialism — calls for absolute and strict unity of will ... How can strict unity of will be ensured? By thousands subordinating their will to the will of one.'

What of discussion and initiative at shop floor level? The idea was summarily dismissed. 'The revolution demands,' Lenin wrote, 'in the interests of socialism that the masses *unquestioningly* obey the single will of the leaders of the labour process.' No nonsense here about workers' management of production, about collective decisions, about government from below. Nor are we left in any doubt as to who the 'leaders of the labour process' were to be. There was, Lenin said, to be 'unquestioning obedience to the orders of individual representatives of the Soviet government during work time' — iron discipline while at work, with unquestioning obedience to the will of a single person, the Soviet leader.'

Lenin's oft-repeated views on labour discipline did not go unchallenged. Opposition developed within the Party itself. Early in 1918, the Leningrad District Committee published the first issue of the 'left' Communist paper *Kommunist*. This was edited by Bukharin, Radek and Ossinsky (Obolonsky and Smirnov were later to join the editorial board). The journal issued a far-sighted warning: 'The introduction of labour discipline in connexion with the restoration of capitalist management of industry cannot really increase the productivity of labour, but it will diminish the class initiative, activity and organization of the proletariat. It threatens to enslave the working class. It will rouse discontent among the backward elements as well as among the vanguard of the proletariat. In order to introduce this system in the face of the hatred prevailing at present among the proletariat for the "capitalist saboteurs", the Communist Party would have to rely on the petty-bourgeoisie, as against the workers, and in this way it would ruin itself as the party of the proletariat.'

Lenin reacted violently. He called such views 'a disgrace', 'a complete renunciation of communism in practice', 'a complete desertion to the camp of the petty-bourgeoisie'. ('Left-wing Childishness and Petty-bourgeois Mentality', *Selected Works* Vol. VII 374.) The Left were being 'provoked by the Isuvs (Mensheviks) and other Judases of capitalism'. He lumped together leaders of the 'left' and open enemies of the revolution, thus initiating the technique of the political smear which was to be used so successfully by Stalin in later years. A campaign was whipped up in Leningrad which compelled the *Kommunist* to transfer publication to Moscow, where the paper reappeared in April 1918, first under the auspices of the Moscow regional organization of the Party, later as the 'unofficial' mouthpiece of a group of comrades.

The controversy smouldered on throughout 1918. *Kommunist* repeatedly denounced the replacement of workers' control by 'labour discipline', the increasing tendency for industrial management to be placed in the hands of non-Communist 'specialists' and the conclusion of all sorts of unofficial deals with previous owners 'to ensure their cooperation'. It pointed out that 'the logical outcome of management based on the participation of capitalists and on the principle of bureaucratic centralization was the institution of a labour policy which would seek to re-establish regimentation of workers on the pretext of voluntary discipline. Governmental forms would then evolve towards bureaucratic centralization, the rule of all sorts of commissars, loss of independence for local Soviets and, in practice, the abandonment of government from below'. 'It was all very well,' Bukharin pointed out, 'to say as Lenin had (in *State and Revolution)* that "each cook should learn to manage the State". But what happened when each cook had a commissar appointed to order him about?'

The conflict between the Leninists and the 'left' Communists came to a head during May and June 1918, during the First Congress of Economic Councils. Lenin spoke out strongly in favour of 'labour discipline', of 'one-man management' and of the need to use bourgeois specialists. Ossinsky, Smirnov and Obolensky, supported by numerous provincial delegates, demanded 'a workers' administration ... not only from above but from below'. They urged that two-thirds of the representatives on the management boards of industrial enterprises should be elected from among the workers. They succeeded in getting a Congress sub-committee to accept this resolution. Lenin was furious at this 'stupid decision'. Under his guidance a plenary session of the Congress 'corrected' the resolution, decreed that no more than one-third of the managerial personnel should be elected, and set up a complex hierarchical structure vesting veto rights in a Supreme Economic Council, at the apex of an administrative pyramid.

A split occurred at this time among the 'left' Communists. Radek was willing to make a deal with the Leninists. He was prepared to accept the 'one-man management' principle in exchange for the extensive nationalization decrees of June 1918, which heralded the period of War Communism, and which in his opinion would ensure the proletarian basis of the régime. Bukharin also broke with Ossinsky and rejoined the fold. The ideas developed by the left Communists continued to find an echo, however, despite the defection of most of those who had first advocated them. Ossinsky and his supporters formed the new opposition group of 'Democratic Centralists'. Their ideas on workers' management of production (and those of the original group of 'left' Communists) were to play an important part in the development, two years later, of the Workers' Opposition.

Writing in the second issue of the *Kommunist,* Ossinsky was to issue a prophetic warning: 'We stand,' he wrote, 'for the construction of a proletarian society by the class creativity of the workers themselves, not by ukases from the "captains of industry" .. . We proceed from trust in the class instinct, and in the active class initiative of the proletarait. It cannot be otherwise. If the workers themselves do not know how to create the necessary prerequisites for the socialist organization of labour — no one can do this for them, nor can the workers be forced to do it. The stick, if raised against the workers, will find itself either in the hands of another social force ... or in the hands of the soviet power. But then the soviet power will be forced to seek support against the proletariat from another class (e.g. the peasantry), and by this it will destroy itself as the dictatorship of the proletariat. Socialism and socialist organization must be set up by the proletariat itself, or they will not be set up at all; something else will be set up: state capitalism.'

These prophetic phrases, and the reception they were given by Lenin and Trotsky, should put an end to all the 'revolutionary' arguments that it was Stalin the Terrible alone who perverted socialism into a bureaucratic dictatorship.

Thus it was Trotsky, not Stalin, who, towards the end of 1919, submitted to the Central Committee the famous thesis 'transition from war to peace'. The most important of his propositions was the call for the 'militarization of the proletariat'.

Trotsky did not believe that these propositions would go further than the Central Committee; like all good bureaucrats he liked to take the most important decisions behind closed doors. But by 'mistake', Bukharin published its text in *Pravda* of 17 December 1919. According to Isaac Deutscher, this indiscretion caused an extremely tense public controversy and one that continued for more than a year, as the working class seized on this unexpected opportunity of discussing its own fate. Trotsky defended his views before the Ninth Congress of the Bolshevik Party in 1920: 'The workers must not be allowed to roam all over Russia. They must be sent where they are needed, called up and directed like soldiers. Labour must be directed most intensely during the transition of capitalism to socialism.' We might add, in parenthesis, that since this transition has not yet been made, and never will be made unless there is another revolution, Soviet workers must prepare to settle down to a further spell of forced labour. 'It is essential,' Trotsky went on, 'to form punitive contingents and to put all those who shirk work into concentration camps.'

Stalin, who as Trotsky himself has repeatedly pointed out, lacked theoretical imagination, did in fact very little more than pursue the theoretical and practical path opened up by Trotsky. In particular, Trotsky introduced Stakhanovism when he offered special bonuses for extra effort 'worthy of socialist emulation'; he also spoke of the need to adopt the 'progressive essence of Taylorism' — at that time the most extreme form of capitalist exploitation. Lenin's thesis of one-man management and 'work discipline' were adopted at this Congress.

After the Ninth Congress, Trotsky wrote: 'The young workers' state requires trade unions not for a struggle for better conditions of labour ... but to organize the working class for the ends of production, to educate, to discipline the workers ... to exercise their authority hand in hand with the State, to lead the workers into the framework of a single economic plan...' (Trotsky: *Dictatorship vs. Democracy,* page 14.) 'The unions should discipline the workers and teach them to place the interests of production above their own needs and demands.' Of the militarization of labour Trotsky said: 'This term at once brings us into the region of the greatest possible superstitions and outcries from the opposition.' *(ibid.,* page 14.) He denounced his opponents as Mensheviks, and 'people full of trade unionist prejudices'.

'The militarization of labour,' he declared at the Third Congress of Trade Unions, '... is the indispensable basic method for the organization of our labour forces.' This use of the word 'our' when referring to the labour forces of the working class fully justifies Debord's remark: 'Its claim to a monopoly of the representation and defence of the workers, turned the Bolshevik Party into what it is today: the masters of the proletariat...' (*La Société du Spectacle.*)

'Was it true,' Trotsky asked, 'that compulsory labour was always unproductive?' He denounced this view as 'wretched and miserable liberal prejudice', learnedly pointing out that 'chattel slavery, too, was productive' — and that compulsory serf labour was in its times 'a progressive phenomenon'. He told the unions that 'coercion, regimentation and militarization of labour were no mere emergency measures and that the workers' State *normally* had the right to coerce *any* citizen to perform *any* work at *any* place of its choosing'. A little later he proclaimed that the 'militarization of the trade unions and the militarization of transport required an *internal, ideological* militarization'.

And this was precisely what Stalin achieved, when he stepped into the shoes of that great strategist who later became his bitterest opponent. Trotsky, who had already 'disciplined' the army by abolishing the soldiers' soviets, early in 1920 took over the Commissariat of Transport, in addition to his defence post. The Politburo offered to back him to the hilt, in any course of action he might take, no matter how severe. Once in charge of Transport, Trotsky was immediately to implement his pet ideas on the 'militarization of labour'.

The railwaymen and the personnel of the repair workshops were put under martial law. There was a major outcry. To silence his critics, and with the full endorsement of the Party leadership, Trotsky ousted the elected leaders of the union and appointed others who were willing to do his bidding. He repeated the procedure in other unions of transport workers.

Perhaps it is of these men he was thinking when he wrote: 'It is a general rule that man will try to get out of work. Man is a lazy animal.' And in his 'Terrorism and Communism', a piece of Trotskyist writing if ever there was one, he proclaimed: 'Those workers who contribute more than the rest to the general good have every right to receive a larger share of the socialist product than layabouts, idlers and the undisciplined.'

The last battle over the militarization of work was fought inside the party in 1920–21. Those opposed to Trotsky's ideas formed the 'Workers' Opposition', whose history has been recorded by Alexandra Kollontai. A Party conference held in Moscow in November 1920 showed that the 'Workers' Opposition' was growing rapidly in strength. 'They, the Centralist Democrats and the Ignatov group (closely associated with the "Workers' Opposition") obtained 124 seats as against the 154 obtained by the supporters of the Central Committee.' (Daniels: *The Conscience of the Revolution.*)

The Party leadership took fright and introduced a whole series of counter-measures, some of which were so scandalous that the Moscow Committee passed a resolution publicly censoring the Petrograd Party 'for not observing the rules of correct discussion'. The Central Committee, too, was criticized and instructed to 'ensure that the allocation of printed matter and speakers was such that all points of view can be honestly represented'. At the Tenth Congress, Alexandra Kollontai nevertheless felt impelled to protest that the distribution of her pamphlet, *The Workers' Opposition,* had been deliberately sabotaged.

Lenin denounced the Workers' Opposition at the very beginning of the Congress, calling it 'a menace to the Revolution.' The atmosphere of the Congress was electric, particularly when Kollontai, Ignatov and many others attacked the bureaucracy, its class character, and the transformation of the Party into a non-proletarian one by the influx of new elements. What the 'Leftist' Communists had foreseen in 1918, what Voline and the anarchists had prophesied all along, had become reality: 'The party had become the springboard for bureaucratic careerists.' Lenin and Trotsky were to triumph over the Workers' Opposition, and when they had done so, the last voice to speak up for the Soviet working class was silenced. The Congress ordered the dissolution of all factions within the Party — having squashed freedom of expression outside the Party leaders now finished off the opposition within. Nor was it simply a struggle of ideas — it was the very fate of the working class that was at stake in this battle. While ostensibly attacking the Left-wing Communists, the Centrist Democrats and the Workers' Opposition, it was in fact the working class itself that was being clubbed down, that lost every right to manage its own destiny.

At the Congress, Trotsky accused the Workers' Opposition of putting forward dangerous slogans. 'They turn democratic principles

into a fetish. They put the right of the workers to elect their own representatives above the Party, thus challenging the right of the Party to
affirm its dictatorship, even when this dictatorship comes into conflict
with the evanescent mood of the workers' democracy. We must bear in
mind the historical mission of our Party. The Party is forced to maintain
its dictatorship without stopping for these vacillations, nor even the
momentary falterings of the working class. This realization is the mor-
tar which cements our unity. The dictatorship of the proletariat does not
always have to conform to formal principles of democracy.'

And Lenin mocked at the Workers' Opposition: 'A producers'
Congress! What precisely does that mean? It is difficult to find words to
describe this folly. I keep asking myself, can they be joking? Can one
really take these people seriously? While production is always necessary,
democracy is not. Democracy of production engenders a series of radically false ideas.'

Lenin should not have laughed quite so loudly at all this 'folly', for
it was precisely what he himself had written in 1917, in his *State and
Revolution.* Every phrase of that book is a denunciation of the Bolshevik
policy in 1920–21, for it was written at a time when the masses forced
Lenin to be an anarchist rather than a Bolshevik. When it suited him,
Lenin buried the *State and Revolution.* And even while Trotsky was still
thundering on about the Workers' Opposition, Lenin was forced, and
not by words only, to correct 'the temporary falterings of the working
class'. This he did at Kronstadt, where the bullets of the Party finally settled 'the conflict between its dictatorship and the evanescent moods of
the workers' democracy.'

4. Kronstadt

At the end of February, 1921, the workers of Petrograd, who had been making an enormous productive effort despite the short rations they were allowed, went on strike against their intolerable conditions. The Party and Zinoviev, who was responsible for the defence of Petrograd, could think of only one answer: to send a detachment of the Koursanty (cadet officers) against the strikers, and to proclaim a state of siege in Petrograd. In *The Kronstadt Commune**, Ida Mett tells what happened next.

On 26 February the Kronstadt sailors, naturally interested in all that was going on in Petrograd, sent delegates to find out about the strikes. The delegation visited a number of factories. It returned to Kronstadt on the 28th. That same day, the crew of the battleship *Petropavlovsk,* having discussed the situation, voted the following resolution:

'Having heard the reports of the representatives sent by the General Assembly of the Fleet to find out about the situation in Petrograd, the sailors demand:

'(1) Immediate new elections to the Soviets. The present Soviets no longer express the wishes of the workers and peasants. The new elections should be by secret ballot, and should be preceded by free electoral propaganda.

'(2) Freedom of speech and of the press for workers and peasants, for the anarchists, and for the Left Socialist parties.

'(3) The right of assembly, and freedom for trade union and peasant organizations.

'(4) The organization, at the latest on 10 March 1921, of a Conference of non-Party workers, soldiers and sailors of Petrograd, Kronstadt and the Petrograd District.

---

* Ida Mett: *The Kronstadt Commune,* Solidarity Pamphlet No 27 published by Solidarity, 53a Westmoreland Road, Bromley, Kent, November, 1967.

'(5) The liberation of all political prisoners of the Socialist parties, and of all imprisoned workers and peasants, soldiers and sailors belonging to working class and peasant organizations.

'(6) The election of a commission to look into the dossiers of all those detained in prisons and concentration camps.

'(7) The abolition of all political sections in the armed forces. No political party should have privileges for the propagation of its ideas, or receive State subsidies to this end. In the place of the political sections, various cultural groups should be set up, deriving resources from the State.

'(8) The immediate abolition of the militia detachments set up between towns and countryside.

'(9) The equalization of rations for all workers, except those engaged in dangerous or unhealthy jobs.

'(10) The abolition of Party combat detachments in all military groups. The abolition of Party guards in factories and enterprises. If guards are required, they should be nominated, taking into account the views of the workers.

'(11) The granting to the peasants of freedom of action on their own soil, and of the right to own cattle, provided they look after them themselves and do not employ hired labour.

'(12) We request that all military units and officer trainee groups associate themselves with this resolution.

'(13) We demand that the Press give proper publicity to this resolution.

'(14) We demand the institution of mobile workers control groups.

'(15) We demand that handicraft production be authorized provided it does not utilize wage labour.

The workers and sailors of Kronstadt were, in fact, defending the power of the soviets against the power of the Party.

The Kronstadt resolution had the merit of stating things openly and clearly. But it was breaking no new ground. Its main ideas were being discussed everywhere. For having, in one way or another, put forward precisely such ideas, workers and peasants were already filling the prisons and the recently set up concentration camps.

And while all this was going on, Radio Moscow kept spreading lies and calumnies against the workers. Thus when Stalin accused Trotsky a few years later of conspiring with a White Guard officer of the Wrangel Army, he was merely using the same smear campaign Trotsky had used against the Kronstadt sailors.

On 3 March, for instance, Radio Moscow launched the following appeal:

'Struggle against the White Guard Plot ... Just like other White Guard insurrections, the mutiny of ex-General Kozlovsky and the crew of the battleship *Petropavlovsk* has been organized by Entente spies. This is clear from the fact that the French paper *Le Monde* published the following message from Helsingfors two weeks before the revolt of General Kozlovsky: "We are informed from Petrograd that as the result of the recent Kronstadt revolt, the Bolshevik military authorities have taken a whole series of measures to isolate the town and to prevent the soldiers and sailors of Kronstadt from entering Petrograd."'

'It is therefore clear that the Kronstadt revolt is being led from Paris. The French counter espionage is mixed up in the whole affair. History is repeating itself. The Socialist Revolutionaries, who have their headquarters in Paris, are preparing the ground for an insurrection against the Soviet power. The ground prepared, their real master the Tsarist general appeared. The history of Koltchak, installing his power in the wake of that of the Socialist Revolutionaries, is being repeated.'

Faced with all these lies and also with an imminent attack by the Central Government, local Bolsheviks deserted their party en masse. To appreciate just how strongly they felt, we need only read some of the letters they sent to the Kronstadt *Izvestia*. The teacher Denissov wrote: 'I openly declare to the Provisional Revolutionary Committee that as from gunfire directed at Kronstadt, I no longer consider myself a member of the Party. I support the call issued by the workers of Kronstadt. All power to the Soviets, not to the Party!'

A military group assigned to the special company dealing with discipline also issued a declaration: 'We the undersigned joined the Party believing it to express the wishes of the working masses. In fact the Party has proved itself an executioner of workers and peasants. This is revealed quite clearly by recent events in Petrograd. These events show up the face of the Party leaders. The recent broadcasts from Moscow show clearly that the Party leaders are prepared to resort to any means in order to retain power.

'We ask that henceforth, we no longer be considered Party members. We rally to the call issued by the Kronstadt garrison in its resolution of 2 March. We invite other comrades who have become aware of the error of their ways, publically to recognize the fact.

'Signed: GUTMAN, YEFIMOV, KOUDRIATZEV, ANDREEV.'
(*Izvestia* of the Provisional Revolutionary Committee, 7 March 1921.)

Every attempt to settle matters peacefully was rejected out of hand by the government; Trotsky ordered his troops 'to shoot the Kronstadt "rebels" down like partridges', and entrusted the task to Toukhatchevsky, a military expert taken over from the Old Régime. On 6 March, Trotsky addressed the following radio appeal to the Kronstadt garrison over the radio:

'The Workers' and Peasants' Government has decided to reassert its authority without delay, both over Kronstadt and over the mutinous battleships, and to put them at the disposal of the Soviet Republic. I therefore order all those who have raised a hand against the Socialist Fatherland, immediately to lay down their weapons. Those who resist will be disarmed and put at the disposal of the Soviet Command. The arrested commissars and other representatives of the Government must be freed immediately. Only those who surrender unconditionally will be able to count on the clemency of the Soviet Republic. I am meanwhile giving orders that everything be prepared to smash the revolt and the rebels by force of arms. The responsibility for the disasters which will affect the civilian population must fall squarely on the heads of the White Guard insurgents.

'Signed: TROTSKY, President of the Military Revolutionary Council of the Soviet Republic.
'KAMENEV,* Glavkom (Commanding Officer).'

* This Kamenev was an ex-Tsarist officer, now collaborating with the Soviet Government. He was a different Kamenev from the one shot by the Stalinists in 1936.

No matter how often the workers of Kronstadt affirmed their loyalty to Soviet Socialism, Kronstadt, like Carthage, was destroyed; its appeal to the truth went unheard:

'TO ALL, TO ALL, TO ALL'

'Comrades, workers, red soldiers and sailors! Here in Kronstadt we know full well how much you and your wives and your children are suffering under the iron rule of the Party. We have overthrown the Party-dominated Soviet. The Provisional Revolutionary Committee is today starting elections to a new Soviet. It will be freely elected, and it will reflect the wishes of the *whole* working population, and of the garrison — and not just those of a handful of Party members.

'Our cause is just. We stand for the power of the soviets, not for that of the Party. We stand for freely elected representatives of the toiling masses. Deformed soviets, dominated by the Party, have remained deaf to our pleas. Our appeals have been answered with bullets.

'The workers' patience is becoming exhausted. So now they are seeking to pacify you with crumbs. On Zinoviev's orders the militia barrages have been withdrawn. Moscow has allocated ten million gold roubles for the purchase of foodstuffs and other articles of first necessity. But we know that the Petrograd proletariat will not be bought over in this way. Over the heads of the Party, we hold out to you the fraternal hand of revolutionary Kronstadt.

'Comrades, you are being deceived. And truth is being distorted by the basest of calumnies.

'Comrades, don't allow yourselves to be misled.

'In Kronstadt, power is in the hands of the sailors, of the red soldiers and of the revolutionary workers. It is *not* in the hands of White Guards commanded by General Kozlovsky, as Moscow Radio lyingly asserts.

'Signed: The Provisional Revolutionary Committee.'

Kronstadt, as Voline has rightly pointed out, was a genuine attempt by the workers to run their own lives, without the help of political leaders, tutors, or shepherds. And Alexander Berkmann added: 'Kronstadt destroyed the myth of the workers' state; it provided the proof of an incompatibility between the dictatorship of the Communist Party and the Revolution.'

The Kronstadt *Izvestia* had this to say: 'Be careful, Trotsky! You may escape the judgement of the people, you may shoot down innocent men and women by the score, but even you cannot kill the truth.'

And on 8 March, the rebels wrote: 'At Kronstadt the foundation stone has been laid of the Third Revolution. This will break the final chains which still bind the working masses and will open up new paths of socialist creation.'

It is in the light of the events of February 1917, and March 1921, that we must read the following text by Trotsky: 'It has been said more than once that we have substituted the dictatorship of the Party for the dictatorship of the soviets. However, we can claim without fear of contradiction that the dictatorship of the soviets was only made possible by the dictatorship of the Party ... In fact there has been no substitution at all, since the Communists express the fundamental interests of the working class ... (In a revolutionary period) the Communists become the true representatives of the working class as a whole.'

Now this is the very essence of Bolshevism: the working class is incapable of socialist consciousness, of making a revolution, of running socialist society — hence the Party must step in on its behalf and, if necessary, ignore the 'temporary aberrations' of the proletariat. What then is the meaning of the phrase *the emancipation of the workers can only be achieved by the workers themselves*? Lenin's answer was that the 'domination by the working class rests on the Constitution, in the new property system'. De Gaulle ought to take a leaf out of his book: enshrine workers' control in the French Constitution but leave the real power with the bourgeoisie as heretofore, since running society, according to Lenin, requires a kind of skill the working class does not have. Fancy a cook running a ministry!

And so, when the party robbed the workers and the soviets of their powers, they were obviously acting in the best interests of what was no more than an ignorant and illiterate mass.

And if only the Party can wield power for them, only the Party must be allowed to wield power. Let us listen to Trotsky again: 'But who will guarantee, some evil tongues have asked, that your party alone represents the cause of historical development? In suppressing or overshadowing the other parties, they say, you have rid yourself of political rivals, and hence prevented any chance of evaluating the correctness of your own line of conduct.' Before looking at Trotsky's reply to his own rhetorical question, we must repeat that not only had the Bolshevik leaders squashed all opposition outside the Party, but that they had also outlawed all opposition *within* the Party — as Trotsky himself was to discover when his turn came to challenge the authority of Stalin. But let us hear what he said at the time: 'This question reflects purely liberal ideas on the progress of the revolution. At a period when all antagonists came out into the open and when the political struggle becomes transformed into Civil War, the party in power has other statistics for evaluating the correctness of its line of conduct than the circulation figures of Menshevik journals ... Noske tried to squash the Communists but their numbers kept growing, whereas we succeeded in demolishing the Mensheviks and the Social Revolutionaries until nothing remained of them. This criterion suffices us.'

It suffices us as well. The German Social Democrat Noske did smash the German Revolution while the number of Communists kept increasing, but all this proves is that Trotsky was good at figures and not necessarily at political analysis. In fact, the German Communist Party enjoyed full parliamentary immunity in the Weimar Republic. However, as soon as Hitler took power in 1933, not only the number of Jews but also that of German Communists diminished by leaps and bounds. Is this a justification of Hitlerism? Again, the number of Trotskyists in Russia dwindled to almost nothing from 1923 to 1940. Is this a Trotskyist justification of Stalinism? All it proves is the power of the repressive system.

In 1921, the fate of the Russian Revolution was finally sealed and the bureaucracy triumphed. Henceforth it would grow daily in strength. It is not surprising that the working class, having been weakened by years of civil war and famine and then by the destruction of the soviets, should have stood by passively while Trotsky himself was 'liquidated'. Stalin could even permit himself the indulgence of calling Trotsky 'the patriarch of all bureaucrats'.

As far as we are concerned there is no break between the ideology of the old Bolshevik Party and that of the new bureaucracy.

'The direction of the proletariat, acting through a clandestine and disciplined party, and run by intellectuals turned professional revolutionaries, had no need to come to terms with other managerial classes, and so became the absolute dictator of society.' Guy Debord: *La Société du Spectacle.)*

Now, while it is undeniable that the Russian Revolution took place in a backward country — one in which the peasantry was predominant, that it was isolated, largely due to the failure of the German revolution, and that it was severely weakened by the Civil War, these general factors can in no way explain the specific turn it took. For instance, like the Commune of 1871 or like the German revolution, it might have been smashed from without and replaced by the old capitalist system. Even the introduction of state capitalism might have taken quite different forms than it did, in fact, take in the Soviet Union. Moreover, backwardness and isolation have long been overcome: today the Soviet Union is a powerful industrial giant with an empire that covers more than half of Europe. No, the specific failure of the Russian Revolution must be laid squarely at the door of the Bolshevik party. That failure was far more significant even than the defeat of the French Commune at the hands of reaction, of the Spanish Revolution at the hands of Franco, or the Hungarian uprising by Krushchev's tanks — simply because the Russian Revolution had triumphed over the forces of external reaction only to succumb to the bureaucracy the Revolution itself had engendered. It forces us to reflect on the nature of workers' powers and on what we mean by socialism. What is specific in the degeneration of the Russian Revolution is that, while the 'revolutionary' party retained power, the working class itself lost it; that it was their own party that defeated the workers, and not the classical forces of the counter-revolution. What Rosa Luxemburg had to say about the German revolution, just before her death, applies in full to the Russian Revolution as well: 'In all previous revolutions, the contenders were ranged on two clear sides, class against class, programme against programme. In the present revolution, the defenders of the old order do not fight under the banner of the ruling class, but under the social democratic banner.'

The only difference is that in Germany, the Social Democrats served as a front for the bourgeoisie, while in Russia, the Bolshevik wing of the Social Democratic Party took the place of the bourgeoisie. From 1918 to 1921, the Bolsheviks were concerned to give Russia a well-organized economy based on the then capitalist model, i.e. State capitalism. This is a term that kept recurring in Lenin's writings. And what he and Trotsky said time and again was that Russia must learn from the advanced capitalist countries, that there is only one way of developing production: the application of capitalist ideas on management and industrial rationalization. Trotsky, for example, believed that the actual organization of the army did not matter so long as it fought on the right side. Thus an army is not bourgeois because of its structure (e.g. hierarchy and discipline) but only if it serves the bourgeoisie. Similarly an industrial system is not considered bourgeois because its discipline, hierarchy, and incentives (bonuses, piece work, etc.) are those used by the bourgeois system. All that matters, apparently, is whose power is enshrined in what Lenin so proudly referred to as his 'constitution'. The idea that the same means cannot serve different ends, that neither the army nor a factory are simple 'instruments' but socialist structures embodying productive relationships and hence the real power — this idea, so obvious to Marxists, was completely 'forgotten'. True, the Bolsheviks abolished private property, and 'the anarchy of the market', but the practical reorganization of capitalist production when it came, took none of the forms the Russian Social Democrats had envisaged during twenty years of debate. 'The revolutionary bureaucracy which directed the proletariat and seized the State machine imposed a new form of class domination on society.' (Guy Debord: *La Société du Spectacle.*)

The most unshakeable belief of the Communist Party, indeed of every party of the Bolshevik type, is precisely that it must direct the Revolution as well as the economy. The only Communists to challenge this view at the time were a handful of clear-sighted comrades, including Rosa Luxemburg, Anton Pannekoek and the far-left German KAPD who, before and after the Revolution, stressed the fact that centralization was bound to dampen the spontaneity and self-confidence of the masses. The reason why the Bolshevik Party was able to usher in a counter-revolution, is because it has crushed, rather than led, the proletariat; because no organization can represent the proletariat; whenever a minority acts in the name of the proletariat it acts only to betray them in the end. The defeat of all the opposition groups inside the Party — the Left-wing Communists in 1918, the Centralist Democrats in 1919 and finally the Workers' Opposition in 1921 — are so many nails in the coffin of the Russian proletariat. The Workers' Opposition, despite its theoretical confusion and weakness, was nevertheless right to assert that the workers must rebuild the social edifice from top to bottom. The Workers' Opposition was the last voice inside the official Marxist movement to call for direct control, to express confidence in the creative capacity of the proletariat, to proclaim that the socialist revolution must usher in a new period in human history. This was the voice of the Kronstadt workers and so clear and loud was their message that it could only be silenced with cannon.

No matter what Trotskyist historiographers may tell us today, it was not in 1927 nor in 1923 nor even in 1920, but in 1918 and under the personal leadership of Trotsky and Lenin that the social revolution became perverted — a fact Trotsky could never understand — simply because he himself was one of its prime architects. Thus twenty years later, when Trotsky founded the Fourth International in opposition to Stalinism, he conveniently forgot that he himself had fired on those who grasped its horrors as early as 1920. At that stage he still saw fit to assert:

'There is good reason for believing that the KAPD (German Communist Workers' Party) under its present adventurist and anarchist leadership, will not submit to the decisions of the International, and finding itself out in the cold, will probably try to form a Fourth International. In the course of this Congress, Comrade Kollontai has sounded this very note, although rather muted. It is no secret to anyone that our Party alone is the true mainspring of the Communist International. However, Comrade Kollontai has depicted conditions in our party in such a way that, if she were right, the workers, with Comrade Kollontai at the head, must sooner of later start a 'third revolution' and establish a true soviet system. But why the third revolution and not the fourth, since the third revolution in the name of the 'true' soviet system has already been made in Kronstadt, during February? There are quite a few left-wing extremists left in Holland, and perhaps in other countries as well. I cannot tell if all of them have been taken into consideration; what I do know is that their number is not very great, and they are unlikely to swell into a torrent inside a Fourth International, if perchance it should ever be established.'

(Trotsky, quoted in *Nouvelle Étape.*)

If we have tried to show how stuck the Bolshevik Party was in the old rut, and how mired down, it was only to stress that, for this reason alone, it was incapable of emancipating the workers. 'Forty years of consistent counter-revolution go to make up the history of modern

Bolshevism. The Bolsheviks are wrong because it is no longer 1920, and even in 1920 they were wrong.' *(De la misère en milieu étudiant.)*

We have digressed at such length on the Russian Revolution because it highlights all the problems and conflicts besetting the working-class movement even in our day. It is highly important not only because it shows how a revolution was made, but also what a revolution should not be.

V

By Way of Conclusion

C'est pour toi que tu fais la révolution

There is no such thing as an isolated revolutionary act. Acts that can transform society take place in association with others, and form part of a general movement that follows its own laws of growth. All revolutionary activity is collective, and hence involves a degree of organization. What we challenge is not the need for this but the need for a revolutionary leadership, the need for a party.

Central to my thesis is an analysis of the bureaucratic phenomenon, which I have examined from various viewpoints. For example, I have looked at the French workers' unions and parties and shown that what is wrong with them is not so much their rigidity and treachery as the fact that they have become integrated into the overall bureaucratic system of the capitalist state.

The emergence of bureaucratic tendencies on a world scale, the continuous concentration of capital, and the increasing intervention of the State in economic and social matters, have produced a new managerial class whose fate is no longer bound up with that of the private ownership of the means of production.

It is in the light of this bureaucratization that the Bolshevik Party has been studied. Although its bureaucratic nature is not, of course, its only characteristic, it is true to say that Communists, and also Trotskyists, Maoists and the rest, no less than the capitalist State, all look upon the proletariat as a mass that needs to be directed from above. As a result, democracy degenerates into the ratification at the bottom of decisions taken at the top, and the class struggle is forgotten while the leaders jockey for power within the political hierarchy.

The objections to Bolshevism are not so much moral as sociological; what we attack is not the evil conduct of some of its leaders but an organizational set-up that has become its one and only justification.

The most forceful champion of a revolutionary party was Lenin, who in his *What is to be done?* argued that the proletariat is unable by itself to reach a 'scientific' understanding of society, that it tends to adopt the prevailing, i.e. the bourgeois, ideology.

Hence it was the essential task of the Party to rid the workers of this ideology by a process of political education which could only come to them *from without*. Moreover, Lenin tried to show that the Party can only overcome the class enemy by turning itself into a professional revolutionary body in which everyone is allocated a fixed task. Certain of its infallibility, a Party appoints itself the natural spokesman and sole defender of the interests of the working class, and as such wields power on their behalf — i.e. acts as a bureaucracy.

We take quite a different view: far from having to teach the masses, the revolutionary's job is to try to understand and express their common aspirations; far from being Lenin's 'tribune of the people who uses every manifestation of tyranny and oppression ... to explain his Socialist convictions and his Social Democratic demands', the real militant must encourage the workers to struggle on their own behalf, and show how their every struggle can be used to drive a wedge into capitalist society. If he does so, the militant acts as an agent of the people and no longer as their leader.

The setting up of any party inevitably reduces freedom of the people to freedom to agree with the party.

In other words, democracy is not suborned by bad leadership but by the very existence of leadership. Democracy cannot even exist within the Party, because the Party itself is not a democratic organization, i.e. it is based upon authority and not on representation. Lenin realized full well that the Party is an artificial creation, that it was imposed upon the working class 'from without'. Moral scruples have been swept aside: the Party is 'right' if it can impose its views upon the masses and wrong if it fails to do so. For Lenin, the whole matter ends there. In his *State and Revolution*, Lenin did not even raise the problem of the relationship between the people and the Party. Revolutionary power was a matter of fact, based upon people who are prepared to fight for it; the paradox is that the Party's programme, endorsed by these people, was precisely: All power to the Soviets! But whatever its programme, in retrospect we can see that the Party, because of its basic conception, is bound to bring in privilege and bureaucracy, and we must wash our hands of all organizations of this sort. To try and pretend that the Bolshevik Party is truly democratic is to deceive oneself, and this, at least, is an error that Lenin himself never committed.

What then is our conception of the role of the revolutionary? To begin with, we are convinced that the revolutionary cannot and must not be a leader. Revolutionaries are a militant minority drawn from various social strata, people who band together because they share an ideology, and who pledge themselves to struggle against oppression, to dispel the mystification of the ruling classes and the bureaucrats, to proclaim that the workers can only defend themselves and build a socialist society by taking their fate into their own hands, believing that political maturity comes only from revolutionary struggle and direct action.

By their action, militant minorities can do no more than support, encourage, and clarify the struggle. They must always guard against any tendency to become a pressure group outside the revolutionary movement of the masses. When they act, it must always be with the masses, and not as a faction.

For some time, the 22 March Movement was remarkable only for its radical political line, for its methods of attack — often spontaneous — and for its non-bureaucratic structure. Its objectives and the role it could play became clear only during the events of May and June, when it attracted the support of the working class. These militant students whose dynamic theories emerged from their practice, were imitated by others, who developed new forms of action appropriate to their own situation. The result was a mass movement unencumbered by the usual chains of command. By challenging the repressive nature of their own institution — the university — the revolutionary students forced the state to show its hand, and the brutality with which it did so caused a general revulsion and led to the occupation of the factories and the general strike. The mass intervention of the working class was the greatest achievement of our struggle; it was the first step on the path to a better society, a path that, alas, was not followed to the end. The militant minorities failed to get the masses to follow their example: to take collective charge of the running of society. We do not believe for a single moment that the workers are incapable of taking the next logical step beyond occupying the factories — which is to run them on their own. We are sure that they can do what we ourselves have done in the universities. The militant minorities must continue to wage their revolutionary struggle, to show the workers what their trade unions try to make them forget: their own gigantic strength. The distribution of petrol by the workers in the refineries and the local strike committees shows clearly what the working class is capable of doing once it puts its mind to it.

During the recent struggle, many student militants became hero-worshippers of the working class, forgetting that every group has its own part to play in defending its own interests, and that, during a period of total confrontation, these interests converge.

The student movement must follow its own road — only thus can it contribute to the growth of militant minorities in the factories and workshops. We do not pretend that we can be leaders in the struggle, but it is a fact that small revolutionary groups can, at the right time and place, rupture the system decisively and irreversibly.

During May and June, 1968, the emergence of a vast chain of workers' committees and sub-committees by-passed the calcified structure of the trade unions, and tried to call together all workers in a struggle that was their own and not that of the various trade union bureaucracies. It was because of this that the struggle was carried to a higher stage. It is absurd and romantic to speak of revolution with a capital R and to think of it as resulting from a single, decisive action. The revolutionary process grows and is strengthened daily not only in revolt against the boredom of a system that prevents people from seeing the 'beach under the paving stones' but also in our determination to make the beach open to all.

If a revolutionary movement is to succeed, no form of organization whatever must be allowed to dam its spontaneous flow. It must evolve its own forms and structures.

In May and June, many groups with these ideas came into being; here is a pamphlet put out by the ICO, not as a platform or programme for action, but as a basis for discussion by the workers:

'The aim of this group is to unite those workers who have lost confidence in the traditional labour organizations — parties and trade unions.

'Our own experiences have shown us that modern trade unions contribute towards stabilizing and preserving the exploitative system.

'They serve as regulators of the labour market, they use the workers' struggle for political ends, they are the hand-maidens of the ruling class in the modern state.

'It is up to the workers to defend their own interests and to struggle for their own emancipation.

'Workers, we must try to understand what is being done to us all, and denounce the trade unions with their spurious claims that they alone can help us to help ourselves.

'In the class struggle we intervene as workers together, and not on the basis of our job, which can only split our ranks. We are in favour of setting up committees in which the greatest number of workers can play an active part. We defend every non-sectarian and non-sectional claim of the working class, every claim that is in the declared interest of all. We support everything that widens the struggle and we oppose everything that tends to weaken it. We are in favour of international contacts, so that we may also get in touch with workers in other parts of the world and discuss our common problems with them.

'We have been led to question all exploitative societies, all organizations, and tackle such general problems as state capitalism, bureaucratic management, the abolition of the state and of wage-slavery, war, racism, "Socialism", etc. Each of us is entitled to present his own point of view and remains entirely free to act in whatever way he thinks best in his own factory. We believe in spontaneous resistance to all forms of domination, not in representation through the trade unions and political parties.

'The workers' movement forms a part of the class struggle because it promotes practical confrontations between workers and exploiters. It is for the workers alone to say how, why and where we are all to struggle. We cannot in any way fight for them; they alone can do the job. All we can do is give them information, and learn from them in return. We can contribute to discussions, so as to clarify our common experience, and we can also help to make their problems and struggle known to others.

'We believe that our struggles are milestones on the road to a society that will be run by the workers themselves.

(Information et Correspondance Ouvrières).

From the views expressed by this and other groups, we can get some idea of the form that the movement of the future must take. Every small action committee no less than every mass movement which seeks to improve the lives of all men must resolve:

(1) to respect and guarantee the plurality and diversity of political currents within the revolutionary mainstream. It must accordingly grant minority groups the right of independent action — only if the plurality of ideas is allowed *to express itself in social practice* does this idea have any real meaning;

(2) to ensure that all delegates are accountable to, and subject to immediate recall by, those who have elected them, and to oppose the introduction of specialists and specialization at every step by widening the skill and knowledge of all;

(3) to ensure a continuous exchange of ideas, and to oppose any control of information and knowledge;

(4) to struggle against the formation of any kind of hierarchy;

(5) to abolish all artificial distinctions within labour, in particular between manual and intellectual work, and discrimination on grounds of sex;

(6) to ensure that all factories and businesses are run by those who work in them;

(7) to rid ourselves, in practice, of the Judaeo-Christian ethic, with its call for renunciation and sacrifice. There is only one reason for being a revolutionary — because it is the best way to live.

Reaction, which is bound to become more and more violent as the revolutionary movement increases its impact on society, forces us to look to our defences. But our main task is to keep on challenging the traditional bureaucratic structures both in the government and also in the working-class movements.

How can anyone represent anyone else? All we can do is to involve them. We can try and get a few movements going, inject politics into all the structures of society, into the Youth Clubs, Youth Hostels, the YMCA and the Saturday Night dance, get out on to the streets, out on to all the streets of all the towns. To bring real politics into everyday life is to get rid of the politicians. We must pass from a critique of the university to the anti-university, open to all. Our challenge of the collective control of knowledge by the bourgeoisie must be radical and intransigent.

The multiplication of nuclei of confrontation decentralizes political life and neutralizes the repressive influence of the radio, television and party politics. Every time we beat back intimidation on the spot, we are striking a blow for freedom. To break out from isolation, we must carry the struggle to every market place and not create Messianic organizations to do the job for us. We reject the policy committee and the editorial board.

In the event, the students were defeated in their own struggle. The weakness of our movement is shown by the fact that we were unable to hold on to a single faculty — the recapture of the factories by the CRS (with the help of the CGT) might well have been halted by the working class, had there been a determined defence of a single 'red base'. But this is mere speculation. What is certain is that the movement must look carefully at its actions in May and June and draw the correct lessons for the future. The type of organization we must build can neither be a vanguard nor a rearguard, but must be right in the thick of the fight. What we need is not organization with a capital O, but a host of insurrectional cells, be they ideological groups, study groups — we can even use street gangs.

Effective revolutionary action does not spring from 'individual' or 'external' needs — it can only occur when the two coincide so that the distinction itself breaks down. Every group must find its own form, take its own action, and speak its own language. When all have learnt to express themselves, in harmony with the rest, we shall have a free society.

Reader, you have come to the end of this book, a book that wants to say only one thing: between us we can change this rotten society. Now, put on your coat and make for the nearest cinema. Look at their deadly love-making on the screen. Isn't it better in real life? Make up your mind to learn to love. Then, during the interval, when the first advertisements come on, pick up your tomatoes or, if you prefer, your eggs, and chuck them. Then get out into the street, and peel off all the latest government proclamations until underneath you discover the message of the days of May and June.

Stay awhile in the street. Look at the passers-by and remind yourself: the last word has not yet been said. Then act. Act with others, not for them. Make the revolution here and now. It is your own. *C'est pour toi que tu fais la révolution.*

Appendix

I am a megaphone...
Daniel Cohn-Bendit

St Nazaire, 18th May

If you say the students are sons of bourgeois you are right. But a minority of them have made a complete break with their class. They are ready to join up with the workers. Where? In the street, where we can argue and can act. People talk about civil war. But on one side there are the workers, the peasants, the students, on the other the bourgeois. The bourgeois will not fight in the streets. And their police are tied down in Paris. There are not enough of them to go round. The first phase of the advanced struggle we are leading must be the occupation of the factories. Then the setting up of revolutionary councils. We must find new forms of management. We must be masters of the means of production. Equality of wages, that is very important. Wages must be equal in an egalitarian society.

It is not a question of attacking the trade union movement, but of creating the conditions for a worker's democracy, where each, whatever his slogans or his banners, can have his say. I attack the leaders of the union organisations, I do not attack the ordinary union members. Unity of the labour movement will be achieved by the young. Shop by shop the young unionists must unite. Unity won't come from the top.

Frankfurt, 23rd May

Q: How do you describe your political position?
A: Basically I am an anarchist ... a Marxist-anarchist.
Q: Some journalists have described you as the leader of the revolution.
A: Let them write their rubbish. These people will never be able to understand that the student movement doesn't need any chiefs. I am neither a leader nor a professional revolutionary. I am simply a mouthpiece, a megaphone.

Q: What is the reason for your expulsion from France?

A: I don't begin to understand why de Gaulle had me expelled. Can he really be so stupid?

Q: You talk as if you have a personal hatred for General de Gaulle ...

A: It is a tactic, naturally. Above all to defend myself against the accusations of the Party, which wants to pass me off as an agent-provocateur of the regime. And this is because at the moment they do not want de Gaulle to be defeated.

Q: Would you support a Popular Front?

A: A Popular Front at the moment would be an extremely positive step in clarifying the situation: the masses would end up by understanding better the nature of the trade-union bureaucracy and the traditional working-class parties and then an alternative on the left of the Communist Party could very easily be formed.

Q: Isn't that a little bit of an over-simplification?

A: Not at all. Look, there are two extreme possibilities: on the one hand the victory of the fascist-type reaction and the relative defeat of the proletariat for at least a decade. On the other hand there might be the development of a situation like that in Russia at the beginning of this century: 1905 or else February 1917. If it turns out to be a February 1917 situation, say we have a so-called Popular Front with a Kerensky by the name of Mitterand or Waldeck-Rochet. Certainly there is no shortage of Mensheviks: the difficulty is to find any Bolsheviks!

Q: But is it possible to have a French revolution in a vacuum?

A: No. The revolution in one country is certainly not feasible. Also from an economic point of view. An economic crisis, caused for example by social conflict, cannot remain isolated in one country. Nor a financial crisis, a dollar crisis, transcends as you know all countries. The system is international. However we have to begin by undermining each particular part of it, and in Paris that's what we have begun. In Paris the situation could truly be described as pre-revolutionary.

Q: What is the role of the Communist Party in all this?

A: The Party is one of the two power-structures which at the moment are propping each other up. De Gaulle and his State on the one defensive, and he is defending his position of power in the State. The Party is on the defensive becaus it is obliged to defend its position of power within the working-class movement. Our action, by contrast, is offensive: that is its advantage. All these intermediate and transitory objectives arising from the present situation, all the strong pressures from below, are pushing away at the old structures of power. You know, in this situation, the Party hasn't very much will to take the reins of the bourgeois state into its hands. Moscow is certainly against it: they have very much more reliance on the General than on the little bureaucrats of the French Communist Party.

Q: Consequently a Popular Front would detach the masses from the Party?

A: Yes, that's more or less the idea, but don't forget that in reality the whole thing is very much more complex. The existence of the Party is an objective reality, one can't decide from one day to another to eliminate it. It is thanks to the Party and the CGT that the concept of the class-struggle has kept its significance in the working-class consciousness. Our accomplishment will be to make conscious the divisions which exist between the declarations of the Party and its actual reformist politics. In the struggles of the last few days we have made enormous strides.

Q: But the workers haven't let you enter the factories.

A: It's not true. The functionaries of the Party have only partially succeeded in closing the factory gates on us. They have had to do this so as not to lose their positions of power, but this has cost them and is going to cost them a great deal.

Q: Do you think of the student movement as a new International?

A: At the moment there are individual contacts and group contacts on an international level, but it is not yet possible to speak of common action. Action is born from below, from the actual situation. It's just the same as in the struggle against capitalism.

Q: Are you thinking, then, of intensifying contact?

A: Certainly, but that is not the central problem. Co-ordination would be a positive gain, but a Student International doesn't interest me. It doesn't interest me at all. What we need to form is a new revolutionary left, of which the student movement would be a component. Otherwise the student movement will remain isolated, within the limits of a movement of protest. But we may already be overcoming this. In France, in Italy, and to some extent in Germany, there are already links with the working class, even if they are only at a local level.

Q: What do you think will be the organisational form of the new revolutionary movement?

A: It isn't yet possible to say ... We are creating groups at the bottom: workers and students who collaborate for local action. But I don't think it's possible to be more precise than this.

Q: Perhaps they are already the Bolsheviks of the new revolution, perhaps they have already decided to institute the dictatorship of the proletariat?

A: No, not the dictatorship of the proletariat. We are against all authority.

London, 12th June

Q: What exactly do you stand for? Are you a communist?

A: I am supporting those who form workers' councils, for self-determination for workers and for students. If this is communist you can call me a communist. But I do not agree with Russian politics. Politics today is not so simple. I am somebody who fights for the self-government of the workers. But when I say that I disagree with the policy of the government in Russia, remember that I disagree also with the policy of the governments in Britain, France, Germany, the USA, etc.

Q: Danny, you are regarded as the leader of the student movement in France ...

A: Excuse me, I will never lead anything. I will never tell people what to do. What they want to do they will do, and what they don't want to do they won't.

Q: It has been reported that you said you want to seek political asylum in this country.

A: It's true I said this. It is a matter of political finesse. I said before that in France there is a pre-fascist situation. Now there was another man who came to this country and asked for asylum when France had a pre-revolutionary situation. This was in 1940 and his name was de Gaulle. He wanted asylum ...

Q: De Gaulle was a Frenchman. Now Danny, you are not a Frenchman.

A: I do not want to compare myself with de Gaulle, you understand. With the young people it does not matter if you are a Frenchman or a German. We don't bother about borders. I was born in France and I lived there, and I consider myself in this sense a Frenchman. This is how young people think. It is important to me that sixty to seventy thousand people all shouted "We are all German Jews".

Q: But Danny, I may be thick, but I still don't understand what sort of government you want.

A: We want a workers', peasants', and students' self-government: the people in the factories to control the place where they work and the students to control the place where they work.

Q: But in the Sorbonne you have got what you were after. Why are the students still demonstrating?

A: The students are supporting the working-class. One and a half million workers are still on strike, and they are not striking for the money, they want control of what they do.

Q: What is your reaction to the way you have been received in England?

A: Well, not astonished. It seems that all the governments want to show that we are right in saying that we live in a repressive society. I arrive in England and they don't want to let me in. Two years ago I came here and nobody said a word. Strange. I don't have to ask Mr. Wilson and his Home Office if I want to see some people in England.

Q: You wouldn't want to give the students here some advice on how to make a revolution?

A: You don't export revolution. No, you don't export protestation against society. You can explain what has been done in France but it's not advice, you only explain it. You can exchange information about how to play soccer, but you don't export soccer games.

Q: It was said in the House of Lords that you had the intention of using force to carry out plans in this country.

A: A lot of people know more than I know. It's very interesting how all sorts of people know what I'm doing and organising. I must really be better than Batman or Superman, just travelling around and organising world revolution. I think it's because people are afraid because of the situation in England. And then they are afraid that a little thing can explode because people are not happy in this country. Perhaps this is the problem.

(taken from *The Raven Anarchist Quarterly 38* (vol 10, no 2; Summer 1998), which in turn borrowed this piece from *Anarchy*, July 1968)

MOINS
DE
21ANS
voici votre
bulletin de
VOTE